MW01233408

CANDACE OWENS PRESENTS
AN INVESTIGATION BY XAVIER POUSSARD

BECOMING
BRIGITTE

PART I

"BRIGITTE" IN POWER

"The old world is dying, the new world is slow to appear, and in this chiaroscuro monsters emerge."

Antonio Gramsci, *Prison Notebooks*, 1948.

1
2017

An "antidote to the patriarchal social and political codes"

On May 14, 2017, Emmanuel Macron, 39, came to power in France. A year earlier, he was completely unknown to the public.

The campaign had been marked by the torpedoing of right-wing candidate François Fillon. As a former Prime Minister, he should have succeeded François Hollande as part of the alternation between Socialists and Gaullists, a frequent feature of French political life until then. François Fillon had triumphed in the right-wing primary thanks to the support of conservative Catholic networks that had become structured and dynamized in the movement opposing same-sex marriage legalized by the Socialist government in May 2013.

To scuttle Fillon, an offensive was launched by the press and the judiciary at the end of January 2017, four months before the presidential election. It targeted him through his wife Pénélope, while the mainstream media unanimously touted the couple of "Brigitte" and Emmanuel Macron... A peculiar couple: Emmanuel Macron had met his wife, "20 years older than him", when he was in high school.

To sell this improbable story, intense propaganda was deployed across all media: television, radio and the Internet. Books praising "Brigitte and Emmanuel" and glossy magazine covers saturated the public space.

The aim was to subliminally instill minds with storytelling designed by the cream of Parisian specialists of public image. This pulpy narrative told the story of Emmanuel Macron, a precocious and virtuoso student at Lycée La Providence in Amiens – the press compared him to "Mozart" – who won over his teacher, "Brigitte", a dynamic, beautiful and charismatic woman (the women's press was fond of the adjective "solar").

Emmanuel Macron's victory over the conformist frowns of Amiens, a small provincial town, and over the ordinary machismo that would not accept an age difference that no one would have noticed if he had been the older of the two, forged an extraordinary destiny for himself. In his perseverance in imposing "Brigitte", the Balzacian young wolf had developed a steel willpower that led him to power.

After Amiens, Emmanuel Macron moved to Paris to attend the prestigious public Lycée Henri-IV, before entering Sciences-Po. An assistant to the philosopher Paul Ricoeur during his studies, he was one of the top-ranked graduates of ENA (2004), the school of the French nomenklatura, joining the Inspectorate General of Finance, one of France's largest government bodies. After becoming the youngest managing partner at Rothschild & Cie (2010), the social-liberal banker joined the campaign team of Socialist candidate François Hollande, who, once elected President, appointed him as his Deputy Secretary General in charge of the Economy at the Élysée Palace (2012), then as his Minister of Economy and Finance (2014). Having emancipated himself from the Socialist tutelage, at the end of 2016 he had announced his candidacy for the presidential election, presenting himself as a new man who would be the bulwark against the populist wave that, blow after blow, had prompted Brexit to the UK and brought Donald Trump to the White House.

The story of the couple formed with "Brigitte" was indeed the foundation of the Macronian saga. No less than 60 daily or weekly newspaper covers were devoted to "Brigitte" between April 2016 and June 2018 [1]. To date, *Wikipedia*'s page on *Paris Match* lists 13 covers devoted to "Brigitte", behind Nicolas Sarkozy (17 covers), but ahead of François Hollande (12), Claude Pompidou (10) and Bernadette Chirac (8).

On April 14, 2016, when *Paris Match* devoted its first cover to "Brigitte", the attentive reader learned that "one day, in her heart, everything secretly changes. She attends Milan Kundera's play Jacques et son maître, in which one of the ninth-graders, Emmanuel Macron, is the hero. He's already got his eagle eye"…

Paris Match's first cover devoted to "Brigitte" touts an "intimate album". The second shows "Brigitte" in a swimsuit. When suspicions arise about her real identity, the Élysée would invoke respect for privacy to sweep any questions under the carpet, and denounce an unwarranted "injunction to show photographs"…

Once Emmanuel Macron was installed in the Elysée Palace, "Brigitte" was consecrated internationally as a leading icon and personality by *1843*[2], the supplement to the elitist *The Economist*, in a portrait bizarrely titled *Brigitte Macron, agent provocatrice,* and presented her as the "new role model for French women" and an "antidote to the patriarchal social and political codes".

An *"official legend"*

Contrary to what was suggested by the intensity of the propaganda surrounding the couple, biographical resources relating to "Brigitte" and Emmanuel Macron remained very scarce. Journalist Hervé Algalarrondo, who tried unsuccessfully to investigate Emmanuel Macron's youth,[3] summed it up: "Yes to magazine covers with Brigitte; little or nothing about the actual story of their relationship.

To tell the lives of "Brigitte" and Emmanuel Macron, the word "legend" came up like a leitmotiv. In an article in which the President was presented as a "great actor" under an "influence", *Le Monde*[4] went so far as to describe his biography as an "official legend". The term "legend" was used by two journalists in a book about "Brigitte" and whose title, *Madame la présidente*[5], revealed right away her political influence: "A legend with high proximity. [...] The most inventive authors had not thought of it, but the Macrons did. She is the emotional component, and he is the intellectual component. But the brain integrates things through emotion. [...] Emmanuel Macron likes to shine in his wife's eyes. To perfect the score he plays, he relies on her sharp eye [...]. Her comments are invaluable. Implacable, she criticizes and corrects him. [...] Are they constantly acting? When are they sincere? Those who have known Emmanuel Macron in his former life have little doubt: [...] "If you don't have the key to acting on stage, you can't understand anything there." [...] Sheltered from prying eyes, far from her slick image, she is a very peculiar special advisor, with a weight that the presidential cabinet methodically strives to minimize. Yet it is with her that the President tests many of his ideas. She's the only one who dares to speak so frankly to him, to have the last word on the agenda. [...] [During the 2017 presidential campaign], early political supporters, most of them elected Socialists, discovered, not without surprise, that she knew everything, from the smallest newcomer to the exact level of donations. "Madame Macron", as they still call her, receives all the strategic notes from the advisors surrounding her husband."

The story served up to the public could be summarized in a few lines: it told the life of Brigitte Trogneux, born on April 13, 1953 in Amiens (Somme), the youngest daughter of a family of confectioners who prospered in Picardy and Northern France. After a strict education with the Sacré-Coeur sisters and an adolescence marked by the liberation of morals, this baby-boomer married in 1974 André-Louis Auzière, a bank executive, at the age of 21, and had three children with him: Sébastien (1975), Laurence (1977) and Tiphaine (1984). Following in her husband's footsteps, she began her career in Lille (Nord) as a press officer at the Nord-Pas-de-Calais Chamber of Commerce (1982). She switched to teaching in the mid-1980s, first in Strasbourg (Alsace) as a literature teacher at the Lucie Berger Protestant College, then in La Providence, the Jesuit school in her native Amiens, in 1991. There, she fell head over heels in love with a brilliant student, Emmanuel Macron, and began a clandestine affair. She eventually married him the year she was transferred to the upscale Parisian lycée Saint-Louis-de-Gonzague in 2007, a year after her divorce from André-Louis Auzière in 2006. In a genuine taboo, this first husband – the cuckold of the story – remained hopelessly untraceable. There were no photographs of him. "Brigitte's" children even seemed to have taken "Emmanuel's" side against their father: their own children held up posters reading "Daddy" (sic) in reference to their young father-in-law.

A fake resume

However, when trying to merge the various accounts of the story orf "Brigitte's", there are mismatches. Starting with his professional resume. According to her official biography[6], "Brigitte" had obtained a literary baccalaureate with *mention Très bien* [first-class honors], then a Master's degree in Modern literature thanks to a dissertation on *L'Amour courtois*. Then, to become a French and Latin teacher, she got a CAPES diploma in Modern Literature. There is a first inconsistency here: mastery of Latin generally leads candidates to stand for the CAPES in Classics, which is both more prestigious and easier to obtain (as there are fewer candidates) than the CAPES in Modern Literature. Additionally, "Brigitte" had only taught in private schools under governmental contract, for which there is a specific diploma, CAFEP.

It was later established that Brigitte Trogneux had in fact obtained a literary baccalaureate a year later, at the age of 19 (not 18), with a mention *Assez bien* (not *"Très bien"*)[7], that she had only obtained a mere Certificate in Literature (a *certificat de Lettres*, not a *"Maîtrise"*)[8]. His date of entry into the teaching profession remained unclear – sometimes it was quoted as 1984, sometimes as 1986. As for "Brigitte's" CAPES (or CAFEP), *Vanity Fair* journalist Sylvie Bommel found no trace of it[9].

A golden address book

This lack of a diploma is surprising, to say the least, especially considering that from the 2007-2008 school year until the end of her career in 2015, "Brigitte" taught at Saint-Louis-de-Gonzague, one of Paris's most prestigious schools. This private high school, nicknamed "Franklin" after the street in the 16th arrondissement where it is located, attracts the children of the elite. In the period when "Brigitte" taught there, the school was run by Viviane Fradin de Belâbre, the mother of politician Bruno Le Maire. After betraying François Fillon, and co-opted onto the Trilateral Commission, Le

Maire become Emmanuel Macron's Minister of the Economy. A writer in his spare time, he sometimes publishes books about how his wife masturbates him in the bathtub[10], or about his interest in sodomy[11]...

Franklin is no ordinary high school. Studying there requires both excellent academic results and membership of the upper-middle class, that of the heirs. Compiling the available information on this period, we discover that "Brigitte" was the French teacher of the children of many of Emmanuel Macron's future supporters. These include Jean-Pierre Jouyet[12], Henri de Castries[13], Renaud Dutreil[14], lawyer and academician François Sureau, and most importantly billionaire Bernard Arnault, CEO of LVMH. "Brigitte" was the teacher of his two children, Alexandre and Jean, from Arnault's second marriage to pianist Hélène Mercier.

Later, "Brigitte" would be a close friend of his eldest daughter Delphine, and the Arnault family would become "Brigitte's" clothing provider through stylist Nicolas Ghesquière, the artistic director of Louis Vuitton's women's collections and, over the past decade, the main promoter of transgender fashion models[15].

Emmanuel Macron will therefore be relying in part on "Brigitte's" copious address book in his conquest of power: "Another influential connection to add to Brigitte Macron's roster is Jacques Attali16, François Mitterrand's former advisor, whom she arranged for Emmanuel to meet. She was also the one who personally asked Attali to introduce her young husband to François Hollande", reports journalist Marc Endeweld[17], revealing "Brigitte's" anteriority in the couple's links with Jacques Attali, who had already spotted the young man at ENA, as had Michel Rocard, Alain Minc and David de Rothschild[18].

A reversal of sides in official history

So the psychology of "Brigitte", her perceptible hold over Emmanuel Macron and her considerable political influence did not fit with the story of a mother seduced by a precocious, vigorous and conquering young man. Journalist Michaël Darmon[19] reports that "in fact, the couple function opposite to the official story: it is not Brigitte softening Emmanuel, as the conventional image pushed to the media would have us believe, but rather the First Lady teaching the President how to be inflexible in crucial moments. Emmanuel is emotional; Brigitte is the tough one."

"He doesn't do anything without asking for her opinion. From hiring a collaborator to the choice of a suit or haircut", as early as 2016, *Le Nouvel Obs*[20], the weekly magazine of the Parisian left-wing intelligentsia which, having failed to unravel the mystery, wrote a few months later: "The problem with Emmanuel Macron is that no one, apart from his wife, can say to this day who he is"[21]. For her part, "Brigitte" muddles some more by declaring: "When I read about our relationship, I always feel as if I am reading someone else's story. In fact our story is so simple"[22].

This enigma creates some embarrassment for the couple's interlocutors, as perfectly described by writer Michel Houellebecq[23]: "He's weird; we don't know where he comes from. I tried to interview him[24]... People who speak quite well... Frankly, it's hard to get them to say anything, any kind of truth."

Former president Nicolas Sarközy shares the same concern about Emmanuel Macron: "He's ambiguous, I don't understand this guy"[25]. And he adds: "What should I think about it? He's cynical, and he is part man, part woman – it's the fashion of the moment. Androgynous. What you like about Macron is that you always like those who don't force you to choose"[26]. Eric Stemmelen, former director of programming at France 2, notes that "despite the recurrent display of [their couple's story] in hundreds of articles, reports and books – which forces us to mention it – we know nothing about the exact nature of their relationship ("sensitive closeness"?), either then or since. And if hearts and minds are to be probed, the truth may well come from Emmanuel's mother. When she wants to demonstrate the couple's stability and her son's fidelity, she says something that is more revealing than she thinks: "You could undress Laetitia Casta in front of him and it wouldn't have any effect on him"[27]. And what about the confidence of Jean-Baptiste de Froment, his fellow student at Henri-IV, that he "didn't give the impression of being interested in girls"?

In fact, this ambiguity – the sincerity of the couple, *and at the same time* [NB: a favorite expression of Macron's] the gripping feeling that there's *something* going on – provokes a sharp uneasiness in those who have had to deal with "Brigitte and Emmanuel": "The tidy young man, capable of mad passion, also talks a lot about himself, is quite touching, but says little. And he doesn't necessarily reveal what he feels. A Socialist politician went so far as to express surprise, paradoxically, at the way he "doesn't look at women like other politicians". [...] "He has an asexual side", she says daringly. The same applies to men. "He doesn't look at them any more", asserts a journalist who is following him. A prominent Socialist puts it bluntly: "He has no affects" [...] A man who is always out to charm, to delight his audience, but who would be terribly cold inside"[28].

However, David de Rothschild, who made Emmanuel Macron the youngest managing partner of Rothschild & Cie before pushing him toward François Hollande, provides some answers, explaining that "Brigitte is a very important part of his life. Enormously. It's a form of psychological reference"[29]. Alain Minc, ubiquitous advisor of French capitalism and unofficial HR director of David de Rothschild, says it all: "Brigitte is essential to understanding Emmanuel Macron. She plays a particularly important role at his side"[30]. And he says as a confidence: "If anything happened to Brigitte, Emmanuel would be devastated..."[31]. Emmanuel Macron confirms this by proclaiming: "Brigitte is me and I am her"[32]. When talking about the couple who seduced him before betraying and humiliating him, former president François Hollande has this sobering phrase: "They are each other's roots"[33].

15

On the fact that "Emmanuel" is "not interested in girls", but, *at the same time*, that his relationship with "Brigitte" is unanimously described as genuine. Writer Emmanuel Carrère writes: "She is his element of truth"[34]. This was for many an unsolvable enigma. To find the key to this enigma, all you had to do, as so often, was *look for the woman*.

----

1. Count from the program *C à vous*, France 5, June 13, 2018.

2. *1843*, September 11, 2018.

3. *Deux Jeunesses françaises*, Hervé Algalarrondo, Grasset, 2022.

4. *Les Présidents et leur père, une histoire compliquée*, Le Monde, January 2, 2021.

5. *Madame la présidente*, Nathalie Schuck and Ava Djamshidi, Plon, 2019.

6. *Brigitte Macron. L'Affranchie*, Maëlle Brun, L'Archipel, 2018.

7. *Il venait d'avoir dix-sept ans*, Sylvie Bommel, JCLattès, 2019.

8. *Deux Jeunesses françaises*, Hervé Algalarrondo, Grasset, 2021.

9. *Qui est vraiment Brigitte Macron*, RTL, May 7, 2019.

10. "I let myself be invaded by the warmth of the bath, the light of the lagoon floating on the glass of the door, the green tea soap, and Pauline's hand gently caressing my sex", *Le Ministre*, Grasset, 2004.

11. "She turned her back to me; she threw herself on the bed; she showed me the brown bulge of her anus. "Are you coming, Oskar? I am more dilated as ever"", *Fugue américaine*, Gallimard, 2023.

12. General Secretary of the Elysée under François Hollande.

13. Former CEO of AXA and Chairman of the Bilderberg Group Steering Committee, currently Chairman of Institut Montaigne.

14. Former minister under Jacques Chirac, and former head of LVMH's US affiliate.

15. *Diversity in Modeling Should Include All Gender Identities*, WWD, 30 octobre 2020.

16. Jacques Attali, right-hand man of Guy de Rothschild at the *Fonds Social Juif Unifié*, then "sherpa" (in charge of preparing for G7/G20 summits) of President François Mitterrand, boast that he has been the unofficial HR director of French politics for forty years. He arranged for Emmanuel Macron to be the auxiliary general rapporteur of the "Commission for the Liberation of French Growth" set up by President Nicolas Sarkozy in 2007, not hesitating to declare: "Emmanuel Macron? I'm the one who spotted him. I'm even the one who invented him" (quoted by Anne Fulda in *Un Jeune homme si parfait*, Plon, 2017).

17. *Le Grand manipulateur*, Marc Endeweld, Stock, 2019.

18. *Madame la Présidente*, Nathalie Schuck et Ava Djamshidi, Plon, 2019.

19. *La Politique est un métier, dans les coulisses de la machine élyséenne*, Michaël Darmon, Humensis, 2019.

20. *L'Obs,* September 1, 2016.

21. *L'Obs*, January 5, 2017.

22. *Elle*, August 18, 2017.

23. *France 2*, January 17, 2017.

24. Published in *Les Inrocks*, June 2016.

25. Quoted by Marc Endeweld in *L'Ambigu Monsieur Macron*, Flammarion, 2015.

26. *Le Point*, May 12, 2016.

27. *Opération Macron*, Éditions du Cerisier, 2019.

28. Testimonials quoted by Caroline Derrien and Candice Nedelec in *Les Macron*, Flammarion, 2017.

29. Quoted by Marc Endeweld in *Le Grand manipulateur*, Stock, 2019.

30. Quoted by Anne Fulda in *Un Jeune homme si parfait*, Plon, 2017.

31. Quoted by Corinne Lhaïk in *Président cambrioleur*, Fayard, 2020.

32. Quoted by Maëlle Brun in *Brigitte Macron. L'Affranchie*, L'Archipel, 2018.

33. Quoted by Gaël Tchakaloff in *Tant qu'on est tous les deux*, Flammarion, 2021.

34. *The Guardian*, October 20, 2017.

2

"BRIGITTE", THE RED THREAD OF EMMANUEL MACRON'S REIGN

"A political ambition stronger than him"

"A couple at Élysée" headlined *Paris Match*[1] when Emmanuel Macron became President of the Republic. And *The New York Times* raved: "By all accounts, she was present at every stage of his political evolution [...]. She is the one he turns to for an unsparing critique. He treats her as an equal partner [...]. To some, Mr. Macron, 39, is a welcome antidote to past hypermasculine French politicians"[2]. Despite the praise of America's leading progressive daily, Emmanuel Macron has always been reluctant to define himself as a liberal-libertarian, although he did hint at his deeper vision when he told the president of the Catholic Family Associations: "Your problem is that you believe a father is necessarily male"[3].

"I don't do politics, "Brigitte" says recurrently. However, her political clout is notoriously out of range from that of his predecessors. Power exercised in a total legal vacuum… *De jure*, there is no "*Première dame*" in the French Republic. But, faced with the centrality of "Brigitte" in the scheme, Emmanuel Macron has tried to give the function a legal standing.

Supposedly outlining "Brigitte's" mission, the text evasively states that her role is to "represent France alongside the Head of State at summits and international meetings, respond to requests from

French citizens who wish to meet her, supervise official receptions at the Élysée Palace and support charitable, cultural or social causes that contribute to France's international influence."

As a result, "Brigitte" has an office staffed by two associates attached to the President, a full-time assistant for these two advisors, and an assistant shared with Emmanuel Macron's 'memory' advisor (Bruno Roger-Petit), who is de facto assigned to "Brigitte". Officially, Brigitte "does not have a representation budget for her clothes, nor a budget allowing her to use outside consultants or private service providers". However, the *Cour des Comptes* [equivalente of the Government Accountability Office], which publishes annually the expenses incurred by the Presidency of the Republic in connection with "Brigitte's" activity, notes a constant increase in this budget: €291,826 euros in 2020, €292,454 in 2021, and €315,808 in 2022.

And yet, even if "Brigitte's" eminently political role is not asserted, or is constantly downplayed or even denied, it shows between the lines in press articles and books devoted to the couple. According to confidential information collected by journalist Marc Endeweld, "Brigitte" is even involved in every stage of Emmanuel Macron's career: "It was during a dinner at Alain Minc's home in the summer of 2014 that the future first lady felt that her husband should plunge into the deep end of the presidential race as early as 2017, and not wait until 2022, as many people were advising him at the time, because her age, she said, would become an insurmountable handicap for the couple: "We can't wait until 2022, because we have a huge problem. The problem is me, it's my looks. So we need to speed things up." [...] "They're one and the same", remarks a close friend of the couple. "She surely has a stronger political ambition than he does", says another. These confidences speak volumes about her actual role, far removed from the PR plans drawn up for the celebrity press and TV channels. Many campaign participants quickly realized this. One of them goes even further: "Brigitte created the man, the envy, the being that he is. The Macron machine was thought up by her. She sensed his potential when he was young, and gave him a destiny.

He owes it all to her." Emmanuel Macron was no different, when he thanked his wife on the evening of the first round, with a compliment that sounded like a line from a soap opera: "To Brigitte, always present and even more so, without whom I would not be me""[4].

"A puppet whose strings she would pull"

Prior to her installation at the Élysée Palace, *L'Express*[5] described "Brigitte" as "omnipresent in the candidate's wake, acting as an accompanist, coach, proofreader, facilitator or organizer. She is her husband's "non-negotiable part" [...]. Within [his political movement] En Marche! - some are annoyed at seeing her so often, and fear the effects on public opinion of mixing private and public life, a confusion of genres that the Macron couple have made a specialty".

On her arrival at the Élysée Palace, *RTBF*[6] reported the unequivocal statement of a former student: "It would be as she was becoming president herself. Her husband gives me the impression of being her puppet – the she is pulling her strings. In fact, I recognize her pugnacity and perfectionism in him: I think it was she who shaped him to get to where he is today".

Françoise Degois, a political columnist and former advisor to Ségolène Royal, has perfectly described the functioning of this couple who "worked intensely to [reach the summit of power], in symbiosis and with method, to seduce, reassure, flatter, convince, enthrall and draw their interlocutors into their dance [...]. In this fusional, exclusive relationship, others have very little place. Apparently, they have no real friends. [...] A couple described as "diabolical" by the disappointed, those who stopped being in their first circle, convinced that they have succeeded in penetrating intimacy, of having been admitted into the very private circle… and realizing, a little too late, that there remains between them and this fusional couple an invisible, impalpable glass pane that prevents any deep, healthy or lasting relationship. [...] This is a genuine couple, quite fusional, but with so much marketing that it becomes a burden. One could call them "The fiends" or "the diabolical" as their mode of seduction, emotional and friendly packaging functions with two voices. A sort of small company that enchanted a large part of artistic and political Paris."[7].

For journalists Caroline Derrien and Candice Nedelec, "She is the cornerstone of the couple – its foundation, its bedrock. Some believe she is rather the weak point in it – his weak point. [...] The French were told that they embodied "transgression", that they would bring "disruption". Brigitte and Emmanuel Macron are somewhat all that. [...] In the fall of 2015, he had his own personal solution: imposing his wife on his staff, as well as on the world, with the same baffling naturalness"[8]. According to journalist Maëlle Brun, "Brigitte" even has the gift of ubiquity: "The 'queen of debriefing', as she calls herself, is maneuvering more than ever. The place of choice in meetings is next to Brigitte rather than next to her husband", some scoff. The woman who had pledged to "preserve their life together" is above all a much-heeded advisor. As a result, she is involved in the hiring process, increasingly interviewing candidates. [...] Coach, rehearsal expert, diary keeper, messenger, headhunter, spin doctor... She has had all these roles at one time or another. From the corridors of Bercy [the French ministry of Economy] to the offices of En Marche!, she was even one of the only women of influence in his entourage"[9]. A few weeks after the couple settled at the Élysée Palace, *Valeurs Actuelles*, a weekly magazine of the conservative right, takes note of "Brigitte's" power grabbing: "The truth is, many advisors don't really exist. Everything goes through Brigitte. Everyone knows it and calls her. [...] Brigitte Macron is not just another advisor. She's the first. Or even a "vice-president" in the shade. [...] In the palace, the First Lady is feared by advisors and ministers alike. "If she has you in her sights, you're out", says one of the President's aides. She does not hesitate to invite herself to meetings with ministers on subjects close to her concerns or areas of interest. "It freezes the ministers, who see it as the eye of Moscow [as in the Cold War]", confides a presidential advisor"[10].

From her job interviews at the Élysée Palace to form the cabinet of the President of the Republic[11] to the dissolution of the National Assembly on June 9, 2024[12], the political influence of one for whom the French never voted has never wavered and never ceased to grow.

During Emmanuel Macron's first term in office, her influence was on full display in the ministry of Education, with the appointment of Jean-Michel Blanquer, whom she recruited and constantly guided. "Brigitte" also supported the appointment and successive reappointments as Minister of Justice of Éric Dupond-Moretti, the controversial criminal lawyer who built his reputation by discrediting and rendering inaudible the words of the victims of pedocriminals during the Outreau affair[13]. Nicknamed "the ogre of the North", he also distinguished himself by invoking "consensual incest", even "happy incest" in the Mannechez affair to justify the repeated rapes of his two daughters by Denis Mannechez, who, after walking out free from the Amiens assize court in 2012, ended up murdering the daughter with whom he had had a son[14]…

"Brigitte" does not hesitate to accompany Jean-Michel Blanquer or Éric Dupond-Moretti on their travels, and to speak for them to the press. Her name comes up every time a new government is formed, when journalists list those who owe their ministerial careers to her. These include Marlène Schiappa[15], Sabrina Agresti-Roubache, Muriel Pénicaud, Olivier Klein, Françoise Nyssen, Sophie Cluzel and others. She has also taken advantage of the rise of Gabriel Attal and Sébastien Lecornu (her pet characters) or the return of Rachida Dati to the government, never hesitating to point out that Gérald Darmanin enjoys "her favor". Her takeover of the Ministry of Culture was described by former Macronist MP Frédérique Dumas: "Emmanuel and Brigitte Macron believe they are the embodiment of culture. [...] Françoise Nyssen, as well as Franck Riester and Roselyne Bachelot later, 'consult' Brigitte Macron"[16]. At the French Ministry of Education, this was tantamount to abuse of power: the news website *Médiapart*[17] reported on the inspection of a teacher in Bas-Rhin (Alsace) after the rectorate was pressured by "Brigitte's" cabinet… Her tentacles even extend into the strategic economic intelligence sectors, as shown by her closeness to David Layani, founder of Onepoint, once a candidate to take over the IT company Atos[18].

The upper hand in strategic positions

At the end of Emmanuel Macron's first term in office, *Le Monde*[19] drew an extensive psychological portrait of "Brigitte", pointing out that "the role of a kind social event keynote lady (*dame patronesse*) of some of her predecessors is far too narrow for her. Although she denies any desire to interfere in political life, she nevertheless plays a central role with the President, providing her opinion on important appointments [...]. Brigitte Macron has a remarkable skill to distract you, take you somewhere else, suddenly telling an amusing anecdote, then going off-topic with a burst of laughter. Cautiously, she avoids any pitfalls, staunchly denies any political role with "Emmanuel". [...] This skilfully cultivated posture of humility contrasts with the considerable importance of Brigitte Macron in the presidential set-up. Distrustful, vertical and solitary, her husband only really relies on two people: his loyal right-hand man Alexis Kohler, and his wife. [...] Both coach and watchdog, Brigitte Macron rereads all her husband's speeches, which he rehearses in front of her in the evenings, just as she like when she was giving acting lessons at the Lycée La Providence in Amiens. [...] "She's the president's broom wagon", explains Jean-Marc Dumontet, a theatrical actor and friend of the couple. He's a magnet, and she's a gateway." [...] Her role is sometimes akin to that of a human resources director with the upper hand in strategic positions".

After the beginning of Emmanuel Macron's second term, *RTL* reports on "The omnipresence in the corridors of power" of the "secret advisor to the President of the Republic"[20]. *Le Nouvel Obs* says the same[21]: "From a five-year mandate to the next... As before, she receives ministers who ask to see her, and newcomers who want to introduce themselves. [...] She still has her favorite people in the government. [...] Cautious as usual, she doesn't say anything publicly, but evaluates everyone. [...] As a true professional in communications and social relations, she has no par to handle journalists, writers, documentary filmmakers and scriptwriters who would like to penetrate further than she has decided. Always charming and urban, she never turns anyone away. It's no use: she knows that the curious will quit, tired of sollicit from sources which are so silent. The intruders or circumstantial "friends" who tried to reach into the fortress all experienced this. [...] Apart from her official agenda, which is always disclosed post hoc to avoid the paparazzi, the First Lady receives many guests: ministers in office, former ministers, MPs, senior civil servants, or the staff of the Élysée Palace... They all talk to her and pass messages to her. The salon des Fougères is first and foremost a place for confidences. "Brigitte being sidelined? If you think so, you don't know the Macron couple well", says a close friend. This is past the electoral campaign, but make no mistake: she remains her husband's main informant".

Le Monde[22], which refers to "Brigitte's increasingly political voice", describes the atmosphere at the beginning of 2024 at the Élysée: "A few yards from the toilets where Donald Trump and Angela Merkel have washed their hands, one can see ministers waiting for an audience with the First Lady. Brigitte Macron, eagerly courted by all those who expect something from the Élysée, is a red thread of the presidential mandate"[23].

1. *Paris Match*, May 18, 2017.

2. *France's First Lady, a Confidante and Coach, May Reshape an Evolving Role, The New York Times*, May 12, 2017.

3. Emmanuel Macron to Pascale Morinière, January 26, 2020, quoted in *Valeurs Actuelles*, January 29, 2020.

4. *Le Grand Manipulateur*, Marc Endeweld, Stock, 2019.

5. *L'Express*, March 1, 2017.

6. *Brigitte Macron: de la professeur « adorée » à la « première dame"*, RTBF, April 26, 2017.

7. *L'Homme qui n'avait pas d'amis*, Plon, 2022.

8. *Les Macron*, Caroline Derrien and Candice Nedelec, Fayard, 2017.

9. *Brigitte Macron. L'Affranchie*, Maëlle Brun, L'Archipel, 2018.

10. *Valeurs Actuelles*, July 20, 2017.

11. *Le Solitaire du palais*, Laurence Benhamou, Robert Laffont, 2022.

12. *Crépuscule de la Macronie. De la disruption à la destruction, Libération,* June 29, 2024.

13. Éric Dupond-Moretti's methods were denounced on January 16, 2018 by expert psychiatrist Gérard Lopez during a hearing at the National Assembly: "You know that Mr. Dupond-Moretti questioned a seven-year-old child in Saint-Omer for six hours. He questioned a seven-year-old child for six hours. And he found it inconsistent! This is what changed the Outreau trial. Remember that this was a case in which all the children were recognized as victims. All of them: 12 out of 12. So, you see, a guy like Dupond-Moretti should not be tolerated... I'm an expert, he doesn't scare me, I've been an expert on the assize courts for thirty years, but imagine a kid, imagine little Delay, who's been through horrors, with this bear yelling at him, and the president saying nothing at all! "On the subject of the Outreau affair, one can read the works of Marie-Christine Gryson-Dejehansart, expert psychologist at the Douai Court of Appeal (*Outreau, la Vérité abusée, 12 enfants reconnus victimes,* Hugo & Cie, 2009), Jacques Thomet, former editor-in-chief at *Agence France Presse* (*Retour à Outreau, contre-enquête sur une manipulation pédocriminelle,* KontreKulture, 2013), Serge Garde, former senior reporter at *L'Humanité* (*Outreau, l'autre vérité,* Ligne de Front, 2013) and Jacques Delivré (*Outreau, angles morts, ce que les Français n'ont pas pu savoir,* Éditions du Pétiole, 2019).

14. Betty Mannechez, the survivor of Denis Mannechez's daughters, gave an edifying testimony to *L'Obs* (March 18, 2021), denouncing in particular Éric Dupond-Moretti's role in the affair: "Today, Betty holds a grudge against one man in particular: Éric Dupond-Moretti. He was her and Virginie Mannechez's lawyer, helping to tell the story of "consensual incest" at the first two trials, in Beauvais and Amiens, where the victims' voices were stolen. "Under pressure from my father, we came up with this story where it was just our own fault – girls vying to sleep with him..." [...] When Betty learned of her ex-lawyer's appointment as Minister of Justice, she choked. "When I hear him talk about age of sexual consent, it drives me crazy. That makes me mad. Protecting victims? What a joke!" Why did "Acquittator" find himself on the side of the civil parties, having always denounced the "victim-side" era and explained that "victims didn't need to be defended since they weren't accused of anything"? This originates from a rather ugly "arrangement" in the form of the reconstitution of an illegal group: that of the lawyers from the Outreau trial. From the outset, it was lawyer Hubert Delarue, one of the leading figures in the Outreau trial, who defended Denis Mannechez. "And it was Denis who chose Dupond-Moretti for Virginie and me", says Betty. [...] "The first time we saw Dupond-Moretti", Betty remembers, "he just said: "What does Bébert say?" [Hubert Delarue]. [...] Virginie and Denis had been living together since 2004, so as the lawyers were afraid it would be discovered, they decided to assume and plead consensual incest", says Betty. I felt dirty being part of it all. But I had no choice." The comedy works well, too well. A psychiatric expert expressed surprise that the children had never received any follow-up care, and when pushed by Hubert Delarue, he slipped up: "There may be cases of happy incest." The verdict obtained was even more lenient than in the first trial: five years, two of which were suspended for Mannechez. At the end of the trial, a judge shaked hands with the incestuous father. "He said to him: "Monsieur Mannechez, I wish you happiness", Betty recalls. In the

corridor, I heard Dupond-Moretti congratulate Delarue: "This has never been seen before in French justice!" I was shocked. At that moment, I said to myself: "You don't give a damn about us." The gendarmes told me this should earn a life sentence. I had too much faith in justice, I thought they would be my saviors. In fact, they destroyed me." In 2014, when Virginia was murdered, Betty expected a gesture from the lawyer. "Not a word. He should have defended us. Everything was all in the file."

15. Marlène Schiappa, the author of erotic books for Éditions La Musardine, has also, in her position as a minister, imported to France in 2021 the "International Day of Transgender Visibility", designed by "transactivist" Rachel Crandall Crocker.

16. *Ce que l'on ne veut pas que je vous dire - Récit au cœur du pouvoir*, Frédérique Dumas, Massot Éditions, 2022.

17. *Mediapart*, April 26, 2022.

18. *Emerging French Tech champions battle for the DGSI's big data contract*, *Intelligence Online*, September 9, 2021.

19. *M Le Monde, Brigitte Macron, la coach de l'Élysée*, November 13, 2021.

20. *Focus, RTL*, July 21, 2022.

21. *L'Obs*, December 8, 2022.

22. *Le Monde*, January 14, 2023.

23. *Le Monde*, March 20, 2024.

3

BRIGITTE AND THE CONSERVATIVE RIGHT: AN ACT OF SOCIAL SLEIGHT OF HAND

The sacred union of gays in circles of power

Analyzing the networks of "Brigitte" and Emmanuel Macron is like delving into the gay *Tout-Paris*[1]. The few women admitted to their entourage[2] generally belong to the category of "gay icons", whom former Culture Minister Frédéric Mitterrand called "madonna(s) of fags"... The LGBT tropism of the Macronie is no secret. In fact, she claims it. Under Emmanuel Macron, the number of ministers who have come out has exploded[3].

The names of other persons are being circulated, but they have not made their homosexuality official, and in France "outing" them would be considered a breach of privacy. It is a privilege that the LGBT network enjoys over all others, whether regional (Auvergnat, Breton, Corsican), denominational (Protestant high society, Jewish), initiatory (Freemasons) or familial (remaining families of the French nobility): revealing membership against the person's will is a matter for the 17th chamber of the criminal court at Paris [specializing in the press], and could lead to social exclusion, even for merely wondering about the incredible rise in power of this network in Paris over the past thirty years.

This is why 'wild' outing comes mainly from the LGBT network itself, in maneuvers consisting of ratting out people to shame – those homosexuals who haven't come out of the closet, as soon as they are not aligned with the LGBT political agenda[4]. A milieu which is a special target of blackmail, the LGBT network paradoxically exercises internal social control through blackmail.

This blackmail is the key to "Brigitte" and Emmanuel Macron's rise to power, i.e. the kind of coup of 2017 – the 'Fillon affair', an operation in the areas of media and judicial (and possibly more), with months of constant harassment of the right-wing candidate regarding his wife. Since then, the right-wing opposition, especially conservative Catholic circles, have kept a surprising low profile. Explanations: as left-wing journalist Marc Endeweld has perfectly described[5], this manipulation had its roots when, in the mid-2010s, militant homosexual circles became aware of the high political potential of the *Manif' pour tous*, the movement opposing same-sex "marriage". This realization has given rise to a kind of sacred union of gays of power[6], who then aligned behind Emmanuel Macron's candidacy. The unspoken message is a muted revenge against Socialist President François Hollande, who they consider guilty of having put them at odds by using "marriage for all" as a political tool to fracture the right.

This centrality of homosexual networks explains the insidious allusions to the supposed homosexuality of François Fillon, the conservative right-wing candidate, throughout the 2017 election campaign in parallel with the media and judicial offensive on his wife. In March 2017, *Vanity Fair* published a portrait of Fillon's godfather in politics, Joël Le Theule, entitled *L'homme qui a initié Fillon*, with a sour subtitle: "This story won't please the organizers of *Manif pour tous*, who are demonstrating behind François Fillon on Sunday, March 5, 2017. Their "martyrdom to the system" went political under Joël Le Theule, MP for the Sarthe department and several times minister, whose supposed homosexuality was constantly branded by his enemies. Two days before the Pénélope affair, François Fillon told Claude Askolovitch all about it."

30

It was at this time that *Paris Match* published several covers to promote the Macron couple in contrast to the Fillon family.

In a mirror image, the Macron/Brigitte couple strategically coaxed the conservative Catholic right to neutralize it. Emmanuel Macron proclaimed "I am not a Socialist", standing near the sovereignist and conservative politician Philippe de Villiers during a visit to the Puy du Fou theme park on August 19, 2016, then deplored, in the left-wing press, that the part of France in tune with the *Manif' pour tous* "had been humiliated"[7].

Is Brigitte (really) right-wing?

These signals sent out by candidate Macron alongside the attacks on candidate Fillon were a salvo of contradictory injunctions (double bind) causing a state of cognitive stress in the conservative right, which was gradually losing its footing. The cornerstone of this high-precision social engineering operation is none other than "Brigitte". Catholic circles are constantly told that "she is one of you" and that "Brigitte" doesn't have "left-wing ideas"[8], and that she is "clearly right-wing"[9]. And her official biography supports this view.

After all, doesn't she come from the provincial bourgeoisie? Hasn't she had a career in elitist private Catholic schools, first as a student, then as a teacher? However, "Brigitte" is careful not to confirm this. "Brigitte" lets assumptions go: "People pigeonhole me on the right based on my background and upbringing... but no one actually knows"[10].

As France shifts towards "right-wing", "Brigitte's" role is to blandish conservative circles by "treating" their main opinion leaders individually, detecting in each one the sensitive chord, the narcissistic flaw before flattering their vanity. This high-precision act of social engineering, in which "Brigitte" is a master, consists in letting people think that the door is always open. But this door isn't just double-locked, it is a *trompe-l'oeil*. And when "Brigitte's" interlocutors understand this, it is often too late. After the charming show comes public humiliation.

Take Nicolas Sarközy. On the vanity side, "Brigitte" told him at their first dinner in 2017, that she was one of his fervent voters. After telling everyone about it, he was publicly humiliated when "Brigitte" denied the information in the press: "She has always denied that she voted in 2007 for the former president, who bragged about it in Tout-Paris. "Even my husband doesn't know who I voted for," she repeats in private [...] She claims to be much more liberal than her husband on issues of morality and society"[11].

To Philippe de Villiers, an influential link in traditionalist circles that the Macrons have added to their roster, the couple suggested that he would be the "shadow" political advisor, the *eminence grise* of their reign. Everywhere in Paris, their emissaries repeated that "Brigitte adores Villiers" and that he is their "close friend"[12]. Unfortunately, this turned sour. And when Philippe de Villiers describes Emmanuel Macron's "hallucinated look - well, a little more than usual", giving "the physical impression of a young man not well-rounded yet" during a tense dinner at the Elysée, which he will recount in 2021 in *Le Jour d'après*[13], Philippe de Villiers incurred the wrath of State television (tightly controlled by the presidency), slinging mud at him by shamelessly attacking his family[14]...

The couple is more in line with societal progressivism, as shown by the confidences gathered by journalists Nathalie Schuck and Ava Djamshidi: "She's a right-wing woman, but on a right-wing MoDem line in a slightly more liberal vein," says an insider. [...] Right-wing, yes, but not on societal issues. While she is careful to never speak out publicly on medically-assisted procreation (MAP) or euthanasia, to avoid any form of political recuperation, Brigitte Macron says she does not understand how a life choice can be imposed on others. Fundamentally liberal, she herself has chosen to live out her relationship with Emmanuel Macron"[15].

In 2023, the magazine *Le Point*[16] looked into this popular idea that "Brigitte" is right-wing and concluded: "Brigitte Macron has always been annoyed that people think her convictions are necessarily right-wing, out of determinism. [...] A woman who has always wanted to choose her own life, she is in fact more liberal than most people think about societal issues. Many have fallen for it, assuming she had to be right-wing by atavism. [...] Many thought they had an ally in the Elysée Palace. The most conservative were even secretly dreaming of revenge on François Hollande and "marriage for all". [...] When we met Macron, baptized as a teenager, he'd say "My wife adores you". Vanity did the rest. What a mistake to fall for it! The front door was a *trompe-l'oeil*."

In fact, the Macrons are at the forefront of the LGBT agenda. Confirmation came from their former Minister of Culture, Roselyne Bachelot, who revealed that "Brigitte" had submitted her project for rebuilding the spire of Notre-Dame de Paris "a sort of erect sex, surrounded at its base by gold balls"[17].

"Brigitte" and the magic wand. Looking at this photograph published in Paris Match *(August 11, 2016), the reader, looking at the picture from left to right, is induced to follow Emmanuel Macron's gaze in the direction of the naturist's (hidden) sex, disregarding "Brigitte". Prestidigitators – the Macrons are social prestidigitators – call this cognitive process "misdirection". For this maneuver, which involves directing the spectator's eye to perform the manipulation, magicians use their magic wand.*

1. Fluctuating as it may be, the Macrons' entourage includes a strong homosexual slant. Albin Servian, leader of the presidential party in London, helped relaunch the homosexual magazine *Têtu*, in a liaison with TV presenter Marc-Olivier Fogiel, another close friend of "Brigitte" who, in 2019, was promoted to the head of *BFMTV*, France's leading news channel, after disclosing his "marriage" to a male photographer and his recourse, in order to have children, to surrogate motherhood, a practice prohibited in France. *Pink TV* boss Pascal Houzelot, singer Mika, presenter Stéphane Bern, stylist Olivier Rousteing, etc. are also on the list.

2. These include Claire Chazal, Line Renaud and Roselyne Bachelot.

3. These include Clément Beaune, Stéphane Séjourné, Olivier Dussopt, Gabriel Attal, Franck Riester, Sarah El Haïry, Mounir Mahjoubi, Guillaume Kasbarian and others.

4. Former French Minister of Culture Renaud Donnedieu de Vabres had to pay the price for opposing the PACS (a civil union contract open to homosexuals). When he was Marine Le Pen's right-hand man, Florian Philippot was also "outed" on the cover of the celebrity magazine *Closer*.

5. *Le Grand Manipulateur*, Marc Endeweld, Stock, 2019.

6. From gay socialists in Paris City Hall and the *Mouvement des Jeunes Socialistes* to right-wing gay circles such as the Sarkozyst *La Diagonale* and the liberal GayLib.

7. *L'Obs*, February 16, 2017.

8. *Brigitte Macron. L'Affranchie*, Maëlle Brun, L'Archipel, 2018.

9. *L'Ambigu Monsieur Macron*, Marc Endeweld, Flammarion, 2015.

10. Quoted in *Le Monde*, November 13, 2021.

11. *lepoint.fr*, January 12, 2024.

12. *Marianne*, May 20, 2018.

13. *Le Jour d'après*, Philippe de Villiers, Albin Michel, 2021.

14. *Histoire, argent, pouvoir : les vrais secrets du Puy du Fou, Complément d'enquête*, France 2, September 7, 2023.

15. *Madame la présidente*, Nathalie Schuck and Ava Djamshidi, Plon, 2019.

16. *Le Point*, February 9, 2023.

17. *682 Jours*, Roselyne Bachelot, Plon, 2023.

4

THE MACRONS' TASTES

The French were soon intrigued by the artistic tastes of "Brigitte" and Emmanuel Macron and by their proactive attitude about the design and decoration of the Élysée Palace, in which they were the first to dwell since Bernadette and Jacques Chirac. Amid the popular revolt of the *Gilets jaunes*, French discovered the result of the six-week work costing of €600,000 of taxpayer money[1]. The presidential palace had been completely redesigned.

The historic furniture was put aside to make way for furniture or artworks in the gaudiest "contemporary" style, tapestries by Pierre Alechinsky (Cobra group) and works by these upstarts' favorite sculptor, Richard Orlinski, who had been contacted by the Macrons to host, along with the Ivorian zouglou band Magic System, the party organized under the Louvre pyramid after Emmanuel Macron's victory in 2017...

This superimposition of the conceptual on the classic often intrigued visitors; the French edition of *Vanity Fair* pointed out the "bad taste" of the Macrons[2]. In the corridors of power, ironically, one of the only people to rave about the decoration of "Brigitte's" office by androgynous designer Matali Crasset was... color-blind.

Namely, this was Frédéric Michel, a former lobbyist for Rupert Murdoch's group, and Emmanuel Macron's strategy and communications advisor between 2022 and 2023. Reporting the anecdote, the magazine *L'Express*[3] gave a description of the *"aile Madame"*, the part of the palace occupied by "Brigitte", nicknamed the "wing of secrets": "In the mysterious and isolated east wing of the Palais, around Brigitte Macron, people are wary of the outside world and especially of the President's advisors. When the new ¨PR advisor Frédéric Michel arrived at the palace in the early days of Emmanuel Macron's second mandate, he was astonished. So much grace in this Madame corridor, like a cottony pearl-gray jewel case, [...] the tapestries dotted with luminous ferns in Brigitte Macron's office and the two French windows opening onto the rose garden. "A party!" marveled the communicator, just back from rainy London. He knows that some visitors find the modernized place to have an air of "Amiens sub-prefecture", mocking "the aesthetics of 1970's executives who think that beauty comes from superimposing the new and the old", thinks that they are too stupid to appreciate the charm [...], and he is ecstatic, even enchanted by the walls' radiant hues: 'What beautiful colors!'. Then he laughs – Frédéric Michel is color-blind."

The French had been already stunned when Emmanuel Macron's office was unveiled shortly after the Macrons moved into the Elysée Palace, during a TV interview[4].

They left the *Salon doré*, the traditional office of French presidents for the *Salon d'angle*, traditionally assigned to the main political advisor. Journalists who follow the French presidency have suspected that the advantage of this was to lead directly to the private apartments, making it possible to move unnoticed by the personnel, into a discreet secondary exit.

Nicknamed "the office that drives you crazy", this room had been completely refurbished by "Brigitte", with a decoration saturated with symbols. Firstly, on the floor of the presidential office, the carpet that "Brigitte" had personally picked from the *Mobilier National* collections a piece entitled *Soleil noir* [*Black Sun*] by the visual artist Claude Lévêque.

In 2021, "Brigitte's" attraction to this artist became embarrassing for the presidential couple, forcing them to remove *Soleil noir* from the presidential office[5] when multiple legal procedures against Claude Lévêque for statutory rape came to light[6], and the press revealed the strong pedophile overtones in the works[7] of this man who, through public commissions, was a quasi-official artist of the French Republic[8]. On this occasion, *Le Monde* noted that "Claude Lévêque refers to the teenagers around him as his godchildren, nephews, assistants, and even 'sons'.

These cuddly toys and teddy bears that he carries around the world, that he takes out for meals, that he displays in every nook and cranny of his two homes, were, according to the artist in his interviews, "given to him by friends – memories too intimate to talk about". His obsession with the world of childhood is seen as an "artistic sublimation", the fantasy of someone who is far more at ease with children than with the world of adults. [...] The visual artist describes his sexual tastes and his relationships with young boys as "linked

to libertarian thought and the punk movement". [...] If you look closely, allusions to these forbidden relationships are found throughout Lévêque's works: here, a quotation from Michel Tournier's *Le Roi des Aulnes* (which revisits the myth of the ogre); there, a reference to *The Night of the Hunter* (with Robert Mitchum as a diabolical preacher stalking two innocent children); plus countless allusions to Visconti's cult film *Death in Venice*, where beautiful teenager Tadzio is idolized by an aging man. Other allusions are more cryptic, such as this press clipping that appears in his book *Holidays in France* (2001), and alludes to Jacky Kaisersmertz, a pedocriminal schoolteacher on rampage in the Nièvre from 1970 to 1997 with more than 70 victims, eventually sentenced in 2001 to eighteen years' imprisonment"[9].

Was Claude Lévêque's world also that of "Brigitte"? In 2020, along with actress Andréa Bescond, "Brigitte" spoke out against "violence against children" on the cover of an issue of the *Elle*[10] magazine featuring this "fight by two committed women". But a year later, disillusioned Andréa Bescond explained: "I met Brigitte Macron and we talked a lot about child abuse. Some work has been done, and promises have been made – promises that have not been kept. That's what is so destabilizing: they pretend to listen to us. I don't go for the idea of a conspiracy where they're all doing it on purpose, but I can't figure it out...".

1. *Brigitte Macron veut dépoussiérer la décoration de l'Élysée. Le Monde*, December 1st, 2018.

2. *Le président a-t-il mauvais goût?, Vanity Fair*, December 2022.

3. *L'Express*, April 13, 2023.

4. *TF1*, October 16, 2017.

5. Announced by Culture Minister Roselyne Bachelot on *Public Sénat*, January 27, 2021.

6. *Le Monde* (January 12, 2021) then *Mediapart* (January 13, 2021) reveal that a preliminary investigation was launched in the spring of 2019 following two complaints lodged against Claude Lévêque at the Bobigny (Seine-Saint-Denis) and Nevers (Nièvre) courts for "rape of minors under 15" and "sexual assault of minors under 15" by sculptor Laurent Faulon, who accused him of abusing him between the ages of 10 and 17, also mentioning similar practices with eight other minors, including his two brothers (one of whom eventually committed suicide), over four decades and until recently.

7. *Lumière crue sur l'œuvre de Claude Lévêque, Beaux-Arts magazine*, March 2021.

8. *Mediapart*, November 23, 2022.

9. *Le Monde*, January 12 and 16, 2021.

10. *Elle*, September 11, 2020.

PART II

THE ENCOUNTER

"It only takes one encounter to save a child."

Brigitte Macron, *RTL*, February 26, 2023.

"All history was a palimpsest, scraped clean and re-inscribed exactly as often as was necessary."

George Orwell, *1984*, 1949.

5

BOY, 14

The false argument of the age difference

As the encounter with "Brigitte" was a highly problematic episode in Emmanuel Macron's biography, the strategy was to silence any questions by focusing on the age difference, and on the fact that this age difference was similar to that between Melania and Donald Trump, for example.

The spin doctoring was first exposed by Éric Stemmelen, in *Opération Macron*[1], whose release went completely unnoticed even though its author's[2] high professional profile in the media should have opened wide the doors of the media for promotion. Originally, the book was due to be published by Le Seuil, but the manuscript was suddenly blacklisted in Paris, and the author had to fall back on a small publisher in Brussels. In September 2019, an insider of the Élysée Palace whispered to me: "In the Castle, they are worrying about a book... I don't know what it is. It was published in Belgium...".

I spotted and bought the book, a chronological press review of Emmanuel Macron's rise between his appointment at the Élysée palace with François Hollande in 2012 and his election to the presidency of the Republic in 2017. I discovered why the Macrons had been worrying over it and why its release had been made invisible by the media.

By superimposing dozens of accounts of the encounter between "Brigitte" and Emmanuel Macron, Éric Stemmelen highlighted the fact that, from 2012 onwards, "the press repeated over and over that his wife was 'almost twenty years' older than him, when in fact they were nearly twenty-five years apart. It was claimed everywhere that, when they met, "she was 36 and he was 17". In fact, in 1992, Emmanuel Macron was 14 years old (born on December 21, 1977) and finishing his third year at Lycée La Providence in Amiens, when he starred in Milan Kundera's play *Jacques et son maître*, staged by him and his friend Renaud Dartevelle. Brigitte Auzière, then aged 39 (born on April 13, 1953), was enthusiastic about the boy's talent (although he would never be a student in her French class). At the start of the new school year, she welcomed him into her theater workshop, in which he would participate for two years. [...] So Brigitte Auzière was not 36 when they met; at 36, she was living in Strasbourg, and when Emmanuel turned 17, he had already left Amiens and was a student at the Lycée Henri-IV in Paris. These facts are rather easy to check, even for a French journalist… This is therefore not an error over details, but deception. With good reason: a 36-17 woman-meets-boy could become a romantic idyll worthy of Stendhal, but a 39-14 pair would arouse suspicions of pedophilia. [...] The ploy accustomed the public to this unusual couple, by disguising an all-too-crude truth, which will only be revealed little by little, in successive snippets, in 2016. [...] the Macron operation, starting with a lot of false information, deemed more acceptable by public opinion, was carried out by PR professionals who rewrote the story and delivered it to lazy, complacent scribblers who did not double check at all. This is a fine example of the systematic diffusion of misstatements designed to mislead public opinion – *fake news*, as the thought police says when it goes counter its lines. [...] This is an unprecedented operation in French electoral history, a monstrous fraud, and here I must retrain my wording, to avoid labelling it an organized swindle. [...] For two years, most media offered the candidate Macron free advertising space, equivalent to tens of millions of euros in editorial advertising, plus free comparative advertising via articles and reports gunning down some of his competitors."

Cited as an example by the Pedophile International

Long unconditionally laudatory about the French presidential couple, the Western press is beginning to introduce nuances. In the spring of 2024, under the pen of Suzanne Beyer, *Der Spiegel*[3] ran the headline *"Emmanuel and Brigitte Macron. No, this love story is not a model."* The editorial highlights "a huge problem with him and his wife. The issue is private – the public has been looking away for years, and the Macrons themselves obviously shun it. But there is also a socio-political aspect". After pointing out that "Suggesting the authenticity of feelings is a trick used by many attackers" so that "the Macrons make it easy for dishonest commenters to make them role models", *Der Spiegel* evasively concluded that all this was a "private matter that touches on current political issues"…

In France, the subject remains taboo in the public debate. Anne Hidalgo, the Socialist mayor of Paris, had a bitter experience of this. After declaring that, "unlike others", she "could never have fallen in love with a teenager"[4], she was pressured to apologize, and "clarified" her point: "Neither in the question I was asked, nor in my answer, was there any connection with the beautiful story of Emmanuel and Brigitte Macron. That's neither my morals nor my ethics."

And, for the general public, the sedimentation of the various layers of rewriting the encounter between "Brigitte" and "Emmanuel" has installed a cloud of vagueness in the minds of the French. This vagueness is perpetuated by the double lie of the 20-year age gap (vs 24) and Emmanuel Macron's 17-year age (vs 14), for example, on the pop-up banner displayed automatically upon accessing the *Closer* magazine website.

Elle y fait la rencontre d'Emmanuel Macron en 1995.

Il est alors son élève, de plus de 20 ans son cadet.

Despite this, the French version of Brigitte Macron's Wikipedia page states that "their relationship could fall under article 227-27 of the French Penal Code, on sexual abuse of a minor".

Yet the presidential couple is cited as an example in *Positive memories*, a publication by International Pedophile and Child Emancipation (IPCE), which lists "positive loving relationships with children"…

1. *Opération Macron*, Éric Stemmelen, Éditions du Cerisier, 2019
2. Éric Stemmelen, trained as a statistician, was the Director of enquiries at Sofres (an opinion polls company) before joining the public broadcasting service at France Télévisions, where he was head of Broadcasting and Programing of the *France 2* channel.
3. *Der Spiegel*, April 16, 2024.
4. Quoted in *Closer*, March 18, 2022.

6

THE MYTH OF MACRON
AS A WRITER

"And I keep his manuscripts"

In the first version of the story of "Brigitte" and Emmanuel Macron (as told between June 2012 and April 2016), the setting for the encounter was not the theater workshop of La Providence run by "Brigitte" but the classroom, as alleged in *Le Parisien*[1] in 2014: "It was around this time that he started a relationship with his French teacher, Brigitte Trogneux, 36, twenty years his senior. [..] Former alumni of La Providence still smile about the budding love affair between the teacher and her pupil, who used to meet in evening classes. "In class, she was always citing him as an example," recalls one. "She was totally captivated by his writing skills. He wrote poems all the time and she read them in front of everyone," adds another".

It has now been established that Emmanuel Macron never had "Brigitte" as a French teacher. The students' testimonials were invented. Afterwards, when the public accepted that for Emmanuel Macron, the theater had been a real "revelation"[2] and the opportunity to collaborate with his stage director ("Brigitte"), PR inevitably turned to their writing work as the actual occasion to meet, since a candidate for the presidency of the Republic could hardly present himself as a mere actor. Additionally, a political trajectory rooted in a theater workshop might recall Roman Polanski's explosive story in *The Ghost Writer*...

The effect was that the second version of the couple's "official legend" was once again focused on writing. In this version, it was love at first sight during the adaptation of a play to assign additional roles to all the students enrolled in "Brigitte's" workshop. In fact, the play in question, *The Art of Comedy* by Italian playwright Eduardo De Filippo, is premonitory by confusing the audience, between the notables of a town about to be received by a prefect, and the members of a theater troupe with usurped identities.

To support this new version launched in the spring of 2016, the legend had to be endorsed from above by featuring Emmanuel Macron in the presence, or under the pen, of internationally renowned writers such as Michel Houellebecq[3], Emmanuel Carrère[4] and, later, Simon Liberati[5].

This is also the reason why "Brigitte", who presented herself to the French for the first time in real life on the cover of *Paris Match* in April 2016[6], mentions E. Macron as a writer: "My workaholic husband is a knight in shining armor, a character from another planet who combines rare intelligence with exceptional humanity. Everything is in the right place in his head. He's a philosopher, an actor turned banker and politician, a writer who hasn't published anything yet. And I keep his manuscripts."

"Scenes of human sacrifice"

From then on, it was necessary to bring these mysterious, unpublished writings into existence, Journalist Claude Askolovitch was called upon in *Vanity Fair*[7] to tell that Emmanuel Macron had written a novel bizarrely entitled *Babylone Babylone*, at the Lycée Henri-IV while preparing for the exams to the prestigious higher education establishments. This improbable novel, supposedly submitted to, and rejected by, publisher Jean-Marc Roberts (who was unable to deny it because he died in 2013…), was a picaresque fresco about Latin America at the time of Hernán Cortés. Reportedly, a school friend of Emmanuel Macron read it and was "blown away" by his "extreme mastery of language": "There were terrible passages, scenes of human sacrifice; everything was told with a lavish of gripping detail"[8]. But a few months earlier, in the documentary *La Stratégie du Météore*[9], "Brigitte" had been presented as the only reader of this manuscript (the prep-school comrade and Jean-Marc Roberts had not yet been associated to the storytelling...) and a second one, a thriller. In his interview with literary critic Jérôme Garcin, Emmanuel Macron declared: "As a confidence, I'll tell you that I have written two other novels and some poems too...". He claimed artistic inspiration from the pedophile writer André Gide[10]: "Gide shows me the path that leads from the cerebral to overflowing sensuality".

In 2020, the myth of the writer Macron was definitively debunked by journalist Corinne Lhaïk[11]: "When he discovered François Sureau's *Le Chemin des morts*, he wanted to write a similar text, with the same sincerity: in his own book, Sureau speaks of a personal tragedy. [...] The publication of *Révolution* [Note: the only book signed and published by Emmanuel Macron], at the end of November 2016, was preceded by a secret attempt: in the spring of 2016, he completes a book about himself, his roots, his grandmother, his preparatory classes, and his attitude toward education. The four or five members of the inner circle who have seen it all agree that the text is very self-centered, with no obvious literary qualities. The future candidate does not insist. [...] Sureau recommends a personal book and a prestigious publisher, Antoine Gallimard. He will have neither: Macron prefers Bernard Fixot, better known in the world of supermarkets. Only the first two chapters tell something about the candidate's life; the rest consists of contributions by experts on Africa, security, pensions"...

"We had always known each other"

Rereading *Révolution*[12], Emmanuel Macron's only known opus, we are perplexed about the story of his encounter with "Brigitte", presented as "a sensitive continent to which only the fragile have access and where they can find themselves": "We talked about everything. And I discovered that we had always known each other".

In his book, Emmanuel Macron talks very little about his family except his maternal grandmother Germaine Noguès. On the other hand, he explicitly makes "Brigitte's" family his own: "We were married in 2007. It was the official consecration of a love that was at first clandestine, often hidden and misunderstood by many before finally imposing itself on them. I may have been stubborn. To fight against the circumstances of our lives where everything would act to keep us apart. To oppose the order of things that condemned us from the very first second, [...] At least I hope that we have built another family; somewhat out of the way, and certainly different; but where the strength of what binds us is even more invincible. [...]. There is not a day without Sébastien, Laurence and Tiphaine calling her, seeing her, consulting her. She is their compass. Gradually, my life was filled with her three children, their spouses Christelle, Guillaume and Antoine, and our seven grandchildren Emma, Thomas, Camille, Paul, Élise, Alice and Aurèle, They are the ones we are fighting for."

As if there were nothing to hide, the film of "Brigitte" and Emmanuel Macron's wedding was broadcast on French television in the documentary *La Stratégie du Météore*.

Everything there is strange, from the sleeveless and particularly short dress worn by "Brigitte" to Emmanuel Macron's pink tie, not to mention the *pièce montée* wedding cake possibly evoking the horns of a Baphomet. Strangely, this wedding did not appear in the local weekly *Les Echos du Touquet* for October 20, 2007: the only event mentioned at the town hall is a christening.

1.*On l'appelle le "Macron d'Amiens", Le Parisien*, October 19, 2014.

2. *Un Jeune homme si parfait*, Anne Fulda, Plon, 2017.

3. *Les Inrocks*, June 2016.

4. *The Guardian*, October 20, 2017.

5. *Grazia*, March 8, 2019.

6. *Paris Match*, April 14, 2016.

7. *Vanity Fair*, February 2017.

8. *Les Macron*, Caroline Derrien and Candice Nedelec, Fayard, 2017.

9. *La Stratégie du Météore*, Pierre Hurel, *France 3*, November 21, 2016. About this hagiographic documentary, *Le Nouvel Obs* (January 5, 2017) writes: "*La Stratégie du Météore* is a must-see. Some scenes are so astonishing – for example the farewell meeting with his colleagues, the announcement of his resignation to the press – that the viewer wonders at times whether this is a documentary or a fictional remake of Jacques Audiard's *Un Héros très discret*, the story of a man inventing his own destiny as a Resistance fighter during the *Libération*. This is exactly the question voters are asking: Is Macron for real?"

10. *L'Obs*, February 16, 2017.

11. *Président cambrioleur*, Corinne Lhaïk, Fayard, 2020.

12. *Revolution*, Emmanuel Macron, XO Éditions, 2016.

7

BALZACIAN YOUNG WOLF
OR EXFILTRATED TEENAGER?

"The romance that appeals so much to the female electorate"

On November 13, 2015, Emmanuel Macron's first attempt to really become visible as a candidate for the 2017 presidential election went completely unnoticed due to the wave of attacks in Paris that evening. On the occasion of a laudatory portrait in *Le Monde*[1], E. Macron, then Minister of the Economy, was showcased by *Canal+*'s flagship program *Le Supplément*, recorded on November 13 but broadcast the following day. Introducing this "new face", the report's *voiceover* tells that he and "Brigitte Macron, his wife, met in high school. He was in the *première* class (eleventh grade). She was his literature teacher", Emmanuel Macron corrects, conceding that he "knew her shortly before he turned 16" when "she was [his] drama teacher", and vigorously denies having been yanked out of his family home as reported in *Le Monde*: "When Emmanuel Macron was 16, an 11th grade student and winner of the Concours Général de Français [a nationwide competition], he fell in love with his French teacher, Brigitte Trogneux, mother of three and twenty years his senior. All of France is now familiar with the romance that appeals so much to the female electorate. Less well known is the fact that Emmanuel had to leave the family home and go into exile in Paris, protected by his grandmother Germaine, a former school principal. She found him a place to stay in the capital for his final year at the Lycée Henri-IV". This is a far cry from arriving in Paris with the "devouring ambition of Balzac's young wolves" that Emmanuel Macron then described in *Revolution*[2]...

This exfiltration of the teenager by his parents was also denied by "Brigitte" in *Paris Match*[3]: "I then asked him to go to Paris, to Lycée Henri-IV, for his final high school year. He assured me he would be back. It was heartbreaking. We didn't cut the thread; on the contrary, it became passionate and, at 17, Emmanuel told me: "Whatever you do, I'll marry you!"". These words were repeated by "Brigitte" for the camera of *France 3*[4]: "Love swept everything in its path and drove me to divorce. It was impossible to resist."

In the run-up to the presidential election, Emmanuel Macron's low-profile parents[5] will be called upon to deny to journalists that their teenage son had been exfiltrated[6]. But at the same time, Emmanuel Macron explained his failure at the admission exam to *École Normale Supérieure* by his sentimental situation: "I entered *khâgne* [preparatory section] without conviction. I had just left Amiens, where my love life had made my situation unmanageable"[7].

The fatal words: "statutory rape"

Across the Channel, the *Daily Mail*[8] investigated the reality of this episode with the testimony of Christian Monjou, Emmanuel Macron's English teacher at Henri-IV[9], who explained that his father had put him there to keep him away from "Brigitte": "Jean-Michel Macron personally contacted the management of Henri-IV to ask if they would accept his son with the guarantee that he would be separated from Madame Trogneux. Principal Patrice Corre kept the family secret". In the same article, Benoît Delespierre, a journalist with *Courrier Picard*, tells how, for "Brigitte's" family "it was a huge scandal. Frankly, they don't really like to talk about it. All this embarrassed them enormously."

Journalist Sylvie Bommel, who worked extensively on "Brigitte", finally spilled the beans: "During the presidential campaign, when it was necessary to provide some details about the circumstances of their encounter, the Macron couple did everything they could to ensure that the fatal words 'statutory rape' ('*détournement de mineur*') would never be uttered"[10]...

In *Les Macron*, one of the hagiographies of the presidential couple, we read: "The case, which was equivocal, did not have the outcome one might have expected, *a fortiori* in a private religious school. In any high school in France, this kind of story is like the sky falling on your head – it is simply inconceivable! [...] Sexual majority is eighteen, not fifteen, if the adult has some authority over the minor. This means that teachers are not legally authorized to enter into intimate relationships with their pupils. [...] In certain respects, this teacher-student diptych borrows from the tutelary relationship between parent and child"[11].

---

1. *Le Fantasme Macron*, *Le Monde*, November 13, 2015.

2. *Révolution*, Emmanuel Macron, XO Éditions, 2016.

3. *Paris Match*, April 14, 2016.

4. *La Stratégie du Météore*, Pierre Hurel, *France 3*, November 21, 2016.

5. In *Le vieil homme et le (futur) président*, published on November 9, 2016, *Le Monde* notes that Emmanuel Macron's parents "hover like ghosts over his biography".

6. ""We did not push him out" says Emmanuel's father, visibly tired of reading about these accusations in the press. We had been planning for a long time that he and his brother would go and study in Paris" , he adds, eager to tell the truth." (Quoted by Caroline Derrien and Candice Nedelec in *Les Macron*, Fayard, 2017); "According to Jean-Michel Macron, who always planned for his children to study in Paris, it was Emmanuel who wanted to study during his *terminale* year [before *baccalauréat*] in the capital: "It was his wish" he says. "Encouraged by Brigitte." [...] And his mother adds: [...] We had intended to register him in Paris from 10th grade. This decision was unrelated to his relationship with Brigitte." (quoted by Anne Fulda in *Un jeune homme si parfait*, Plon, 2017).

7. Interview with Jérôme Garcin, *L'Obs*, February 17, 2017.

8. *Emmanuel Macron exiled to Paris 'to escape Brigitte'*, *Daily Mail*, 28 avril 2017.

9. This testimony must be taken with a grain of salt. It may have been a communications ploy, as Emmanuel Macron had an ongoing relationship with Christian Monjou at the time. "Christian Monjou, his former teacher with whom, since he has been at the Élysée, he exchanges messages every week" (*Le Monde, Les Infortunes du jeune Macron*, March 3, 2018). *Le Point (Christian Monjou, prof principal du président de la République*, June 29, 2018) also describes an "affective" relationship between Monjou, a specialist of US civilization, as such well-connected in transatlantic networks, and his former pupil, who tenderly calls him "Bibiche"...

10. *Il venait* d'avoir *dix-sept ans*, Sylvie Bommel, JCLattès, 2019.

11. *Les Macron*, Caroline Derrien and Candice Nedelec, Fayard, 2017.

8

THE SHADOW
OF THE PEDOPHILE LOBBY

The Great Manipulation

"I have a personal conviction that I want to share with you. We need to align the age of consent with that of sexual majority, at 15, for the sake of consistency and the protection of minors". Since Emmanuel Macron's announcement on November 25, 2017, the unease has never dissipated, and, like the ever-sticking plaster on Captain Haddock's face in Tintin, the issue has resurfaced at regular intervals, with its PR impact, but mostly its implicit aspects.

Emmanuel Macron's announcement came after the media coverage of two legal scandals in the fall of 2017, one in Pontoise (Val-d'Oise) on September 25 and the other in Meaux (Seine-et-Marne) on November 7. What the two cases have in common is that the French justice system has concluded that 11-year-old girls had consented to sexual relations with adults. In Pontoise, the public prosecutor's office downgraded the qualification of rape to sexual assault, making it a misdemeanor punishable not by the assize court (federal district court in the US) but by correctional court (sentencing court). In Meaux, the rapist was acquitted by the assize, deeming there was consent.

59

Faced with the wave of indignation in public opinion, the government, through the voice of Nicole Belloubet, then Minister of Justice, had launched a campaign of smoke and mirrors by putting forward the idea of a sexual majority at age 13, which would be the threshold for an "irrefragable" presumption of non-consent, i.e. irrefutable[1]. The measure was obviously presented as a "bill to better protect women and minors against sexual violence". In fact, the goal consisted in advancing an old request of the pedophile lobby: the lowering of the age of sexual consent.

In France, sexual majority is defined as "the age at which a minor can validly consent to sexual relations (with or without penetration) with a person who is major of age, provided the latter is not in a position of authority over the minor". Since 1945, this age has been set at 15, but extended to 18 if the adult is a person with authority over the minor. This is a clear definition of sexual majority, and Nicole Belloubet, then Minister of Justice, could not have been unaware of it since it had been confirmed in 2015 by the Constitutional Council while she was a member of it.

And Emmanuel Macron gives himself the best role, presenting as a "personal conviction" and a concern for "protection" the "alignment of the age of consent with that of sexual majority, i.e. 15".

In fact, Emmanuel Macron and Nicole Belloubet had launched a major manipulation. As summarized in six points: 1- Consent is already aligned with sexual majority. 2- Sexual majority is already set at 15. 3- The law is simply not enforced. 4- Nicole Belloubet and Emmanuel Macron are well aware of this, and a simple circular reminding the courts of the law would have sufficed. 5- Pretending that there is no alignment between consent and sexual majority and proposing to lower sexual majority to 13, while invoking the protection of minors and launching the pseudo-concept of "irrefragability", is therefore a perverse trick designed to reopen the debate on two subjects: the sexual consent of minors and the lowering of sexual majority. 6- These two items are the historical claims of the pedophile lobby.

The presidential couple trapped by the statute of limitations

The government then argued that the introduction of an "irrefragable" age of non-consent would be rejected by the French Constitutional Council (which, as we have just seen, is false). The Conseil d'État then backed up this fallacious argument by rejecting the threshold of "irrefragable" presumption of non-consent. All this with the support of the (radical) *Syndicat de la magistrature*, whose general secretary Jacky Coulon had declared: "The automaticity of this threshold flouts the presumption of innocence. Including it in a law text would render it unconstitutional"[2].

But at the time, the government was overwhelmed by the media coverage in France of the sexual practices of British photographer and notorious pedocriminal David Hamilton. This is how this sequence led to the inclusion, in the Schiappa law of August 3, 2018, of the extension of the statute of limitations for sexual crimes against minors, from 20 to 30 years from the victim's coming of age, i.e. until the victim reaches the age of 48. Concerning the presidential couple, Emmanuel Macron will turn 48 on December 21, 2025…

As in 2017-2018, the pedophile lobby made another move in 2021 with a new attempt to sneak sexual majority back to 13 by sneaking in the "bill to protect young minors from sex crimes". On January 21, 2021, the Senate passed on first reading an amendment that included "as a sex crime, oral sex committed by an adult on a minor of 13 years of age". Annick Billon, the UDI (*Union des démocrates et indépendants*) senator who tabled the amendment, doesn't even try to hide her thoughts when she explains: "Yes, there may be children who consent, and we must not forget that."[3]

Faced with the outcry, Éric Dupond-Moretti, who succeeded Nicole Belloubet at the Ministry of Justice, tried to put out the fire by repeating, on February 9, 2021, that "any act of sexual penetration, performed by an adult on a minor under the age of 15, will be considered rape"… which is in fact already the case.

This will be reaffirmed by the law of April 21, 2021, which sneaks in two changes to the principle of sexual majority of 1945. 1- Adults will only be liable to criminal prosecution if their age difference with the minor exceeds 5 years. This modification is bizarrely nicknamed the *"Romeo and Juliet* clause".

2- While "incest" (extended to include great-uncles and great-aunts) has now been included in the French Penal Code[4], the exception of a position of authority bringing the age of sexual majority up to 18 now seems to be sought only in the family context, which in essence would mean that this threshold would no longer apply to other "adults in authority", i.e. sports coaches, educators, teachers, theater workshop leaders, etc.

---

1. Interview with Nicole Belloubet, then Minister of Justice in *Le Parisien*, November 19, 2017.

2. Quoted in *Marianne*, May 15, 2018.

3. *BFMTV,* January 22, 2021, 10:29 a.m.

4. In the first Penal Code, drafted during the French Revolution, in 1791, incest was decriminalized in the name of "individual freedom".

9

WHAT WAS BEHIND
THE MATHIEU GALLET RUMOR ?

Tancredi and the two rings

In the spring of 2016, to cover up the rewriting of their encounter, i.e. the change from 17/36 to 14/39, "Brigitte" and Emmanuel Macron lit a powerful counter-fire: the Mathieu Gallet rumor. The idea was that "Brigitte" was just a cover, Emmanuel Macron was gay, pursuing an affair with handsome young Radio France boss Mathieu Gallet and photos were soon to appear in the press.

Mathieu Gallet is a sort of gay Rastignac [the ultra-ambitious character from Balzac] whom Frédéric Mitterrand, Nicolas Sarközy's former Minister of Culture, compared to Alain Delon in *The Leopard*: "Tancredi seduces everyone, and I'm no exception to the rule. It would be exhausting to list all the reasons for this success, but let's just say that his intellectual qualities are just as attractive as his looks. Tancredi is not only handsome and remarkably intelligent, he's also young, cultured, well-mannered, hard-working, valiant and also very ambitious. [...] Tancredi lends himself to everyone and gives himself to no one. He is amiable, attentive, considerate with all, but we know of no liaison dictated by sensual excitement, amusement or interest"[1]. The formula had struck a chord in the *Tout Paris*, and the whiff of an affair between Mathieu Gallet and Emmanuel Macron was soon to become the talk of the "*dîners en ville*".

One detail fueled the rumor mill: Emmanuel Macron wore two wedding rings, one on each ring-finger, a possible hint that he belonged to the homosexual networks of the upper crust of the civil service. Two rings had also been ostensibly worn by Richard Descoings, the emblematic president of Sciences-Po Paris, and companion of SNCF boss Guillaume Pépy after his marriage to Nadia Marik in 2004: "I'm homosexual for those who know and heterosexual for those who don't need to know" proclaimed Descoings, the black prince of gay power and notorious cocaine addict who was found dead in his New York hotel room on the night of April 3 to 4, 2012.

When the Mathieu Gallet rumor was launched, the double-ring detail was on everyone's mind. It had recently been highlighted in *Richie*, the biography of Richard Descoings by *Le Monde's* journalist Raphaël Bacqué. From then on, everyone scrutinized Emmanuel Macron's hands. Journalist Anna Cabana wrote at the time: "His gaze carries the awareness, and the courteous but absolute claim, of his singularity. There are his wife, twenty years his senior [in fact more]; the intertwined ring he wears on his right hand, symmetrical to his wedding ring; and that constantly borderline self-assertion."[2]. While, on the surface, Emmanuel Macron's name has rarely been associated with that of Richard Descoings, Anne-Sophie Beauvais, who knew both at Sciences-Po, saw there a link, explaining that she "can't help being struck by the similarities between Emmanuel Macron and Richard Descoings". She describes Emmanuel Macron as "a true witness to this generation. Ideologically, he represented what this school embodied: economic liberalism and Europeanism. What Natacha Polony, another student in our class, calls "formatting". I prefer the notion of dominant thought. He was a kind of emblem of it."[3]

"We knowingly relayed the story about Mathieu Gallet"

With the combination of Mathieu Gallet and Richard Descoings as symbols, the rumor would catch like a shrub fire and spread far beyond the walls of Paris. And when, in April 2016, the story of the encounter was rewritten, France overall was unreactive, convinced that Emmanuel Macron was gay, that he formed a clandestine couple with Mathieu Gallet and that "Brigitte" was just a cover.

And throughout the presidential campaign, Emmanuel Macron seemed delighted to publicly deny his homosexuality: "I don't have a double life" he exclaims for the first time on November 2, 2016, during an interview with *Mediapart*. Then a second time, on February 6, 2017, on stage, at a meeting at the Bobino theater: "I hear people say I'm duplicitous, that I have a hidden life or something [...] If they tell you I have a double life with Mathieu Gallet, that's my hologram". A *Closer* issue proclaimed "*Non, il n'est pas gay*" (No, he is not gay) across the cover[4], and an interview with the gay magazine *Têtu* provided the assertion: "If I were homosexual, I would say so and live with it openly"[5]. On July 24, 2018, Emmanuel Macron publicly denied homosexuality for the fifth time regarding his controversial bodyguard Alexandre Benalla: "Alexandre was never my lover!". However, Emmanuel Macron never sued Alexis du Réau de la Gaignonnière, who in several *YouTube* videos alleged that in 2013, during one of those private swingers' evenings prized by the elite (politicians, lawyers, businessmen, show business celebrities, etc.) to which he was invited as a porn actor, he sodomized Emmanuel Macron.

The aim with these denials was not to convince, but to stoke a counter-fire about "Brigitte". In fact, in a high-precision social engineering operation, in 2015-2016, during the dinners they organized at the taxpayer's expense[6] at the Ministry of the Economy to enrich their address book, the Macrons themselves fed, if not launched, the rumor, as established in 2019 by journalist Marc Endeweld[7]: "Every dinner at Bercy is an opportunity for Emmanuel and Brigitte to address the issue in front of their guests. "You know, they say Emmanuel is gay... but it's totally false!" protests an indignant Brigitte Macron. [...] As for Macron, when he meets privately with editorial writers or press bosses to prepare for his take-off, he never forgets to mention "the rumor" in these political conversations. He can't help: he has to talk about it. [...] This obsession with denial, in a private setting, ends up being counter-productive, as it only fuels the rumor. [...] A former member of the Macron campaign later confided: "We knowingly relayed the story about Mathieu Gallet"". This fog of war was spread just when their story was being rewritten, as journalists Caroline Derrien and Candice Nedelec had already perceived: "We've heard all kinds of things" sighed someone close to the En Marche! candidate: "that Emmanuel has made mysterious trips to Africa or chooses his lovers at the Paris Opera!". This is a strange confidence from the camp trying to seize on the rumor to better cast its champion as a victim."[8] Later, when another "rumor" arose about the real identity of "Brigitte", the couple was much less talkative, and not amused at all...

1. *La Récréation*, Frédéric Mitterrand, Robert Laffont, 2013.

2. *Macron: et pourquoi pas lui?*, *Le Point*, December 31, 2015.

3. *On s'était dit rendez-vous dans vingt ans*, Anne-Sophie Beauvais, Plon, 2018.

4. *Closer*, February 10, 2017.

5. *Têtu*, February 26, 2017.

6. On this, see *L'Express*, November 16, 2016, *Dans l'enfer de Bercy* by Frédéric Says and Marion L'Hour (JCLattès, 2017) and *Un Ministre ne devrait pas dire* ça... by Christian Eckert (Robert Laffont, 2018): "In addition to the private apartment, all the spaces on the 7th floor of Bercy, which house the Ministry's meeting and reception rooms, were used simultaneously. This strategy enabled Brigitte and Emmanuel Macron to enjoy a cocktail at a reception at the Ministry, then begin a more formal dinner with other guests on the 7th floor, followed by a second dinner at the apartment! A double dinner, in short. [...] In 2016, the entire year's appropriations were spent on entertainment expenses during the first eight months!".

7. *Le Grand Manipulateur*, Marc Endeweld, *Stock, 2019.*

8. *Les Macron*, Caroline Derrien and Candice Nedelec, Fayard, 2017.

10

A PEDOCRIMINAL NEBULA AROUND THE MACRONS ?

Olivier Duhamel

January 4, 2021, 4:52 p.m. Le *Monde*'s website drops a bombshell whose fallout will irradiate the entourage of "Brigitte" and Emmanuel Macron. It is a long article by journalist Ariane Chemin, with an unequivocal title: *Olivier Duhamel, l'inceste et les enfants du silence*, which heralds the release, three days later, of *La Familia grande*[1]. In this book, Camille Kouchner, daughter of former minister Bernard Kouchner, tells how her stepfather Olivier Duhamel abused her twin brother Antoine Kouchner from 1988, when the latter was "13 or 14 years old". The rapes took place at Olivier Duhamel's summer residence, the Mas des Genêts d'Or in Sanary-sur-Mer (Var), where generations of the Duhamel clan had entertained the cream of the French intelligentsia[2] whose morals were now exposed publicly: "In the evenings, kids sometimes have to act out sex scenes in front of their parents", writes *Le Nouvel Obs*[3]. "One evening, the teenagers are asked to tell how they lost their virginity. On another, mothers dress their 12-year-old daughters in provocative outfits, smear them with lipstick and send them off to dance with men thirty years older". "Hardly anyone is offended to see Camille, a teenager, asked to simulate an orgasm in front of adults", adds *Paris Match*[4]. "Hardly anyone is surprised by the photos pinned up on the walls: little Aurore's bottom or Camille's breasts, next to her grandmother's ample ones."

Olivier Duhamel, an archetypal figure of the "caviar left", straddling the worlds of academia, publishing, the media, politics and senior administration, was previously known as a lecturer and guarantor of *pensée unique* (hegemonic thought). This zealous Europeanist and fervent campaigner for voting right of foreigners was a Socialist member of the European Parlament between 1997 and 2004, speaking out at the time "against a white, Christian Europe"[5]. *Le Monde* aptly summed up Olivier Duhamel's personality: "A rough man [who] nonetheless looks cool, with his Brazilian bracelets, his lighter dangling from a cord around his neck and his systematic polo shirts. Even at dinners at *Le Siècle*, the club where the ruling elite meet, he refuses to wear a tie, against a long-time rule. On the one hand, he cultivates his anti-establishment allure; on the other, he navigates the heart of the *nomenklatura* with ease. He is powerful and influential; his tantrums are intimidating, and his manner of humiliating, overwhelming. [...] He loves arranging couples or sponsoring new unions. In his professional life, he has a passion for cronyism"[6].

The main surprise in the Duhamel affair is that while knowledge of the family secret (incest) was disclosed among power insiders from 2010 onwards, while Olivier Duhamel was promoted to the most strategic positions in the French Republic – positions that confer the power to ban or distribute membership cards; in short, to identify those who will be "part of it". This was performed both upstream, with control of the *Fondation nationale des sciences politiques* (Fondapol), which oversees Sciences-Po Paris (hence the selection of future elites), and downstream, via *Le Siècle*[7], the most powerful and secretive club in France, at the head of which he was unanimously elected president in November 2019. In short, Olivier Duhamel "may have benefited from complacent blindness, and even high protection", writes *Libération*[8], which goes on to say: "One man, central to the constitutionalist's life, never turned away from him: Jean Veil, a lawyer the eldest son of former minister Simone Veil. A historic member of the Sanary "family" [...]; Jean Veil, a star of the Paris Bar who has advised Jacques Chirac, Dominique Strauss-Kahn and Société Générale, welcomed Olivier Duhamel to his firm in 2010. [...] A significant boost [...]. Ten years later, the same Jean Veil, an influential member of *Le Siècle* which he himself chaired from 2014 to 2016, worked behind the scenes to elect his friend to the presidency of the cenacle of Avenue de l'Opéra."

In January 2021, the revelation of Olivier Duhamel's incest with his stepson, aged "13 or 14", shook the Elysée Palace: "Ever since the 'Olivier Duhamel affair' broke in early January, Emmanuel Macron has been monitoring each development like milk on the stove", reports *Le Monde* at the time[9]: "Descriptions in the press of the extent of Olivier Duhamel's networks have stunned both the Elysée Palace and former PM Édouard Philippe. A man of power, the constitutionalist, formerly close to the Socialist Party, had woven his web all the way to the Elysée and Matignon palaces. Before celebrating Emmanuel Macron's qualification for the second round of the presidential election on April 23, 2017, at the brasserie *La Rotonde*, he had passed several notes to the candidate and attended a few campaign meetings. Olivier Duhamel did not stop there. After the victory, the former member of the European Parliament is passionate about this young President "of both the right and the left". In his magazine *Pouvoirs*, he compares him to General de Gaulle, and chides the media for call him derisively "Jupiter". [...] Olivier Duhamel also boasts about his meetings at the "Château". [...]. In its January 20 issue, *Paris Match* reported that the lawyer even gave some advice on how to handle the "Benalla affair" in the summer of 2018."

A significative episode was then revealed by the press: the "Sciences-Po lunch"[10] during which, the day after the presidential election, "Brigitte", alongside Olivier Duhamel and Frédéric Mion (Richard Descoings' successor at the head of Sciences-Po Paris), had "casted" Édouard Philippe, Emmanuel Macron's future Prime Minister... This caused interrogation about what could possibly link the provincial "Brigitte", a member of the Picardy bourgeoisie with a career in private Catholic education, to Olivier Duhamel, a Saint-Germain intellocrat at the crossroads of all the networks of power. Was what discretely happened in a provincial theater workshop a peccadillo not worth much attention, or, on the contrary, did it make Emmanuel Macron a pure product of a pedophile nebula of which he would henceforth be the guarantor and protector? Networks that are by their very nature subject to blackmail, sometimes by foreign powers…

Once the incest involving his stepson, aged "13 or 14", was revealed, Olivier Duhamel resigned from all his positions, including the presidency of Fondapol and the *Le Siècle*, as well as his seat on the board of Institut Montaigne, the think tank of the CAC 40 companies [top-ranking companies on the Paris stock exchange].

A year after the resignation, the Institut Montaigne was shaken once again, this time by the fall of its director, Laurent Bigorgne. On December 8, 2022, he was given a one-year suspended prison sentence and fined €2,000 for sneakily drugging his colleague and ex-sister-in-law Sophie Conrad by lacing her drink with a copious amount of MDMA ("three times the recreational dose" according to the expert report - i.e. bordering on overdose). The criminal court ruled that Laurent Bigorgne had used the drug "in order to commit rape or sexual assault against her". *Le Monde*[11] points out that "Laurent Bigorgne, 48, is not well known in the general public. But he is known in the circles of power. Just ten months ago, he was regularly mentioned as a potential minister, should Emmanuel Macron be re-elected". *Libération*[12] reports that he "was everywhere and loved it. He was a favorite figure. Many thought that talking to him was like talking to Macron".

Indeed, Institut Montaigne's influence with Emmanuel Macron had been evident since the launch of his party En Marche! in April 2016[13]. The new political movement was domiciled at Laurent Bigorgne's personal address. This was a family thing, since the latter's companion, Véronique Bolhuis, former director of admissions at Sciences-Po, was also the publishing director of En Marche!'s website.

A key figure in Emmanuel Macron's entourage, Laurent Bigorgne quickly climbed the ladder of power and was co-opted into the

Le Siècle, the Bilderberg Group and the Trilateral Commission. Bigorgne was a pure product of the Richard Descoings stable, which had spotted him during his studies at Sciences-Po Paris and made him its deputy director, in other words, practically the jack-of-all-trades of the trio made up by Richard Descoings, his "wife" Nadia Marik and... Olivier Duhamel. The school of the French elite was not very detailed in the bibliography relating to the presidential couple, but it turned out that pulling on the Sciences-Po thread led to the "deep Macronie".

Elisabeth Guigou and Hubert Védrine

In January 2021, the fallout from the Duhamel affair hit the head of State. Former Socialist Justice Minister Elisabeth Guigou, a regular at the mas de Sanary and a pillar of Olivier Duhamel's gang, has been forced to resign from the Independent Commission on Incest and Sexual Abuse of Children, which she was appointed to head a month earlier as it was set up by the French government.

Chairing a commission on incest while being named in the Duhamel affair was unsustainable. Although she announced her resignation, she was discreetly entrusted by Éric Dupond-Moretti[14] with a mission concerning the presumption of innocence, before being appointed by Emmanuel Macron as a qualified member of the *Conseil supérieur de la magistrature* (CSM).

Even before the Duhamel affair, Elisabeth Guigou's appointment as head of a commission on incest had outraged associations defending victims of incest[15] because of the bitter memory left by her time at the Ministry of Justice between June 1997 and October 2000, which coincided with the "Zandvoort CD-ROMs" scandal, a gigantic pedo-criminal affair during which her attitude was more than ambivalent[16].

The Republican justice system's treatment of the Zandvoort affair, which marked Elisabeth Guigou's time in the Place Vendôme [site of the Justice ministry], finally attracted the attention of the UN,

71

which sent to France a special rapporteur, Juan Miguel Petit. In his conclusions delivered in April 2004, he was astonished by "the surprising way in which the Paris *Tribunal de Grande Instance* [Court of major instance] handled the Zandvoort files case. [...] For over a year, Juan Miguel Petit has been asking for these documents to be passed on to Interpol. France has still not complied with this request"[17].

Elisabeth Guigou, affiliated to the *Le Siècle* and the Trilateral Commission, drafted with Peter Sutherland, then CEO of Goldman Sachs International, a report arguing in favor of a Euro-Mediterranean community (EuroMed) initially, then a Euro-African version (a "Euro-African bloc [of] 3 billion human beings" by 2050), requiring the free movement of goods, capital and people. Elisabeth Guigou, who came from the French Treasury, had been encouraged by François Mitterrand, to whom she had been introduced by her close friend at ENA: Hubert Védrine.

Védrine, Socialist Minister of Foreign Affairs between 1997 and 2002, has also been very much in the news since Emmanuel Macron came to power. In addition to his directorship of LVMH, Bernard Arnault's group, and his membership of the Trilateral Commission and *Le Siècle*, of which he was a director, Hubert Védrine represented France on the group of experts tasked with considering the future direction of NATO set up in the spring of 2020 in the context of the first Trump presidency. On the subject of his relationship with Emmanuel Macron, (but abstaining from criticizing his catastrophic diplomatic record publicly), *Le Monde* reports that "secretly [Hubert Védrine] has access to Emmanuel Macron [who] reads with interest M. Védrine's notes and sometimes invites him to accompany him on trips. Insiders then spotted, in presidential speeches formulas inspired by the guardian of the Mitterrand temple"[18].

Between 1977 and 1995, as part of his political implantation in the Nièvre department, Hubert Védrine settled in the presbytery of Saint-Léger-des-Vignes, which was both the home and photography studio of a priest, Nicolas Glencross, who turned out to be one of the biggest purveyors of pedophile photos in France. This line of inquiry was first raised by journalist Bernard Violet as part of his investigation into the 1990 murder of Joseph Doucé[19], a former Baptist pastor who had established himself in Paris as a focal point for "sexual minorities" via the *Centre du Christ Libérateur* (CCL), a shady platform for homosexuals, sadomasochists, transvestites, transgenders and pedophiles. Glencross sold his photos via the publications of Doucé's nebula. Glencross had been arrested a few months before Doucé's murder. This led Bernard Violet to wonder about a link between the murder of Pastor Doucé and blackmail by the Elysée Palace, for which Hubert Védrine was then General Secretary to François Mitterrand: "The Doucé case? Hubert Védrine has never been particularly interested. He knows it from what he has read in the press. [...] In the same way, he tells me, he was never asked to take part in the Glencross affair. [...] Back to Doucé: was he ever approached by the enterprising pastor? Did he ever meet him, and if so, under what circumstances? The answer to my questions is firm and categorical: 'Never. Never.' Here again, I have to note some discrepancy between the recollections of the Secretary General of the Elysée Palace and a testimony gathered in the course of my research. This is the testimony of Caroline Blanco, a friend and confidant of the deceased pastor, who claims (but her testimony is only indirect and based on the statements of a dead man) that Hubert Védrine and Joseph Doucé saw each other at least once: "I remember that the pastor met him in 1986. He came to the CCL premises. That day, after his visit, I saw Pastor Doucé, who put on his roguish air, a big smile and playful eyes, before saying to me: "I've just had a visit from an important man: Hubert Védrine""[20].

Daniel Cohn-Bendit

Another man also made the connection between "Brigitte and Emmanuel" and Olivier Duhamel: Daniel Cohn-Bendit, a figurehead of May 68. An old buddy of the incestuous stepfather, he shared Olivier Duhamel's passion for European integration.

They co-authored a *Petit dictionnaire de l'euro*[21]. Both admired Emmanuel Macron, had joined the first circle of his couple and had invited to celebrate the first round of the 2017 presidential election at La Rotonde, the renowned brasserie in the Montparnasse district. Daniel Cohn-Bendit is also infamous for his writings and his very explicit pedophile statements[22].

His writings are mainly drawn from an autobiographical work published in 1975, Le *Grand Bazar*[23], in which "Dany" tells about his work as an educator of young children in anti-authoritarian programs *(Kinderladen)* in Frankfurt: "On several occasions, some of the kids opened my pants' fly and started tickling me. I reacted differently depending on the circumstances, but I had a problem with their desire. I asked them: "Why don't you play together, why did you choose me and not other kids?" But if they insisted, I stroked them anyway". "I needed to be unconditionally accepted by them. I wanted the kids to want me, and I did everything I could to make them depend on me". To promote this book, Daniel Cohn-Bendit, in a very serious tone, had explained that "by having experiences with kids, by playing with them, by having emotional and even sexual relationships in the emotional sense, caresses, etc., I learned a lot about myself"[24]. In 1982, on French public television, "Dany" boldly declared: "You know, a kid's sexuality is absolutely fantastic. Frankly. I worked with kids aged between 4 and 6. Well, you know when a little girl of 5, 5 and a half starts undressing you, it's fantastic because it's an erotico-maniac game"[25].

While Cohn-Bendit conceded some "remorse", insisting that this had been mere "provocation", Eckhard Stratmann-Mertens, co-founder of the German Green Party, explained: "I was also a student in Frankfurt when Cohn-Bendit and Joschka Fischer were there. I took part in the same events. And I can tell you that I don't believe a word of Cohn-Bendit's explanations when he says that he made his revelations about his sexual relations with children for the sole purpose of provocation, and presents them as purely theoretical"[26].

Jean-Marc Borello

The Duhamel affair continued to destabilize the Macrons" entourage. Frédéric Mion, who had succeeded Richard Descoings as head of Sciences-Po and had taken part in the "Sciences-Po lunch" with "Brigitte" and Olivier Duhamel, was forced to resign from the school on rue Saint-Guillaume. It was then that he joined Impact Thank, a think tank set up by a Jean-Marc Borello, head of Groupe SOS, in conjunction with the foundation of Klaus Schwab, Chairman of the World Economic Forum.

Sciences-Po once again acted as a bridge: while a professor at Sciences-Po, Jean-Marc Borello got to know Emmanuel Macron and prepared him for the "Social Questions" test in the ENA admission exam. Jean-Marc Borello has since joined the innermost informal circle of the presidential couple, declaring that he finds "Brigitte" "extraordinarily modern"[27] and asserting his "taste for borderline people"[28].

An avowed reader of *Les Amitiés particulières*, the novel by the pedophile writer Roger Peyrefitte, Jean-Marc Borello sits on the board of Emmanuel Macron's party, with a say in the proceedings far beyond his function in the organizational chart[29]. A case in point is this confidence from Louis Gallois, former head of the SNCF: "In some meetings, Mr. Borello sometimes towers over the ministers, cutting them off." An ascendancy that allows him to push his whims: "On the executive board of En Marche!, [...] he advocates taking care of jihad returnees (a structure in his group deals with them), and criticizes inheritance and property rights"[30]. "His influence and address book are highly coveted", adds *L'Express*. He does favors, a lot and often. Because he knows all the local players, he is quite useful on the nomination committees of En Marche!"[31].

Jean-Marc Borello's networking was also evident when Emmanuel Macron visited the Grand Orient de France on July 21, 2016. The meeting was orchestrated by *TF1* journalist Laurent Huberson,

Bertrand Délais (author of documentaries praising Emmanuel Macron for public television) [32], and Éric Moniot, (a senior Socialist civil servant, now implicated in a drug money laundering case)[33], who happens to be a long-standing acquaintance of Jean-Marc Borello, and manages a subsidiary of his group of companies. Among the lodges co-hosting the event on that day was Alètheia, whose grand master was investment banker Emmanuel Goldstein, managing director at Morgan Stanley, organizer of the hottest parties in gay Paris and a pillar of Richard Descoings' entourage[34].

Officially, in 2017 Jean-Marc Borello was in charge of the "social" aspect of Emmanuel Macron's campaign, for which he was the "left-wing guarantor"[35]. At the time, he figured prominently in the French delegation to the World Economic Forum in Davos, which made Emmanuel Macron a *Young Global Leader*. As for Borello, he was awarded the "Social Entrepreneur of the Year" prize by the Schwab Foundation for his work at the head of Groupe SOS – a company involved in a drug affair and a pedophilia scandal that could have ended Jean-Marc Borello's career, had he not been rescued by his networks. Starting with Richard Descoings, who offered Jean-Marc Borrello a professor position at Sciences-Po Paris (1998 and 2003), where he would meet the young Emmanuel Macron.

Flashback. After a mysterious start at the *Protection judiciaire de la jeunesse* (Youth Judicial Protection)[36], Jean-Marc Borello was recruited in 1981 to the *Mission interministérielle de lutte contre la drogue et la toxicomanie* (Interministerial Mission to Combat Drugs and Drug Addiction). In this context, he was asked to found SOS Drogue International. This structure to combat drug addiction, placed under the supervision of the Socialist Prime Minister Laurent Fabius, was promoted by Régine, the Parisian 'queen of the night'[37]. As a result, Jean-Marc Borello quickly became Régine's right-hand man, as the manager of *Compagnie financière du Triangle*, the holding company of Groupe Régine. He took charge of *Régine's*, the Parisian nightclub of the entertainment world, and its franchises in Miami, New York, Saint-Tropez, Deauville, Monaco, etc., to which were added the *Pavillon Ledoyen* on the Champs-Elysées in 1988, and *Le Cheval Blanc Régine's Hôtel* in Nîmes in 1991, and finally, in 1992, the *Le Palace* nightclub, the epicenter of gay Paris in the 1970s and 1980s.

But in June 1995, following a police raid, *Le Palace* was administratively closed. In this affair, Jean-Marc Borello, who had built his career on the fight against drug addiction, was jointly and severally sentenced in 1999 to pay 900 000 francs (€137,000) to the customs administration and to serve a six-month suspended prison sentence for having "facilitated the illegal use of narcotics, by allowing to develop and prosper [...] a narcotics trafficking operation consisting in the visible and notorious resale and consumption of ecstasy"[38]. This did not prevent him from being made a knight of the Légion d'honneur by Prime Minister Lionel Jospin, at the same time as his name appeared in an otherwise sordid scandal: the Tournelles affair.

Also as Régine's right-hand man, and through SOS Drogue International, Jean-Marc Borello sits on the board of the Institut des Tournelles, a structure for the rehabilitation of maladjusted children through "luxury and wonder", inspired and supported by the pediatrician Françoise Dolto. Located in Hautefeuille, a few kilometers from Coulommiers (Seine-et-Marne, north-east of Paris) in the Malvoisine forest, this medical-social center is accredited by the Ministry of Justice, approved by the *Aide sociale à l'enfance* (children's welfare agency) and covered by the Social Security system. It is housed in a 19th-century manor renovated by Jean-Michel Wilmotte and Philippe Starck to four-star hotel standards. Les Tournelles takes in around 50 boys aged 7 to 18 suffering from "behavior and personality disorders".

This program of re-education through "beauty" is accomplished via trips – called "educational transfers" – abroad (to the United States, Morocco, etc.), vacations at Club Méditerranée, stays in Hilton hotels, sumptuous gifts, evenings in the grand hotels of Paris and the Côte d'Azur, but also outings to the nightclubs controlled by Régine and Jean-Marc Borello, to which the boys are transported in luxury cars.

While the program has the support of the political and administrative authorities, what is behind the scenes causes interrogation. In 1989, a psychologist noticed "the presence of naked Moroccan dancers performing a rather libertine act". On March 19, 1997, the scheme began to crack up: the State Secretariat for Emergency Humanitarian Action received an anonymous letter. The author describes his experiences at Les Tournelles: "There are Sundays when some youth are retained, the kindest and cutest – and I'm one of them – to receive celebrities with whom you have to be very nice and let yourself go". Two months later, 17-year-old Jérôme Nivelle-Gens filed a complaint. He claims to have been repeatedly raped as a 14-year-old by the man who runs the institute: Robert Mégel. Mégel was sentenced to eleven years in prison by the Melun Assize Court for rape and sexual assault of two minors under the age of fifteen. The sentence was increased to twelve years on appeal in Paris on May 12, 2006.

During the Melun trial, Jean-Marc Borello "endeavored for three quarters of an hour to dismantle the prosecution's arguments. In the manner of a lawyer - "You are not here to plead!" says the judge -. This former educator [...] talks in particular about his "militant commitment" to Robert Mégel and to the benefits of this unique experience of re-education through luxury. Networks of influence: "Yes, I convinced ministers to help Les Tournelles"; relationships: "I took Danielle Mitterrand there"; gifts: "A meal for 170 people at *Ledoyen*, on the *Champs*". All for the cause of the Tournelles, "a home that has helped hundreds of kids get better". Rape and sexual assault? "Impossible from Robert. I'm absolutely certain of his innocence. The affair unleashed a media avalanche on Les Tournelles, creating an unbearable climate of homophobia""[39].

During the appeal proceedings, the brother of one of the victims testified in court, denouncing a "winning trio" at the head of Tournelles: Robert Mégel, psychiatrist Jean Tremsal and Jean-Marc Borello. He also recalls a conversation in a bar, during which Tremsal extolled the virtues of "his pretty round bed that turns by itself", while Borello made a series of somewhat obscene allusions. "I felt like a piece of meat", he says to sum up the ambience there"[40].

It was when the Tournelles affair broke that Jean-Marc Borello was recruited by Richard Descoings at Sciences-Po Paris and transformed SOS Drogue International into Groupe SOS. The headquarters of the Institut des Tournelles, the Manoir d'Hautefeuille, is still today a vacation spot for Jean-Marc Borello, as *Le Monde* revealed in 2018 in a barely believable description: "The boss travels by chauffeur-driven car. He spends weekends at one of the group's properties, Les Tournelles, in Hautefeuille (Seine-et-Marne), a château with swimming pool, jacuzzi, projection room, and even kangaroos in the park. Signs that do not go down well in the social action world, and in sharp contrast with the treatment of ordinary employees"[41].

Since then, Groupe SOS has grown from 300 employees in 2001 to 2,200 employees and a turnover of 155 million euros in 2010 (ten associations and eleven companies). In 2016, SOS had 15,000 employees and a turnover of 900 million euros. In 2019, SOS will have 17,000 employees, a turnover of one billion euros and a presence in no less than forty countries. By 2022, SOS will have 22,000 employees, 650 facilities and sales of €1.26 billion. The latest internal roadmap aims to double the turnover by 2025. But, as the *Cour des Comptes* (the body auditing public accounts) noted as early as 1998: "Only the continued financing of its activities by the State [is] able to ensure the sustainability of the existing financial arrangements".

In fact, Groupe SOS is a sucker of public subsidies, active in facilities for migrants, the care of convicted terrorists and… in closed educational centers for minors. Groupe SOS has become "a behemoth that everyone is afraid of, given its proximity to political power and its links with the *Protection judiciaires de la jeunesse*" noted *Mediapart* in 2022 in a revealing investigation on Groupe SOS's management of the closed educational center (CEF) for juvenile delinquents in Pionsat (Puy-de-Dôme): "The management is unstable, the staff is poorly qualified, and the team is too young and unqualified", laments a high-ranking gendarmerie officer under anonymity. "It opens the door to compromises, and even inappropriate behavior"[42].

Groupe SOS sales thus doubled between 2015 and 2021, and *Le Monde* was astonished by the number of tenders won by Jean-Marc Borello since his "friend" Emmanuel Macron came to power: "A hospital to straighten out financially, a historic monument to restore, radicalized Islamists to put back on the right track, elected representatives to train, refugees to house... From month to month, SOS never stops winning the most diverse calls for tender, and is growing, growing". And we wonder about the opacity of this empire, which is officially just an association: "No volunteers, no members apart from a hundred or so hand-picked members: magistrates, senior civil servants, medical professors who must be sponsored by the thirty members of the board of directors... whom they have elected themselves"[43].

Jean-Marc Borello, vindicator of the decriminalization of cannabis[44] and signatory of the *Appeal for a Multicultural and Post-Racial Republic*[45], was accused of "sexual harassment and assault in his company" in an investigation published in 2018 by *Libération* which reports on the evening parties of Groupe SOS employees: "The unwritten rule is that Jean-Marc Borello opens the ball, to Caribbean rhythms or, more often, *Gigi l'amoroso*, the cult song by Dalida, France's first gay icon. At the end of the evening, [...] the big boss has also got into the habit of kissing his date, selected from among the trainees or collaborators. On the mouth, in full view of everyone and, in the cases *Libération* has documented, without consent. The scene has become a classic of SOS evenings. [...] Within his cabinet, the Chairman of the SOS Board of Directors surrounds himself with many men. The "*Borello boys*", thirty-somethings with diplomas and ambitions, quickly move into management positions, a sign of the boss's confidence. Significantly younger, the boss's personal trainees also have a nickname: 'kikis'"[46].

Jean-Marc Borello occupies a central position in what is now known as the "LGBT lobby", all the more so as he was once vice-president of Sidaction, the AIDS organization funded and chaired by businessman Pierre Bergé.

Pierre Bergé

Shortly before his death on September 8, 2017, at his farmhouse in Saint-Rémy-de-Provence (Bouches-du-Rhône), billionaire Pierre Bergé had been described as "the most powerful man in France" by American magazine *Town & Country*[47]. Although excessive, this qualification nevertheless reflected the unrivalled influence on contemporary French politics of this media and financial supporter of the Socialist Party, who co-founded the fashion house of the same name with his companion Yves Saint Laurent.

At the end of his life, enthralled by Emmanuel Macron, Pierre Bergé declared himself ready "to find financial support [...], and to help him by any means necessary. [...] My support is obviously logical and natural. I've been supporting Emmanuel Macron for a long time; he and his wife are personal friends. For a long time now, I've been putting my trust in youth, which is not a handicap but an advantage"[48]. In fact, it was Julien Dray, who had also benefited from Pierre Bergé's bounty with SOS Racisme, who spilled the beans by presenting Emmanuel Macron as "a flirt with older people"[49].

Pierre Bergé had recently "married" the landscape architect Madison Cox. The name of Madison Cox, who inherited Pierre Bergé's fortune, will come up in the summer of 2019 when the unexpurgated version of Jeffrey Epstein's *Black Book*, dated 2004-2005, is circulated. Madison Cox, landscaper for international billionaires and decorator of the gardens of Bergé's estates in France and Morocco, has a special place in the address book of the master blackmailer of the world's hyperclass, with a well-documented entry in the section concerning Epstein's island, Little Saint-James... Undisputed and indisputable, this document, which suggests at least a collaboration in the development of the infamous island of pedophilia, was never mentioned by the mainstream press in France.

At the time of pedophile writer Gabriel Matzneff's downfall in 2020, Christophe Girard, who was Yves Saint Laurent's general secretary, gave Pierre Bergé credit as the "generous, unconditional patron of his work" mentioned by Vanessa Springora in *Le Consentement*[50], an autobiographical account in which she tells of her affair with Gabriel Matzneff when she was 14 and he 49[51].

In 2012, a priest in the South of France alerted the French police about cases of cases of "prostitution of minors at the Villa Majorelle, owned by Yves Saint Laurent and Pierre Bergé, where [former Socialist minister] Jack Lang was a regular guest"[52]. An accusation that Pierre Bergé refuted, not without ambiguity, a few months before his death: "Back then, morals were freer than they are today, especially in Morocco. Sexuality was more unbridled, and we paid less attention to it. When they say I was having orgies in Marrakech with Jack Lang and little boys – I wouldn't even have wanted to, because I don't like little boys"[53]…

Fabrice Thomas, a former employee of Pierre Bergé, did not believe this ambiguous denial. Fabrice Thomas, son of an incestuous father who was Pierre Bergé's sex slave, in turn became Pierre Bergé's chauffeur and sex slave… Now living in Canada where he has rebuilt his life with a woman, Fabrice Thomas has recounted his eight years (1984-1992) in the service of the couple formed by Pierre Bergé and Yves Saint Laurent in a totally explosive book[54]. Against a backdrop of "*parties fines* that would have pleased the Marquis de Sade more than the fragile Marcel Proust", Fabrice Thomas tells how he alternates sexual relationships to please Yves Saint Laurent's "masochistic passion" and Pierre Bergé's "sadistic passion".

In an interview with journalist Jacques Thomet, Fabrice Thomas opened up about the extent of Yves Saint Laurent's sadism, first revealing that an episode of coprophagia was responsible for the end of the relationship between Pierre Bergé and Yves Saint Laurent ("one day, after tying [Yves Saint Laurent] to a chair, [Pierre Bergé] forced the fashion designer to swallow his own excrement"), before asserting that Yves Saint Laurent didn't touch minors, but that the latter had "told him over and over that Pierre Bergé was banging kids in Morocco. He was very attracted to prepubescent girls"[55].

His experience and Yves Saint Laurent's confidences prompted Fabrice Thomas to ask himself what interpretation should be given to *La Vilaine Lulu*[56], a character created by Yves Saint Laurent: "He had himself already confessed this publicly, in a way, when he produced the comic strip *La Vilaine Lulu* (*The Ugly Lulu*), a plain-looking, cynical, sadistic and pedophile child character, in a book that is regularly republished. Yet his role was not in sadism. Several times I had asked him why he'd done the comic strip, and invariably he'd flash a sardonic, half-angel, half-demon smile. [...] Whose projection was this heroine?"[57]. Some of the plates in *La Vilaine Lulu* feature child sacrifices "offered to Venus".

Jack Lang

An old and inseparable accomplice of Pierre Bergé, Jack Lang (already mentioned above) has been a central figure in French State culture since the 1980s. Since the arrival of Emmanuel Macron, he has been the undisputed head of the Institut du Monde Arabe (IMA). Twice, in 2020 and 2023, Emmanuel Macron has reappointed this former Socialist Minister of Education and Culture to this golden post combining travel, social events, diplomacy and influence. Jack Lang recently launched the artistic and social career of Laurence Auzière (billed as "Brigitte's" daughter), who until then had just been a cardiologist in

Jack Lang ✔ @jack_lang · 7h
Très heureux d'avoir accueilli @iambilalhassani à l'Institut du Monde arabe.

The embodiment of France in the Arab-Muslim world, Jack Lang poses here at the Institut du Monde Arabe with North African transvestite Bilal Hassani (X, September 19, 2021). Hassani, an "LGBT icon", never misses an opportunity to express his admiration for the presidential couple, going so far as to declare: "Brigitte Macron is my queen, I love her too much. She's a legend"[75].

the Paris chic suburbs. Since Emmanuel Macron came to power, Jack Lang has been present at every event and on every official trip. In short, Jack Lang embodies France in the Arab-Muslim world.

In 1977, Jack Lang was one of the main promoters of a petition aimed at influencing the trial of three men on trial for "non-violent indecent assault on minors under 15", who were remanded in custody for photographing and filming "sexual games" with children aged 12 or 13. Signed by 80 intellectuals who proclaimed "Three years in prison for caresses and kisses, that's enough! "The petition was published simultaneously by *Le Monde* and *Libération*[58].

In January 2020, a year before the Duhamel affair broke out, Jack Lang had been mentioned by one of the petition's signatories, Bernard Kouchner (the absent father of Antoine Kouchner raped by his stepfather Olivier Duhamel) to justify his own signature: "His petition? I haven't even read Matzneff's petition! Daniel Cohn-Bendit and I signed it because Jack Lang asked us to. That was forty years ago. This is a huge mistake. There was clearly a whiff of pedophilia behind it" [59]. A year later, on the radio, Jack Lang was summoned to explain this pro-pedophile petition. He only conceded that he was "carried away by a libertarian vision... a faulty revendication" [60].

Jack Lang is a militant libertarian. He has never concealed it. In 1998, in its "nightclubbing" section, *Libération* [61] reported his presence at the inauguration of the Parisian club *Le Dépôt*: "On Thursday, at 8.45pm, Jack Lang honored the *Cité des Hommes*, visited as a neighbor by Thierry Mugler, with *Le Dépôt* in the basement. A club featuring *"cinémathèque à partouze, go-gos en cage et fistés en sling"* [for the non-initiated: this means that dancers are sodomized with fists in cages where they sit on swings opportunely pierced] are discovered through a labyrinth of sixty booths, moleskin living rooms, holes and bowls and a bluish *dance floor"*. These libertarian activities between consenting adults do not pose a problem... Even if they sometimes go wrong and lead Jack Lang to become a "character witness" for Jorge Lopes da Fonseca, a high-ranking civil servant "hors cadre" (with no fixed assignment) in the Ministry of Culture, sentenced to ten years in prison in October 2000 for strangling the owner of a swinger bar during a sadomasochistic session.

But in the case of the 1977 petition, it concerned "sexual crimes against minors", which he describes as a "faulty revendication". All the more so since, in 2001, when asked about the petition, this time he had fully assumed his responsibilities: "There was a leaden blanket hanging over society in the 1970s, an official society that denied teenagers' sexuality" [62].

In addition to the testimony of the priest from the south of France who had denounced cases of "prostitution of minors at the Villa Majorelle, owned by Yves Saint Laurent and Pierre Bergé, where Jack Lang was a regular guest"[63], there is a note from the notebooks of Yves Bertrand, the former head of the *Renseignements généraux* [the police's intelligence service]: "Lang at La Mamounia in Nov. [2001] did little boys" [64]. On September 2, 1996, Yves Bertrand had also written a note (which went unheeded) warning the Minister of the Interior of the "forthcoming media relaunch of a pedophilia case involving Jack and Monique Lang" [65]: "Following the suicide in 1988 of a 15-year-old resident of the *Centre international de la danse* in Cannes, a pedophile affair broke out involving several of the Centre's managers, including Rosella Hightower and her concubine Rabier, a pedophile painter. [...] Warrant Officer Candela, in charge of the investigation, is said to have privately confided at the time that the wiretaps revealed the names of Jack and Monique Lang, Monique making appointments for her husband with residents of the Center. The gendarmerie officer is even said to have mentioned scurrilous details about the Minister of Culture's proclivities. In one of the wiretaps, Monique asked for a glass table to be set up so that her husband could see his wife having sex with a young teenager. However, the wiretaps were not included in the proceedings. But it is said that the recording tapes should in principle be registered at the Grasse court registry. However, it seems plausible that the instigators of the smothering of the affair took care to remove any trace likely to compromise them, except for questioning Warrant Officer Candela".

Back in the 1980s, when he was François Mitterrand's Minister of Culture, Jack Lang's name came up in a pedophilia scandal about *Le Coral*, a center for troubled children with cases of rape and where an 11-year-old handicapped boy was found dead, sodomized and his head in a bucket of bleach with broken cervical vertebrae[66]. Among the personalities whose names had come to light in this affair was children's judge Jean-Pierre Roseczveig[67], at the time chief of staff to the Socialist Minister for Family, now a supporter of Emmanuel Macron, a member of the National Council for Child Protection and, in 2019, a member of the Independent Commission on Sexual Abuse in the Church. Although the Coral affair was hushed up, one of those in charge of the police investigation, Patrick Riou[68], explained to the judges that he could distinguish "four types of adults who attended

86

Le Coral at the time: 1) blameless individuals who devoted themselves with immense generosity to the hard work; 2) those accused of pedophilia by children and adults, and more or less openly acknowledging it; 3) those accused by children, "who could not have been unaware of what was going on": and 4) avowed pedophiles who came for weekends"[69]. Years later, during a search of a storage box belonging to Commandant Christian Prouteau, founder of the *Groupe de sécurité de la présidence de la République* (GSPR, the French Secret Service) under François Mitterrand, a file entitled *"Coral ballets bleus"* was discovered, including documents in which "the names of several political figures appear, as well as photocopies of very telling photographs"[70]. Christian Prouteau's right-hand man, Captain Paul Barril, explained: "I remember we were told to stop the investigation into the "Coral" pedophile ring, because of the personalities involved"[71].

More recently, a mysterious donation of $57,897 made in 2018 by Jeffrey Epstein to the *Association pour la promotion de la politique culturelle nationale menée dans les années 1980 et 1990 du XXᵉ siècle*, hosted and managed by Jack Lang's close entourage[72], has come to light. The relationship between Jeffrey Epstein and Jack Lang was already largely known and seems to go back a long way. In the first part of the *Black book*, for example, one of the contacts of Ghislaine Maxwell is Jack Lang's youngest daughter Caroline Lang, who began her career in Robert Maxwell's orbit at Maxwell Communication Corporation, then at Maxwell Macmillan Publishing before joining Warner. Jeffrey Epstein's Parisian steward[73] had also mentioned, as early as the summer of 2019, visits to 22, avenue Foch, by ""ministers in office today [therefore under Emmanuel Macron] or who belonged to past governments". Among them is Jack Lang [...] who has invited Jeffrey Epstein to the 30th anniversary celebrations of the Louvre Pyramid in March 2019. The two men met several years ago at a dinner organized in Woody Allen's honor at the Paris home of the Princess of Bourbon of the Two Sicilies. "Epstein was a charming, courteous and pleasant person" says Jack Lang, referring to an "occasional contact". "I have only been to his place on avenue Foch once for lunch. It's true that he was often accompanied by a few pretty women, but they were obviously not minors", says the former minister"[74].

1. *La Familia grande*, Camille Kouchner, Seuil, 2021.

2. In Les Genêts d'Or, generations of Duhamels hosted top-level protaginists of French politicians and intelligentsia: Edgar Faure, François Mitterrand, Simone and Antoine Veil, Marcel Bleustein-Blanchet, Jean-Luc Lagardère, Luc Ferry, Elisabeth Guigou, Jean Veil, Alain Finkielkraut, Marc Guillaume, Nadia Marik, Aurélie Filippetti, François Hollande, etc.

3. *L'Obs*, January 14, 2021.

4. *Paris Match*, January 21, 2021.

5. *France Soir*, April 30, 2004.

6. *Le Monde*, January 15, 2021.

7. A valuable source on the club *Le Siècle* is *Au cœur du pouvoir: Enquête sur le club le plus puissant de France*, Emmanuel Ratier, Facta, 2015.

8. *Libération*, January 11, 2021.

9. *Le Monde*, January 26, 2021.

10. This episode was first narrated in *Olivier Duhamel, son déjeuner avec Brigitte Macron (lexpress.fr*, January 13, 2021), then by *Le Monde* (January 15, 2021).

11. *Le Monde*, December 10, 2022.

12. *Libération*, April 5, 2022.

13. The eminence grise role of Laurent Bigorgne, director of Institut Montaigne during Emmanuel Macron's 2017 campaign, has been widely documented, notably by the *MacronLeaks*.

14. See *Chapter 2*.

15. Cf the press release published on December 11, 2020 by Face à l'inceste.

16. In *Le Livre de la Honte* (Le Cherche Midi, 2001), journalists Laurence Beneux and Serge Garde discovered that even before the affair was brought to light by the press, the Elysée Palace had received the documents – CD-ROMs containing thousands of child pornography files: "In April 1999, the Presidency received these documents and acknowledged their receipt. Logically enough, a presidential advisor quickly forwarded the document to the Chancellery and, given the seriousness of the facts, asked to be kept informed of further developments. This was not done. Why did the Minister of Justice, Elisabeth Guigou, make a call on a television channel, asking us journalists for a document... that her departments had possessed for a year? Above all, we wondered how the country's justice system had dealt with a CD-ROM revealing such heinous crimes perpetrated on children, how the little victims were being searched for... In short, we tried to understand what had happened. And we asked. The answer is incredible. After receiving the CD-ROM from the Élysée, the Chancellery forwarded it to the Paris Public Prosecutor's Office on May 14, 1999 for investigation by the Paris Public Prosecutor. The Minors' Brigade of Paris was called in and informed the public prosecutor's office of the results of its investigations on June 17, 1999. There was a blitz investigation that lasted less than a month!

Finally, on July 7, 1999, the public prosecutor closed the case "in the absence of any criminal offence"! [...] The police had noted the same thing as us: pornographic images of minors. Let's be clear. We're talking about babies being sodomized, very young children being forced to perform fellatio, and all other kinds of sexual acts that definitely rule out any notion of consent, given the age of the victims".

17. *Le Parisien*, April 7, 2004.

18. *Le cavalier seul diplomatique d'Emmanuel Macron*, *Le Monde*, December 14, 2022.

19. *Mort d'un pasteur*, Bernard Violet, Fayard, 1994.

20. *Ibid.*

21. *Petit dictionnaire de l'euro*, Olivier Duhamel and Daniel Cohn-Bendit, Seuil. 1998.

22. Long forgotten, Daniel Cohn-Bendit's pedophile texts resurfaced in *The Observer* (January 28, 2001) after being retrieved by Bettina Röhl, daughter of Red Army Faction co-founder Ulrike Meinhof.

23. *Le Grand Bazar*, Belfond, 1975.

24. *Destins, Télévision suisse romande,* October 7, 1975.

25. *Apostrophes, Antenne 2*, April 23 1982.

26. Interview with *Die Welt*, July 27, 2013.

27. *Le Point*, October 25, 2018.

28. *Mon bonheur, c'est les autres*, Jean-Marc Borello, Débats Publics Éditions, 2022

29. In the latest statutes of Emmanuel Macron's party published in October 2022, Jean-Marc Borello is in charge of the "fight against interference and fake news".

30. Quoted in *Le Monde, Jean-Marc Borello, l'homme qui fait du social un business*, December 6, 2018.

31. *L'Express*, December 18, 2019.

32. Director of *Macron, en marche vers l'Élysée (France 2*, 2017) and *Macron, la fin de l'innocence (France 3*, 2018), Bertrand Delais was later promoted head of *La Chaîne Parlementaire*. The *MacronLeaks* reveal that he co-edited Emmanuel Macron's "board" lecture (*planche*) before the Freemasons of the *Grand Orient de France* in 2016.

33. At the same time as he was organizing Emmanuel Macron's visit to the Freemasons, Éric Moniot was running the programs for *La Chaîne Parlementaire*, which he left in 2018 in strange circumstances, under a judicial investigation opened on February 5, 2022 for drug trafficking and criminal conspiracy. The judicial authorities suspect him of having participated in a money-laundering network linked to this traffic, involving prefect Jean Mafart (who had worked for the DGSE and DGSI before being promoted to Director of European and International Affairs at the Ministry of the Interior's central administration in 2020): "Both, reports *Le Canard enchaîné* (February 23, 2022), are closely linked to 30-year-old businessman Oussama Oualid, who was indicted on February 5. They are suspected

of having participated in the laundering of his income. Oualid had been indicted for transporting, buying and selling cocaine and other synthetic treats (methamphetamine and ketamine) in "quantities too large to correspond to his personal consumption". Listed in the wanted persons file, he was in a civil partnership from 2015 to 2019 with Place Beauvau's current head of international relations, under the noses of the French secret services. [...] Oualid has set up several companies in the import-export, construction and IT sectors. [...] At OML Systèmes, founded in February 2016, the young man is both the president and sole employee. [...] On July 26, 2017, the small company landed an improbable "services contract" with the *LCP-AN* channel [*La Chaîne Parlementaire - Assemblée Nationale*], represented by Éric Moniot... who admitted to the cops that he was having an affair with Oualid. [...] In addition to the initial contract (€ 37,000 excluding taxes), there were a maintenance follow-up and additional services. In the end, *LCP-AN* - whose premises were raided in October - spent over € 92,000, well over the threshold (€ 25,000) requiring a public tender."

34. *Richie*, Raphaëlle Bacqué, *Grasset*, 2015.

35. *Macron's real boss*, Le Point, March 2, 2017.

36. Gérard Luçon, a former civil servant at the Ministry of Justice who became director of the NGO Handicap International in Romania, witnessed Jean-Marc Borello's early career. In a text published online, "For most of the media, for those who follow the career paths of our 'great men', Jean-Marc Borello's life began in 1981 with his appointment in the wake of the French 'Socialists' accession to power. [...] Borello trained as a specialized educator, so in the "private" sector; so far this is nothing very special, except that, during this training, he obtained in 1979-1980 something particularly rare, namely to carry out part of this training at the Ministry of Justice, with the Supervised Education service [*Direction de l'Éducation surveillée*, which became *Protection judiciaire de la jeunesse* (DPJJ) in 1990]. The deal was negotiated between Borello and the director of the ISES (*Internat spécialisé d'éducation surveillée*) in La Roche Verte, Marseilles, apparently without any internship director from his teacher training school. The children housed in this ISES are teenage girls aged 15 until they come of age, and boys aged 10 to 15. The director of this ISES is Roland Pouget, a well-known figure, dynamic, paunchy, with furious fits of anger, and highly autocratic. He is single and lives in an apartment on the same floor as the children. He is accomodating a young adult boy, named "B...u", to whom he allegedly has a liking since his previous position in an institution in north-eastern France, where the youngster was in educational care. Pouget explained to the staff that Borello is from Gardanne, in Provence, therefore a "local" [...]. Borello's internship was of course validated by Pouget, and he evaporated to settle in Paris as a young special educator. In 1981, ISES went through a crisis that was difficult to identify, but which caused seven of its educational staff to request and obtain transfers. A few months later, Roland Pouget was caught up in an ugly case of pedophilia involving youth from ISES. He was immediately arrested, and a local newspaper got hold of this sordid affair and published an article. There was no second article, and the affair was suddenly totally muzzled! [...] Because Pouget had announced that he was going to speak out and that heads would roll,

he was released and, from the position of director of an institution, became deputy departmental director of supervised education in the Essonne department! What did Pouget know? Who were the people and personalities he could bring down? [...] And of course, in view of these events, what were the links between Borello and Pouget, bearing in mind that Borello was later implicated in a nasty affair, again involving officials from the Education Department? "

37. In her autobiography, *Appelle-moi par mon prénom* (Robert Laffont, 1986) Régine Choukroun, née Zylberberg, tells how the Rothschild family helped her build her nightlife empire: "I was talking about the people who allegedly "financed" me; the Rothschilds would have been among them. Let's get one thing straight. I knew the Rothschilds at the time of the Twist club. [...] They found me funny, nicely, rotund and humorous. And I was Jewish. Élie and Éric came first. One day, when we knew each other a little, they said to me: "You're famous, people are talking about you – you can help a lot of people". In fact, yes, it was they who asked me to help them with the charities, not the other way round. But thanks to them, I came out of my unconsciousness and my madness. I realized what I could do to really help the State of Israel in a serious way. [...] The Rothschilds, on the other hand, made me realize the true dimension of the problems, and I began to work for the associations they look after. [...] I don't have the Rothschilds behind me or in front of me, they're next to me and I'm next to them. [...] We have, they towards me and I towards them, very precise places to hold, a game to play, and I believe that each of us plays it to the full".

38. Although he denied having been aware of the trafficking, the court nevertheless ruled that "the material elements [...] gathered make it possible to consider that Mr. Borello was aware of the trafficking and consumption taking place in his establishment. [...] In fact, Mr. Borello appears as the manager of a commercial group [...] of which *Le Palace* was the "flagship", as he put it. This group needed the kind of high sales that only *Le Palace* could provide; the relaunch of *after* parties was part of this business strategy. To achieve this, it was necessary to tolerate the presence of dealers who were also efficient attractors of customers ("locomotives"). Mr. Borello agreed to it, implicitly no doubt, but effectively".

39. *Le Parisien,* December 8, 2004.

40. Quoted in *Libération,* May 11, 2006.

41. *Jean-Marc Borello, l'homme qui fait du social un business, Le Monde,* December 6, 2018.

42. Médiapart, June[1,] 2022.

43. *Jean-Marc Borello, l'homme qui fait du social un business, Le Monde,* December 6, 2018.

44. *Les Echos,* February 4, 2022.

45. Opinion column published in *Le Monde* on January 22, 2010.

46. *Jean-Marc Borello, enquête sur un #MeToo gay, Libération,* December 21, 2018.

47. *Town & Country,* September 2017.

48. Quoted by l'*AFP,* January 31, 2017.

49. Quoted by Anne Fulda in *Un jeune homme si parfait*, Plon, 2017.

50. *Le Consentement*, Vanessa Springora, Grasset, 2020.

51. *A Pedophile Writer Is on Trial. So Are the French Elites*, The New York Times, February 11, 2020.

52. Quoted in *Pédophilie à Marrakech. L'enquête impossible*, *VSD* n° 1857, March 28, 2013.

53. *Le Marrakech de Saint Laurent et Bergé, Stupéfiant!*, France 2, November 23, 2016.

54. *Saint Laurent et moi - une histoire intime*, Fabrice Thomas, Hugo Doc, 2017.

55. Quoted in *La Pédocratie à la française*, Jacques Thomet, Éditions Fabert, 2021

56. *La Vilaine Lulu*, Yves Saint Laurent, Tchou, 1967.

57. *Saint Laurent et moi - une histoire intime*, Fabrice Thomas, Hugo Doc, 2017

58. *Le Monde* and *Libération*, January 26, 1977.

59. *Lepoint.fr*, January 11, 2020.

60. Interviewed by Sonia Mabrouk on *Europe 1*, January 18, 2021.

61. *Libération*, October 26, 1998.

62. *L'Express*, March 1, 2001.

63. Quoted in *Pédophilie à Marrakech. L'enquête impossible*, *VSD* n° 1857, March 28, 2013.

64. *Libération*, July 22, 2011.

65. The authenticity of this note has never been questioned. Yves Bertrand, who headed the *Renseignements Généraux* between 1992 and 2004, even took credit for it before journalists Christophe Deloire and Christophe Dubois in their investigation, published as *Sexus Politicus* (Albin Michel, 2006).

66. *Le Monde*, November 18, 1982.

67. *L'animateur du "Feuilleton du Coral"* a été écroué, *Le Monde*, February 28, 1983.

68. Patrick Riou was deputy head of *Brigade des stupéfiants* (the drugs and pimping squad) at the time.

69. Quoted in *Le Monde*, January 13, 1986.

70. *Le Figaro Magazine*, March 8, 1997.

71. Public hearing, April 29, 1997.

72. See *The Daily Beast* (October 5, 2020) and *Politico* (October 14, 2020).

73. On October 4, 2019, *France Info* opened a track worth exploring by revealing that Jeffrey Epstein's Franco-Brazilian butler, Valdson Vieira Cotrin, was previously in the service of François Dalle, the former L'Oréal boss who, alongside André Bettencourt and Pierre Guillain de Bénouville, formed the clan of François Mitterrand's youthful friends and lifelong loyalists described in *En bande organisée: Mitterrand, le pacte secret* by Sébastien Le Fol (Albin Michel, 2023).

74. *France Info*, August 30, 2019.

75. *Libération, January 21, 2019.*

11

THE AUTHORS
OF THE "OFFICIAL LEGEND"

Formed by covering Dominique Strauss-Kahn's lifestyle

May 14, 2011, New York City, 4:40pm. Dominique Strauss-Kahn, Managing Director of the IMF, is arrested at New York's JFK airport. This prominent Socialist, ahead in the polls for the forthcoming French presidential election, is accused of having sexually assaulted a few hours earlier a chambermaid, Nafissatou Diallo, in suite 2806 of the Sofitel hotel in New York. DSK's addiction to sex and his insistence with women were common knowledge, but the main figures of the Socialist Party feign astonishment on television. In this month of May 2011, everyone is repeating the same language in the form of denial: "I know Dominique. It's not like him".

This was a formula concocted by a team of crisis communicators from Euro RSCG who, have been, for years, organizing and protecting the lifestyle of the libidinous Managing Director of the IMF: Anne Hommel, Stéphane Fouks, Ramzi Khiroun, Gilles Finchelstein and Ismaël Emelien.

This time, their champion's political career is really over. Part of this team will be tasked with building the "official legend" of the Macron couple, as soon as 2012, when Emmanuel Macron took over the Élysée from François Hollande: "Gilles Finchelstein will be working with

DSK to prepare his presidential candidacy step by step. He remembered the kid's name [Emmanuel Macron] [...] A few years later, it was Macron's turn to listen to this brainy young man, who became one of the secret guests of his strategy dinners. Once appointed Deputy Secretary General of the Élysée Palace, he is a frequent guest of the Gilles Finchelstein-Ismaël Emelien duo, reconstituted at Euro RSCG, now Havas. "We were his trusted brainstormers", recalls Fincheslstein, who denies being "his advisor" [...]. But "We were his eyes and ears", says the second. [...] Everyone is required to remain silent after leaving the premises. Gilles Finchelstein often introduces the discussion"[1]. "Brigitte" is both a topic and the cornerstone of the discussions: "Every Sunday evening, the couple hold secret meetings in a room situated in the east wing of the Élysée Palace. [...]"How can I have a public profile?" That's really the question. On the agenda: discussing about of his popularity, his media strategy and his relationship with the press, his relations with the bosses. His wife "Brigitte" is almost always present, and not with an auxiliary role: she gives her opinion, leads the discussion, and moderates it, allocating talking turns"[2].

In fact, the wording for the first misleading version of the encounter (served between June 2012 and April 2016), of their being "almost twenty years apart" in a relationship which began when "she was 36 and him, 17", and of a teacher "troubled" and "captivated" by a "brilliant" student, bore the hallmark of Gilles Finchelstein[3]. His touch can be spotted in three anecdotes told by "Brigitte" and widely echoed by the press: "To those who ask, she simply slips in, in a tone of secrecy, the same three anecdotes that sum up her romance with "Emmanuel": a remark by second daughter, (who first spoke to him at Lycée *La Providence* in Amiens) about a "crazy character who knew everything about everything"; the young prodigy's departure for Paris, swearing he would return to marry her; and her certainty, from the moment they met, that she would always live with him"[4].

And when Emmanuel Macron was appointed Minister of the Economy, Ismaël Emelien, Gilles Fichelstein's right-hand man, joined his cabinet. Emmanuel Macron even presented him as his "closest collaborator" when, in November 2015, the team of *communicants* was reinforced by Joël Benenson, an influential American spin doctor haloed by his success with Barack Obama during the 2008 and 2012 presidential elections[5]. Joel Benenson's specialty: his opinion polls, which helped sell to the US public the Barack and Michelle couple.

Yet the confidential polls commissioned on the "Brigitte" case did not produce the expected results: "Early in 2016, the wife of the future president had gone so far as to canvass several profiles of PR advisors, and meet some of them, to replace Ismaël Emelien", reports *Marianne*[6]: "A few months later, in autumn 2016, it was this time the young advisor who, on the basis of qualitative opinion surveys, advised his boss to put less emphasis on his wife. "She was considered too much into '*show off*'[sic in French], almost too '*bling-bling*' for Macron", an insider explains. However, candidate Macron never ruled against his wife. [...] On the evening of the first round, when the campaign team met at the brasserie La Rotonde [a chic *brasserie* in Montparnasse] – originally "Brigitte's" idea –, Emelien was denied access to the floor where the future president was dining. Brigitte Macron would not admit the man who tried to oust her at the start of the campaign..."

When the couple's media presence was not well established yet, on the rare occasions when discourse was not carefully filtered, "Brigitte", far from the elegant and refined literature-fond woman officially presented, projected an entirely different image, with a series of heavy-handed and often gross innuendos: "Montaigne said: You always have to polish your brain but rubbing it against someone else's. It is very important for progress. So we rub a lot"[7]. [In French, *limer* can be used as a vulgar sexual metaphor]. In a sequence that could have fitted in Sacha Baron Cohen's provocative character *Brüno*, "Brigitte" and "Emmanuel" giggle at homosexual writer Philippe Besson's jokes about the anatomy of "Makao", their Congolese bodyguard[8]...

Later, it was established that the language used to describe Emmanuel Macron as "handsome" and Brigitte as "her husband's charming asset, the embodiment of French glamour" was entirely bogus:

"Several of his advisors [...] point to opinion polls in which French women explain that the almost forty-year-old [...] doesn't thrill them as so charming. Electorally dangerous. Jacques Chirac and Nicolas Sarközy, on the other hand, were perceived by some women voters as sex symbols. At the end of 2016, an extract from a qualitative study by Ipsos on Macron's presidential image provided more evidence for the detractors of the future First Lady. "The covers of *Paris Match* and the spotlight on Brigitte Macron did not cause virulent reactions, but an agreement was quickly reached to enforce greater discretion towards the media about her private life, in particular the visibility of her family," he wrote in highly diplomatic language. *Exit* Brigitte?"[9].

About the tense relationship between "Brigitte" and Ismaël Emelien's team, journalists Nathalie Schuck and Ava Djamshidi write that they "dream of her dying. For them, this grieving widower would be great for PR. They are in love with him. At night, they dream of making her disappear"[10]… Ismaël Emelien left the Élysée in the spring of 2019, allegedly to write an essay on progressivism (a complete failure despite copious media hype). But the real reason for his exit from the scheme was obviously his disagreement with "Brigitte" and the revelations by *Le Monde* of his January 16, 2019 hearing by the *Inspection générale de la police nationale* (IGPN), the '*police des polices*', i.e. the service policing all police services" , during which he sheepishly admitted having coordinated trolling operations and the diffusion of fake news on *Twitter* during the fall of Alexandre Benalla, the Macrons' bodyguard and handyman.

When communication goes wrong

Yet, after trying to oust "Brigitte", Ismaël Emelien was at the helm during the disastrous media sequence in the summer of 2018, a revealing event that was one of the unspoken causes of the popular revolt of the *Gilets jaunes*…

The swerve took place on June 21, 2018. For the *Fête de la Musique*, the presidential couple organized a public evening in the courtyard of the Élysée Palace. The star guests: a troupe of African transvestites dancing on the porch to the music of a DJ with a T-Shirt emblazoned with the words "Son of an immigrant, black and fag". The whole of France watched in amazement as the presidential couple swayed to the sound of this gay rap music: "Tonight, let's burn this house down, let's burn it down completely", "don't sit down, bitch, please", "dance, motherfucker, dance", "you're mad at

me because I've had my d... sucked and my a... licked", and so on. "When I saw the transgenders on the stoop, I thought about Yvonne de Gaulle and Bernadette Chirac. Sixty years ago, Mme de Gaulle banned divorcees from the Élysée Palace, and now we're bringing in a queer DJ and his transgender dancers..." confided a dismayed advisor of the President of the Republic[11].

As a reminder of the evening, this photo, reproduced here on the front page of the Catholic conservative daily *Présent*[12], was posted on *Instagram* by "Brigitte's" cabinet, then consisting of Pierre-Olivier Costa[13] and Tristan Bromet. Their nickname at the Élysée Palace was "the chicks" [*les meufs*: a familiar word for *femmes*].

The *Fête de la Musique* was followed, at the end of September, by Emmanuel Macron's solo tour of the Caribbean (planned and organized by Ismaël Emelien) with the catastrophic image of a President of the Republic giving in to his impulses, groping bare-chested West Indian robbers in front of the stunned French...

Between queer exhibition at the Élysée in June and the West Indian tour endearing delinquents in September, Emmanuel Macron traveled to Nigeria. He has never tried to hide his physical attraction to soccer players Paul Pogba and Kylian Mbappé during several editions of the FIFA World Cup. In his "road trip" to the Nigerian capital Lagos (where he had stayed during his internship for *École Nationale d'Admininstration*), he treated himself to an afrobeat night at the *New Afrika Shrine*, the hot nightclub in town.

In November 2019, when Internet users suspect Emmanuel Macron of having received Serbian conceptual artist Marina Abramović at the Élysée Palace, *Libération*'s website's *Checknews* section [14] insisted that this guest should not be called plainly Marina Abramović "but the artist Rouge Mary, self-defined as non-binary, trigender and, why not, more"…

1. *Emmanuel Macron, en marche vers l'Élysée*, Nicolas Prissette, 2016, Plon.

2. *Le Grand Manipulateur*, Marc Endeweld, Stock, 2019.

3. In *Les Strauss-Kahn* (Albin Michel, 2012), Raphaëlle Bacqué and Ariane Chemin reveal how Gilles Finchelstein crafted his public language with Dominique Strauss-Kahn, from the time of the MNEF affair (a case of personal enrichment and fake jobs affecting the *Mutuelle nationale des étudiants de France*): "Gilles Finchelstein reports that many of them still trust in Dominique Strauss-Kahn. Well-versed in militant argumentation and already experts in producing catch-phrases for public relations, they repeat the very same word to excuse their boss: oversight (*légèreté*), presented not as a flaw but a somewhat inevitable trait of the gifted, brilliant, care-free person who has neither the taste nor the desire to bother with the trivial aspects. They reiterate that "Dominique may have sinned out of oversight, but justice will clear him, and he'll be back". Ten years later, the Piroska Nagy affair [of illicit favors by DSK to an economist of the IMF] broke out: "On October 19, 2008, Anne Sinclair, wife of Dominique Strauss-Kahn, posted on her blog a text largely inspired by this PR pair. "Many of you sent me very kind messages yesterday after the article in the *Wall Street Journal* and the echo it had in France." This touched me." [...] and the crusty punchline: "Everyone knows that these are things that can happen in the life of any couple. As far as I'm concerned, this one-night stand is now behind us. We have turned the page. May I add in conclusion that we love each other as we did on the first day?" "Frankly, we've done very well," says Gilles Finchelstein with satisfaction. "Then, after the Sofitel scandal: "Why did they choose these words that they are all repeating? Jean-Christophe Cambadélis firmly declares: "At this time, I neither want nor can draw hasty conclusions from Dominique Strauss-Kahn's indictment, but this whole story is not like him [*ça ne lui ressemble pas*]." Jean-Marie Le Guen: "We must be careful not to draw any conclusions before Dominique Strauss-Kahn has spoken. And then, most importantly, this case is not like DSK, the man we all know." Pierre Moscovici: "Let us wait for DSK's version of the events. I've known him for thirty years, and this is not like what I know of him." François Pupponi: "Caution must be the watchword here. All I can tell you is that what we're being portrayed as is absolutely nothing like the Dominique Strauss-Kahn I know." Everywhere the same incredulity in the form of denial. And the same recurrent wording: "It's not like him."

4. *Compagne présidentielle*, Le Monde, April 18, 2017.

5. *Ismaël Emelien, le très discret homme du président*, Le Monde, February 2, 2019.

6. *Marianne*, October 27, 2017.

7. *Canal +*, November 14, 2015.

8. "Philippe Besson - Do you have any special protection tonight? Emmanuel Macron: - I've got Makao, a guy who wears shoe size 54. Besson: - It makes you dream about the rest! Macron: - Yeah! (everyone laughs) ." The sequence was aired on TMC's *Quotidien* program on June 3, 2017.

9. *Madame la Présidente*, Nathalie Schuck and Ava Djamshidi, Plon, 2019.

10. *Madame la Présidente*, Nathalie Schuck and Ava Djamshidi, Plon, 2019.

11. *Madame la Présidente*, Nathalie Schuck and Ava Djamshidi, Plon, 2019.

12. *Présent*, June 26, 2018.

13. Pierre-Olivier Costa left the Élysée in October 2022 for the presidency of the *Musée des civilisations de l'Europe et de la Méditerranée* (Mucem) in Marseilles.

14. *Libération.fr*, November 8, 2019.

12

"MIMI", "BRIGITTE" AND
LA LÉGENDE DES SIÈCLES

On the cover of a "Men's Special" issue

To control the public image of "Brigitte" and flood the media with selected pictures, the wannabe presidential couple called on Michèle Marchand, "popess of the celebrity press" in Paris and Monaco. "Mimi", launched by Régine, is another former nightclub owner with good connections among the police. At fifty, she used this underworld

address book to recycle herself in the celebrity press, building a system of not-so-tight sluices leaking some information about some people, while managing and protecting the image of others, notably through staged "paparazzi" sessions or edited photos. With "Mimi" enjoying near-exclusivity over "Brigitte's" public image, the course of their relationship can be tracked via the content of magazine covers, for better (left, "Brigitte Macron – she has won the hearts of Americans"[1]) and for worse (right, "Brigitte" on the cover of a "Men's Special" issue[2])...

The methods of Bestimage, her photography agency, beside this blackmailish approach, range from faking a story (a fictitious interview with Trevor Rees-Jones, Lady Diana's bodyguard, after the fatal accident) to using its connections to produce falsified documents, such as a false Interpol file provided to journalists in order to sink the reputation of the businessman Omar Harfouch[3]...

Through Bestimage, "Mimi" controled "Brigitte's" image from the spring of 2016. It was Xavier Niel, the head of Iliad, who acted as intermediary between the Macrons and her[4]. A key figure in the Macrons' entourage, the telecom tycoon (and son-in-law of billionaire Bernard Arnault) got to know "Mimi" in the early 2000s. They met through their shared lawyer, Caroline Toby, during their respective stays in prison: in Fresnes for "Mimi"[5] and in La Santé for Xavier Niel (remanded in custody for "aggravated pimping" and "concealment of misappropriation of social assets"[6]).

A lot has been written about Xavier Niel[7], the launcher of the *Freebox* and the €2 cellphone subscription plan, today a full member of the global hyperclass, connected to all the Silicon Valley big shots and propelled by Henry Kravis to the board of directors of the powerful American investment fund KKR. However, the role of its storage service, *DL Free*, in hosting child pornography is still too little known, and Free has even been described by the Canadian Centre for Child Protection's *Project Arachnid* as "the largest source of child sexual abuse images"[8].

In June 2024, it was again Xavier Niel who helped out "Mimi", pitching in to save Bestimage, her photo agency. Still in this reciprocal relationship of protection (she is both the "protected" and the "protector") Michèle Marchand is a close associate of another billionaire, Marc Ladreit de Lacharrière[9]. "Mimi's" company is domiciled at 252, rue du Faubourg Saint-Honoré, the address of the Salle Pleyel, owned by Fimalac, Marc Ladreit de Lacharrière's holding company. And it's a small world: Marc Ladreit de Lacharrière never misses an opportunity to make a public appearance with "Brigitte". In November 2022, at the premiere of the musical *Starmania*, its producer Thomas Jolly was recruited, in the presence of "Brigitte"[10], to stage the LGBT-oriented opening ceremony of the Paris 2024 Olympics, culminating in a blasphemous parody of *The Last Supper* by drag queens…

The de Lacharrières' secret

Michèle Marchand's central role and disproportionate importance for the Macrons reached a climax in the spring of 2018, when this photograph of her standing, smiling, gesturing "V" for victory behind the presidential desk was published in the mainstream press[11].

But a few months later, the mood had somewhat cooled, and the Macrons were now trying to distance themselves from her. A biography had just revealed, among other things, that their "Mimi" had blocked the media coverage in 2015 of the judiciary mishap of Marc Ladreit de Lacharrière's eldest son to a thirty-month suspended prison sentence for distributing pornographic images of very young children on the Internet[12]: "In October 2018, the publication of the book *Mimi*, an investigation into her inglorious past [...], finished convincing the presidential couple to take some distance from their "protector", explains *Le Nouvel Obs*[13]. "No more Thursday meetings in the *Madame wing*. Farewell to Mimi's dream of selling Bestimage and having a job at the Élysée Palace. However, the bond was not broken, Mimi told journalists Gérard Davet and Fabrice Lhomme[14]. In March 2019, Emmanuel Macron begged her to retrieve the photos [of Interior Minister] Christophe Castaner in charming company in a nightclub at the height of the *Gilets jaunes* crisis. Mimi kept quiet, only saying "I just shut up" so the president would think twice about it. A few weeks later, a smear bomb exploded in *Closer*: Brigitte was spotted at the entrance to the American Hospital in Paris, for, reportedly cosmetic surgery under general anesthesia. A furious First Lady set a precedent in having the magazine condemned. What game was Mimi playing?"

The day "Mimi" ratted on "Brigitte"

I was puzzled by "Brigitte's" condemnation of *Closer* for breach of privacy, whereas a year earlier, *L'Express*[15] had not been bothered after commenting ironically on "Brigitte's" surgery with Dr Sydney Ohana… What specific information in *Closer's* article[16], admittedly perfidious but totally innocuous for the average reader, could have troubled "Brigitte" so much? The key is the surgeon. Without naming names, *Closer* mentions the American Hospital in Paris, and an "eminent and media-savvy plastic surgeon who would keenly quote Victor Hugo: *"Chair de la femme, argile idéale [Woman's flesh – ideal clay]"* – something that would probably strike a chord with the former French teacher."…

In effect, *Paris Match*[17], in its feature *"Opération rajeunir" [Operation Young again]* published in the wake of the 2017 presidential election, had asked a plastic surgeon at the American Hospital in Paris about the artistic dimension of his work, to which the surgeon responded with a verse by Victor Hugo in *La Légende des Siècles*: *"Chair de la femme, argile idéale"*. Name : Patrick Bui.

Why is *Closer's…* disclosing of Patrick Bui's identity, even obliquely, so embarrassing ? Because he has acquired over more than 25 years a worldwide reputation in "facial morphology" and "volumetric modifications" thanks to his special skill in "feminization of the facial skeleton in transsexualism". Patrick Bui's skills are internationally recognized and recommended for perfecting "male-to-female sex reassignment surgery". In this capacity, for example, he was part of *Team Surgery*[18] magazine's "Special transgender" feature, discussing "Feminizing the face". Why has "Brigitte" called on the services of the world specialist in "feminization of the facial skeleton in the context of transsexualism" ?

In the summer of 2019, via this line from Victor Hug, "Mimi" had launched a scud. In October 10, 2023, at the Élysée[19], "Brigitte" delivered to Bui the medal of *Officier de la Légion d'Honneur*, a high distinction of the French Republic.

1. *Gala*, December 8, 2022.

2. *Gala*, June 15, 2023.

3. *De Voici* à l'Élysée: *Mimi Marchand, la femme d'influence de la République, Complément d'enquête, France 2.* January 13, 2021.

4. *La reine des people au chevet des Macron, Vanity Fair*, April 2017.

5. Michèle Marchand had been jailed in connection with her indictment for aggravated money laundering in the *Voici* magazine slush fund affair. For more on this episode, see *Les Dessous de la presse people* by Léna Lutaud and Thiébault Dromard, Éditions de La Martinière, 2006 and *Les Méthodes choc des paparazzi, Spécial Investigation, Canal+*, November 10, 2009.

6. Although Xavier Niel was dismissed on the pimping charge, but he was found guilty of embezzling 368,000 euros over three years (the tax authorities did not investigate further): he had received part of the sales in cash from the twenty or so peep-show venues and sex shops in which he was a shareholder in Paris and Strasbourg. The alarm had already been raised when he was heard as a witness in a case of pimping organized by two of his associates, the actual managers of New Sex Paradise. When he was received a two-year suspended prison sentence and a € 375,000 fine for misappropriation of corporate assets (he was recovering part of the cash), *Libération* (September 16, 2006) wrote: "Everything is slipping away from him, as are his previous convictions (to mere fines) for false advertising, indecent exposure and hindering the operation of an IT department. On the stand, Niel, who doesn't say much, refers to this "culture of discrete operations": "This instant cash does not give the same feeling of gain as the money I earn in a straight way as a telecom operator. "This episode, which revealed his secret garden, reminds us that Xavier Niel founded Iliad with Fernand Develter, a former Société Générale attorney whom he met "in the mid-1980s at the café Le Petit Ramoneur, which was the meeting place of sex shop employees on rue Saint-Denis" *(Le X, versant obscur du patron de Free, Libération*, September 14, 2006).

7. See, for example, *Xavier Niel - La voie du pirate* by Solveig Godeluck and Emmanuel Paquette, First, 2016.

8. *War Of Words Erupts Over How Billionaire-Owned Telecom Giant Handled Child Pornography Alerts, Forbes.com*, July 23, 2021.

9. A man of shadows and networks, Marc Ladreit de Lacharrière is a graduate of ENA's Robespierre class (which included Jacques Attali, Louis Schweitzer and Philippe Séguin). A close friend of Jacques Chirac and François Hollande, this pillar of the *Le Siècle* club has, by his own admission, a passion: "pulling strings" *(XXI*, December 2011). That's why this Freemason (*L'Express*, April 2, 1998) was president of the French section of the Bilderberg Group (alongside Thierry de Montbrial), co-founder and financier of SOS-Racisme and owner of *Valeurs actuelles*. After failing to take over from François Dalle at the helm of *L'Oréal*, "the man whom the Tout-Paris is courting" (*L'Express*, March 6, 2019) moved into the fold of Rothschild & Cie, via his advisor, Alain Minc, having been one of the sponsors,

with David de Rothschild, of the creation of Euris. Via Fimalac, Marc Ladreit de Lacharrière has long controlled the financial rating agency Fitch, while expanding into the entertainment and digital sectors (Webedia, Allociné, jeuxvideos.com, etc.) via his partner Véronique Morali. Highly committed to the representation of "women and daughters of [big shots]" on various boards of directors, she is a *Young Leader* of the French-American Foundation, Vice-Chairwoman of *Le Siècle*, a member of the Supervisory Board of Edmond de Rothschild, a director of Lagardère and of the Fondation Nationale des Sciences Politiques, the Sciences-Po "holding company" formerly chaired by Olivier Duhamel, of which Marc Ladreit de Lacharrière is a "generous patron"...

10. *Brigitte Macron peut compter sur Mimi*, L'Obs, November 17, 2022 and *Deux hommes et une idée folle*, Le Parisien, July 26, 2024.

11. *Le Point*, May 7, 2018 and *Le Canard enchaîné*, May 9, 2018.

12. The episode was reported by Jean-Michel Décugis, Pauline Guéna and Marc Leplongeon in *Mimi*, the biography of Michèle Marchand published by Grasset in 2018: "When there are children, she never goes there." "Children are her weak point." "She loves children and cannot t stand people who hurt them. She's very family-oriented." Everyone agrees on this, even her detractors: Mimi protects children. On October 7, 2015, in a closed-door trial before the Paris Correctional Court, Jérémie Ladreit de Lacharrière, 38, was given a 30-month suspended prison sentence for distributing pornographic images of children on the Internet. He is a repeat offender after a first final conviction in 2008 for identical offenses. According to the ruling, Jérémie had been registered since January 2011 on a specialized site hosted in Russia. There he presented forty-six albums entitled girls, boys, kids, containing two thousand seven hundred and twenty-eight nude photos of children. Half of the albums were freely accessible and featured photos of children with their faces and private parts blurred out. The others, protected by a password ("warmly shared at the request of other members", as he indicated in the introductory text) showed unblurred images and close-ups of children's genitalia. One album in particular featured eighty-one shots of the same 3-year-old girl. Jérémie Ladreit de Lacharrière exchanged these photos for shots of young teenagers, specifying that he was only looking for "private and original" material. To avoid checks, he used advanced techniques, including concealing pedophile images within non-objectionable photographs. American cyber-crime units had to spot them and report them to their French counterparts, before an investigation could be launched by the Paris juvenile brigade. The children photographed were those of friends with whom he vacationed at his estate every year. Jérémie Ladreit de Lacharrière was arrested at his home on January 9, 2013. During the search, a photo camera, a video camera , two hundred and thirty-five burned CDs and a large quantity of computer equipment were seized. On the network, Jérémie boasted that he had a previous conviction, and described the precautions he was taking, including a USB key containing thousands of other images, so well hidden that his apartment would have had to be demolished from top to bottom to find it. Confronted with this judicial interception, he agrees to bring the incriminating key to the investigators, who discover only banal videos recently downloaded, so heavy that they have overwritten the previous

content. Mimi met Marc Ladreit de Lacharrière, Jérémie's father, in 2013, when [...] negotiations started to acquire Webedia, the company that owns Purepeople. Mimi hasn't been a shareholder since 2010 (as we have seen, she sold her shares for €500,000), but she has negotiated an outside service contract that allows her to oversee the site, and he wanted to make sure she would continue, she told us. Marc Ladreit de Lacharrière refuses a first summons to the juvenile brigade concerning his son, but ends up going to the second, on the advice of the lawyer he has chosen to defend his son: Me Caroline Toby, who, as we have seen, is Mimi's criminal lawyer, notably in the *Voici* case, as well as that of Xavier Niel. On the day of the hearing, two of the three assessors called in sick and had to be replaced at short notice. The brisk brunette lawyer managed to keep Jérémie Ladreit de Lacharrière out of prison. Given the personality of the father of the accused and the age of the victims (very young children), the case should have been widely publicized. But neither *AFP*, which publishes the judicial agenda, nor the *Association de la presse judiciaire* were aware of this. According to a number of converging sources, Mimi has taken charge personally of this dossier to ensure that nothing leaks out. "In January 2022, Jérémie Ladreit de Lacharrière was imprisoned for the first time on January 14, 2022, after forty-eight hours in police custody at the *Brigade de Protection des Mineurs* (BPM) of the Paris Judicial Police, for "importing, recording and possessing pornographic images of minors". A computer engineer and former Microsoft executive, he has turned to organizing shows with children (Pôle Nord Productions) and is a director of Fimalac, his father's holding company; he was subsequently sentenced by the Paris Criminal Court to a year's imprisonment, with an electronic bracelet and an obligation to undergo medical treatment... At his home, the BPM police seized several computers and an external server. The analysis of this equipment revealed 4,000 files depicting minors, including over 700 images and videos of a child pornographic nature: in other words, in sexual contexts.

13. *L'entremetteuse de la République, L'Obs,* December 23, 2021.

14. *Le Traître et le néant*, Gérard Davet and Fabrice Lhomme, Fayard, 2021.

15. *L'Express*, August 15, 2018.

16. *Closer*, August 2, 2019.

17. *Paris Match*, May 24, 2017.

18. *Team Surgery*, September 2011.

19. Patrick Bui, shown here with "Brigitte" and his sister, stylist Barbara Bui.

PART III

THE INACCESSIBLE PAST OF THE PRESIDENTIAL COUPLE

"My innermost self is dissociated from my public activities. This was already true in my childhood".

Emmanuel Macron, *Vanity Fair*, February 2017.

"Another thing must be mentioned, non-systemic, accidental, which I don't like to talk about but which must be talked about: another reason for Macron's preference for disorder and violence is undoubtedly a personality problem, a serious psychological problem. His relationship with reality is unclear. He is criticized for his contempt for ordinary people. I suspect he hates normal people. His relation to his childhood is unclear. Sometimes he reminds me of those excited children testing for the limit, waiting for an adult to stop them. What would be nice would be for the French people to grow up and stop the Macron child. [...] The situation is extremely dangerous because we may have an out-of-control president in a socio-political system that has become pathological".

Emmanuel Todd, *Marianne*, April 6, 2023.

"I needed photos of Brigitte Macron as a young woman, with small children… showing an itinerary, outside of those stamped by the Bestimage agency. What doesn't come out is anything to do with his former life. It's a total blackout".

Virginie Linhart about her documentary Brigitte Macron, un Roman français, *Le Nouvel Obs*, June 7, 2018.

"It's like an episode of Black Mirror, where the President's offices have found a way to penetrate the brains of his former acquaintances and erase everything".

Sylvie Bommel about her investigation of Brigitte Macron's first marriage in *Il venait d'avoir 17 ans*, JC Lattès, 2019.

13

MACRON BEFORE BRIGITTE

"The only one in the class we knew nothing about"

Emmanuel Macron remains a mystery to those who went to school with him. His former classmates describe him as "the only one we didn't know anything about, either where he spent his vacations or what his parents did for a living". A "loner", "not much socialized", "not gathering others around him"[1]. Later, at Henri-IV, he stayed in the background. Elusive. "He maintained an air of mystery, a parallel life of which we knew nothing. [...] No one knows of any close friends among his forty-eight fellow students. [...] "He had a very striking chameleon-like manner""[2].

Emmanuel Macron's early life, before he met "Brigitte", is a black hole. Journalists who have tried to cover the subject have all fallen back on cross-portraits[3], for lack of material (testimonials, photographs, etc.). The information that could be gathered can be summed up in a few lines. Born on December 21, 1977 in Amiens (Somme), Emmanuel Macron spent his childhood on rue Gaulthier-de-Rumilly in Henriville, the upscale district of Amiens, in a house bought in 1982 by his parents, Jean-Michel Macron, a neuropsy-chiatrist at the Amiens University Hospital from a Picard family, and Françoise Noguès, who a pediatrician who became an expert for the Social Security, whose family originates from Bagnères-de-Bigorre (Hautes-Pyrénées). The couple had two more children, Laurent (1979) and Estelle (1982), both physicians, before divorcing in 2010. Emmanuel Macron has a half-brother, Gabriel (2005), from his father's second marriage to Hélène Joly, a psychiatrist at the Institut médico-éducatif de la Somme. He speaks very little about this family, other than saying that this side had a "Mendésist tradition" [relating to the socialist politician Pierre Mendès-France], or that in the area "there was a lot of prejudice to struggle against"[45].

Journalist Sylvie Bommel summed up the impression left by Emmanuel Macron's evocation of his family: "In *Révolution*, Emmanuel devotes five pages to his maternal grandmother, only one to his parents, and two lines to his brother Laurent and his sister Estelle. [...] Nor is there any mention of his half-brother Gabriel, born in 2005 from his father's second marriage, and even less of his father's companion Hélène [...]. Conversely, he scrupulously mentions the first names of Brigitte's three children and their spouses, as well as those of her seven grandchildren (she has since had an eighth one). On the day of the investiture, the Auzières were the only ones to tread the red carpet leading up to the *Palais de l'Élysée*. Tiphaine and Laurence, blonde, slim and elegant [...] and their brother Sébastien, all accompanied by their spouses and children [...]. The estrangement is reciprocal. In 2014, a colleague of his brother Laurent at the hospital asked him if the Macron working with François Hollande at the Élysée Palace was a close relative. "No, he's a vague cousin. Everyone's bugging me about this guy!" "[6]. "As for the sister, Estelle, we hardly ever saw her", assures Nicole, a first-degree cousin of Françoise Noguès"[7].

On May 18, 2017, Paris Match[12] *published the family photographs taken at Emmanuel Macron's inauguration. At the bottom, he appears with the "Brigitte" side; at the top, his own side, without "Brigitte", looks like an unnatural set of motley strangers...*

No photos of Emmanuel Macron as a child with his parents

At first sight, the real mystery is the virtual absence of any snapshots of Emmanuel Macron as a child, in the 1980s and 1990s, a time of massive democratization of photography and family film, the golden age of the Polaroid, the camcorder, typically longish slide sessions and voluminous photo albums. Sylvie Bommel perfectly expresses this strangeness. With the blatant contradiction between a PR plan based on intimacy and a lack of photographs which, logically, could and should have made the "Macron product" endearing: "I had a hard time finding Emmanuel's friends. [...] "He never talked about his family" [...]. We are hard-pressed to find any photos of his early years. When, as a grown-up, he launched his presidential campaign, many political analysts noted that his communication was inspired by Obama – even if this is the case, he has neglected his early childhood. Anyone interested in the former US president can look with emotion at baby Barack in a romper suit, the chubby kid wielding his first baseball bat, the kid with two holes where he just lost his baby teeth... – in short, watching him grow up. Our President's photo album begins in his tenth year. The shot was taken in the choir of the chapel of *La Providence*, with Emmanuel reading a passage from the Bible. Around his neck, a shiny medal, worn for the first time, marks the day of his baptism [at age 12]. [...] Françoise and Jean-Michel have a distant relationship with religion. Of course, they were married in a church to enjoy the pump of the event and gather their families, but they never considered having the baby baptized"[8].

Taken from the *150th anniversary album of the Association des anciens élèves de La Providence*, these three photographs, widely considered to be the first known pictures of Emmanuel Macron, show him, from left to right, at his christening, on the facebook of his 7th grade class, and during a lesson. What happened to the traditional photos of toddlers in short pants? And the ones on the tricycle, surrounded by his parents? For the time being, after 13 years of media coverage, there are no known photos of Emmanuel Macron with his family during his childhood.

On closer inspection, we found three other photographs of Emmanuel Macron in the 1980s (still without his family). These photographs have been disclosed once when he came to power, in issue 3547 of *Paris Match*[9], but have not been republished on the Internet, as is customary. Inexplicably, they were not incorporated into the authorized biographies produced later.

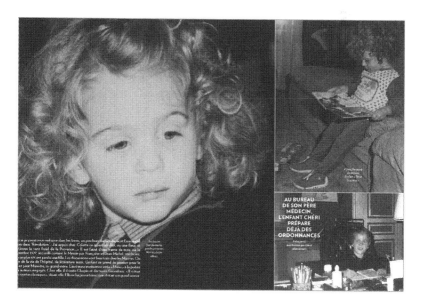

The oldest known photo of Emmanuel Macron with his family can be found in the same issue of *Paris Match*. It is not dated, but seems to have been taken during his studies at ENA, when he had already been away from home for some ten years…

115

Asked in 2016 about this lack of documentation, Jean-Michel Macron and Françoise Noguès answered that Emmanuel was a "replacement child" conceived after a stillborn sister. The purely psychological explanation of the "disappearance of this little girl without a name, this little girl to forget thanks to Emmanuel's mission"[10] was the only explanation offered to all interrogations about the totally undocumented first years of Emmanuel Macron's official biography.

"Brigitte", a bulwark between journalists and the Macron family

Hervé Algalarrondo is the journalist who has gone furthest in his attempt to tell the story of Emmanuel Macron's youth in *Deux Jeunesses françaises*, an investigative book covering simultaneously the destinies of Emmanuel Macron and Édouard Louis, a gay writer from the Picardy proletariat who defines himself by saying: "I realized that, as a gay child, I was a born actor"[11].

On the Macron side, Algalarrondo did not have any success at any stage, even admitting halfway through that his angle might not have been the right one, and that Macron's hallmark was indeed "this loathing for provincial life". Here's a brief overview of the ordeal of Hervé Algalarrondo, the only journalist to have investigated Emmanuel Macron's childhood exclusively.

- His Picard roots. "Authie, the cradle of the Macron family. [...] Not one Macron has lived in Authie for decades, but "there are plenty in the cemetery", the current mayor, Honoré Froideval, told me. [...] Before entering the political field in 2012, Emmanuel Macron considered running for municipal or legislative office on several occasions. Never in Picardy; almost always in Pas-de-Calais, further north. Hence the lapidary judgment of Gilles de Robien [former centrist mayor of Amiens and former minister under Jacques Chirac], who is not a priori unfavorable to the President of the Republic, since he is close to the Trogneux family: "Macron is not an Amiénois, he's a Touquettois!" [a denizen of the seaside resort Le Touquet]. [...] Macron when president has done worse. He skipped the commemoration of the centenary of the Battle of Amiens on August 8, 2018. The Amiens-born Macron was conspicuously absent, while Theresa May, then Prime Minister of the United Kingdom, and Prince William, one of Queen Elizabeth's grandsons, were present; the English had stood shoulder to shoulder with the French in this battle of World War I, the start of the Allies' victorious offensive. [...] Emmanuel Macron didn't attend the celebration, even though his family's birthplace, Authie, was on the front line of another famous battle, the Battle of the Somme, and the castle housed a field hospital. Even though he knows full well, as he has mentioned in several speeches, that Picardy still bears the scars of the wars against Germany. Beyond the 20th century. Dury, the commune near Amiens where his godfather, Jean-Michel Noguès, lived, has erected a stele to commemorate the battle that took place there on November 27, 1870".

- His Pyrenean roots. "During a visit to Andorra, he presented himself as a neighbor, "a child of the Pyrenees". [...] Yet Emmanuel Macron shows little interest in the culture and traditions of Bigorre. This showed in a harshly embarrassing exhange in February 2018 with Xavier Luciani, a Corsican nationalist official, as noted by a journalist from *L'Express*, Michel Feltin-Palas. "I had great-grandparents who were Bigourdan, and they only spoke Pyrenean. Their sole aim in life was that my grandmother would attend a State school [*l'école de la République*] to learn French. Think about it". This exposed an astonishing lack of culture. Several regional languages are spoken in the Pyrenees, from Basque in the west to Catalan in the east. In Bigorre, people speak Bigourdan, a variant of Gascon/Occitan. Pyrenean doesn't exist".

- An untraceable family. "It is even more closed to the outside world than I imagined. Only his teachers and his few friends from Providence are forthcoming, and they have often already spoken to other journalists or biographers. [...] The Amiens family remains locked in. [...] Jean-Michel Macron did not reply to any e-mail message. I could not even get through to Lucette, the widow of Jean-Michel Noguès, Emmanuel's uncle and godfather. To reach his pavilion in Dury, you have to drive down a long driveway. As I step onto the cement terrace, the door opens. A young woman appears, probably one of his two daughters. As soon I have introduced myself, she cuts me off: "We don't receive anyone." and adds with a smile: "From our side, you'll get nothing", and closes the door. The other maternal aunt, Marie-Christine Noguès, was just as prompt. I dropped in unannounced at her ophthalmologist's practice in Vallée des Singes, south of Amiens. "Oh... I must ask if I can talk to you.", she whispers when I approach her between two patients. When I call back – without expecting much – to know the result of her consultation, her secretary curtly tells me that her boss doesn't want "to be bothered anymore". [...] Françoise Noguès shows no interest in meeting me. Having tracked down her mobile number, I sent her several text messages to which she never replied. [...] At this moment I think I've got "the" right idea: to talk to Brigitte. [...] She is the one who manages relations with the Macron family. An official from Bigorre told me of his surprise when the President visited Bagnères. Out of civility, he asked her about her sister, Estelle, who lives nearby. Emmanuel Macron turned to Brigitte to know what to answer"...

1. Testimonials quoted by Sylvie Bommel in *Il venait d'avoir 17 ans*, JCLattès, 2019.

2. *Le Parisien*, January 23, 2015.

3. Hervé Algalarrondo described Emmanuel Macron's youth with that of writer Édouard Louis (also a native of Amiens) in *Deux jeunesses françaises* (Grasset, 2021); in *Vanity Fair* (February 2017), Claude Askolovitch treated the subject by adding the childhood of former Socialist minister Najat Vallaud-Belkacem, on the grounds that she was born in 1977 and had lived in Amiens; In *Les Présidents et leur père, une histoire compliquée*, *Le Monde* (January 2, 2021) dealt with the subject of Emmanuel Macron's father, blending it with the relationships maintained with their fathers by Nicolas Sarközy and François Hollande, the previous two presidents.

4. *Brigitte Macron: L'affranchie*, L'Archipel, 2018.

5. *Revolution*, Emmanuel Macron, XO, 2016.

6. *Il venait d'avoir 17 ans*, Sylvie Bommel, JC Lattès, 2019.

7. *Deux jeunesses françaises*, Hervé Algalarrondo, Grasset, 2021.

8. *Il venait d'avoir 17 ans*, Sylvie Bommel, JC Lattès, 2019.

9. *Paris Match*, May 10, 2017.

10. *Un Jeune homme si parfait*, Anne Fulda, Plon, 2017.

11. Quoted in *Le Soir*, January 25, 2020.

12. *Paris Match*, n° 3548 of May 18, 2017, page 66.

14

« MANETTE »

Goddess of her enchanted world

The only family member mentioned in Emmanuel Macron's child-hood is his maternal grandmother, Germaine Noguès, born Arribet on October 5, 1916 in Tarbes (Hautes-Pyrénées), who died on April 13, 2013 in Amiens (Somme). Emmanuel Macron is said to have spent most of his childhood with the woman he nicknamed "Manette". The journalist Anne Fulda briefly raised the possibility that Emmanuel Macron had "almost been adopted by his grandmo-ther", "goddess of his enchanted world", "queen of his childhood and even of his adult life"[1].

Living just a few blocks from his parents, she has, reportedly, intro-duced him to reading, tutoring him and facilitating his excellent school results. It was also at her home that Emmanuel Macron recounts having "spent all [his] summer and winter vacations at the family home in Bagnères-de-Bigorre. I learned to walk, fish and play rugby with my grandparents"[2].

"Manette", a teacher first posted to Nevers (Nièvre), then to Poix-de-Picardie, ended her career in Amiens as headmistress of the Sagebien middle school south of Henriville, the Amiens neighborhood of the Macrons and Trogneux. The character of "Manette" helps explain the absence of photos and childhood memories of Emmanuel Macron: "So I spent my childhood in books, somewhat out of the world. It was still life. Although he has never officially lived in her home, Emmanuel Macron is sowing doubts: "I remember those early mornings when I would go to her room and she would tell me stories of her wartime friendships. As a child, I would pick up the thread of the interrupted discussion every day and travel through her life as if picking up a novel. And the smell of the coffee she sometimes brewed in the middle of the night. And my bedroom door ajar as early as seven in the morning when I had not yet come to her, exclaiming with feigned concern: "Are you still asleep?"[3]. "According to several witnesses, Manette, once retired, stayed at home, surrounded by books. She hardly ever goes out, and the rooms are bathed in darkness. [...] In Bagnères-de-Bigorre, too, the shutters often remained closed and she was never seen outside"[4].

During his time with François Hollande, the story of "Manette" was used to anchor Emmanuel Macron in the French left. At the time, it was the story of a "grandmother whose life story is a perfect cameo to illustrate the "republican" rise of a lower-class woman"[5]. But as I dug deeper, I realized that "Manette" did not really connect with the left. Under her combined name as a wife and as a maiden, Germaine Noguès-Arribet had in fact co-written, for the publisher Hatier, several textbooks for supplementary classes [6]– now in French "college", equivalent to middle school – including *Géographie de la France métropolitaine et de l'Union française* (classe de 3e), under the direction of geographer Henri Boucau, Inspector General of Public Instruction under Vichy. In it, "Manette" wrote: "When there are few of them, foreigners assimilate fairly quickly. But when they are very numerous, they retain their language and nationality, and form foreign islands in the country: there are Polish villages in the Nord, and Italian villages in the Gers."

After having been used to give Emmanuel a patent for socialism, the story of "Manette" was used for a reversal of roles in the episode of François Hollande's betrayal. Nathalie Schuck and Ava Djamshidi's account of "Manette's" death is a real eye-opener: "A tragedy is about to shatter the friendship between François Hollande and his young advisor. On April 13, 2013, at the age of 96, Emmanuel Macron's beloved grandmother died in his arms as he had come to her bedside in Amiens. [...] Devastated by her death, the young man informs the Élysée Palace that he will be absent for a few days to take part in the funeral. The following Monday, he returns for a morning meeting chaired by François Hollande. The head of State opens the door and calls out to his advisor, seated among other participants. "Ah, you... you're here..." with a hint of a reproach about the prolonged absence. Emmanuel Macron remains inscrutable. François Hollande continues: "Ah yes, that's right, you had a family event [*une histoire de famille*]." Those are clumsy words that burn the heart of this grieving man. A "family event"? Is this the right way to evoke the passing of one of the most important figures in his life? Grief and anger overwhelm him. Political advisor Aquilino Morelle, who has taken a liking to him, takes him out for a coffee. Macron gets angry: "What he did to me there, I'll never forgive!" His empathetic wife is stunned by this lack of humanity [sic]. François Hollande's friends, aware of the episode, try to put it into perspective. "Losing a child is terrible. Her spouse is atrocious. A mother is very hard. But a grandmother over 80 is not unnatural..." apologizes an historic partisan of Hollande, rolling up his eyes: "Hey, we were not going to hold a ceremony at the Élysée Palace and set the flags at half-mast!""[7].

The authors that "Manette" shared with him...

In a relationship that has something of home instruction (now violently opposed by the government), the literature "Manette" allegedly recommended to her grandson is surprising. According to journalists Candice Nedelec and Caroline Derrien, "as a teenager, young Macron escaped by reading. [...] Books by André Gide and Michel Tournier's *Le Roi des Aulnes* are on his bedside table. His beloved maternal grandmother [...] shared a liking for these author with him"[8]. Emmanuel Macron fully embraces the largely pedophile nature of this authors and those works, describing André

Gide as an "irreplaceable companion"[9]. He even had one of Gide's books, *Les Nourritures terrestres*, in his official portrait as President of the Republic. Only the journalist Hélène Devynck has publicly commented on this: "André Gide? To say what? [...] Clumsiness and error are inconceivable in a setting crafted to remain in the historic iconography of the country. Inevitably, someone in the presidential entourage, if not the head of State himself, has read André Gide's autobiography *Si le Grain ne meurt*, where he tells the story of little Mohammed: "How handsome he was! half-naked under his rags, black and slender as a demon". The writer admires "the slenderness of his child's body, the gracefulness of his bare legs peeking out from his baggy pants". He describes how he sodomize the child to (his own) exhaustion. Two years later, he watches his friend Daniel sodomizing Mohammed, now a teenager. [...] What message did the young and dashing President of the French Republic send with this photo posted on the walls of school town halls? [...] What should we understand? That pedocriminals can rest easy?"[10]

The reference to Michel Tournier's *Le Roi des Aulnes* (*The Alder King*)[11] is even more explicit, since it is a classic of pedophile literature. It contains quotes like "Children's buttocks are alive, quivering, always alert, sometimes sunken, and seconds later, smiling and naively optimistic, as expressive as faces". Based on the concept of "malignant inversion", this novel revisits the ogre myth through the character Abel Tiffauges. One might even recognize "Brigitte's" descriptions of the young "Emmanuel" when he talks about "the category of children with surprising intellectual maturity – who seem to have read and understood everything from birth – contradicting a physical immaturity that gives an air of ingenuity to everything they say". When asked in 2021 for his favorite filmmaker, Emmanuel Macron mentioned Pedro Almodovar[12], the Spanish film director whose favorite themes are homosexuality and, beyond, pedophilia and transsexualism.

1. *Un Jeune homme si parfait*, Anne Fulda, Plon, 2017.

2. *La Nouvelle République des Pyrénées*, April 11, 2017.

3. *Révolution*, Emmanuel Macron, XO, 2016.

4. *Deux Jeunesses françaises*, Hervé Algalarrondo, Grasset, 2021.

5. *Un Jeune homme si parfait*, Anne Fulda, Plon, 2017.

6. *Histoire de France de Clovis à Henri IV* (classe de 5ᵉ), *Découverte de la terre* (classe de 6ᵉ) et *Géographie de la France métropolitaine et de l'union française* (classe de 3ᵉ).

7. *Madame la Présidente,* Nathalie Schuck and Ava Djamshidi, Plon, 2019.

8. *Les Macron*, Candice Nedelec and Caroline Derrien, Fayar, 2017.

9. *Révolution*, Emmanuel Macron, XO, 2016.

10. *Impunité*, Seuil, 2022.

11. *Le Roi des Aulnes*, Michel Tournier, Gallimard, 1970.

12. *Quotidien*, TMC, March 15, 2021.

15

FRANÇOISE MACRON-NOGUÈS AND THE TRANSGENDER TRACK

Faced with the wall of Emmanuel Macron's childhood, we decided to screen it meticulously[1], with this question in mind: why did the family refuse to respond to journalists' requests, and why did they need "Brigitte's" approval? A hearing at the French National Assembly caught our attention: that of Sylvaine Télesfort, President of the *Association Maison Intersexualité et Hermaphrodisme Europe* (AMIHE). Born in Beauvais in 1956 under the name Sylvain Télesfort (changed to Sylvaine by a court ruling in Paris on May 15, 2007), he incidentally revealed to the French National Assembly that he had been given administrative support in his gender transition by "a senior doctor at the primary health insurance fund, Dr Françoise Macron", i.e. Emmanuel Macron's mother.

Needless to say, this connection never appeared in the documentation available on the subject: Françoise Noguès-Macron was always presented as only a medical advisor to the Social Security organization (*Caisse Nationale d'Assurance Maladie*), with no further details. We now knew that Françoise Macron had helped Sylvain administratively to become Sylvaine. But had she also coached others to take this kind of step? In 2009, *Le Monde*[2] reported that "in a certificate dated 2003, the physician who follows Sylvain Télesfort [...] stresses that 'his case is out of the ordinary' [which implies familiarity with this type of case]: transsexuals are asking to go to the other side, but Sylvain Télesfort is already mid-way".

This information was confirmed in 2024 in an interview[3] with "Alexandra"[4], an "intersex" person, who described her experience and explained that she had benefited from "waivers granted by the national referral advisor Doctor Françoise Macron-Noguès who – it must be said – is the mother of the current president; she has done a tremendous amount of work, following all kinds of generations of people like me, granting subsidies so that we can have access to the best specialists, so that we can take our time, and so that in everyday life we are not on the margins. If people were rejected by their families, she would find them a small room, and they would receive a disability pension for the duration of the trip. In short, it was very, very well organized. I don't understand why people despise this protocol". In a second interview[5], she explains that Françoise Noguès was concerned with a particular pathology, primary congenital pseudo-hermaphroditism… Needless to say, her focus on this specialty, with which Emmanuel Macron had no doubt been familiar during his childhood, never appeared in the mainstream press in France…

It remains that Françoise Noguès was a well-known figure among those who had to deal with "transidentity", as was Patrick Bui, the surgeon who operated "Brigitte" in 2019. In short, the names Françoise Noguès and Patrick Bui had undoubtedly acted as a coded message that only insiders had received… And what were we to understand when Françoise Noguès, in one of her rare media appearances, explained: "For me, Brigitte is not a daughter-in-law"[6]?

---

1. A character in particular caught our attention: Emmanuel Macron's maternal uncle, Jean-Michel Noguès. He was important: Emmanuel Macron chose him as his godfather when he decided to be baptized; the role of godmother obviously fell to "Manette". Moreover, Jean-Michel Noguès was presented as a sort of "first attempt" by Germaine Noguès to achieve a success story with her son, who had become "only a general practitioner" because of "a troubled youth" *(Deux Jeunesses françaises*, Hervé Algalarrondo, Grasset, 2021). This unsuccessful attempt may have led her to try again with her grandson Emmanuel Macron… Born on December 25, 1940 in Nevers (Nièvre) and died on October 6, 2006 in Amiens (Somme), Jean-Michel Noguès was not a banal general practitioner. He was a prominent member

of the board of the Faculty of Medicine of Amiens, as indicated by his obituary published by his colleagues in *Le Courrier Picard*. He was also the chairman of Domus Medica, a non-trading real estate company (*Société civile Immobilière*) bringing together numerous of local healthcare professional organizations (*Conseil Départemental de l'Ordre des Médecins de la Somme, Association Générale des Médecins de France, Conseil Régional de l'Ordre des Médecins de Picardie*, etc.). He married Lucette Duponchel on December 30, 1964 in Poix (Somme). Lucette was born on July 20, 1939 in Jouy-sous-Thelle (Oise) and died on October 14 in Dury (Somme). Emmanuel Macron attended this elementary school in the Henriville district *(Les Macron,* Candice Nedelec and Caroline Derrin, Fayard, 2017) before moving on to La Providence. When, in 2021, in *Faits & Documents*, I first raised the question of the absence of photos of Emmanuel Macron as a child with his parents, an interview with Jean-Michel Macron on the *lalsace.fr* website (April 18, 2022) published a photo of Emmanuel Macron in primary school, in 1983, at the Delpech school. Later, I managed to consult three other class photos of Emmanuel Macron at the Delpech school where his aunt was a teacher. But there are still no known childhood photos of Emmanuel Macron with his parents. A Google search for "Françoise Noguès jeune" brings up a photograph of this aunt, Lucette Duponchel. But as we dug deeper, we came across a photo of Françoise Noguès at the age of 15 (1965-1966 school year) during her time at the Lycée Mixte d'Amiens. Nothing to report on that front. Born on December 8, 1950 in Poix-de-Picardie (Somme), Françoise Noguès defended her thesis on June 23, 1980 at the Université de Picardie (on *Celiac disease in children, based on 26 observations*). This thesis, which we have been able to consult, is dedicated "To Jean-Michel, Emmanuel and Laurent, with all my love". Laurent, Pierre-Henri, André Macron, born June 21, 1979 in Amiens (Somme), married Sabine, Marie, Juliette, Sonotefa, Aimot on March 21, 2009. His sister, Estelle, Élodie, Françoise Macron, born March 24, 1984 in Amiens (Somme), entered into a civil solidarity pact (PACS) on March 30, 2016 in Toulouse (Haute-Garonne) with Carl Franjou, born January 12, 1983 in Briançon (Hautes-Alpes). Marie-Christine Noguès, the youngest sister of Jean-Michel and Françoise Noguès, was born on June 11, 1952 in Amiens (Somme), where she married Philippe, André, Raymonde Bove on February 10, 1973 (divorce decree issued on October 28, 1992), before marrying Jean-François, Christian, Leprêtre in Le Touquet-Paris-Plage (Pas-de-Calais) on May 23, 2015.

2. *Sylvaine, née Sylvain, Le Monde*, December 2, 2009

3. *Alexandra: Personne intersexe, elle explique son opposition à l'idéologie transgenre*, chaîne *Youtube Femelliste*, 17 juin 2024.

4. Pseudonym of Emmanuelle, Vivianne Delair-Gamain.

5. *Hermaphrodite, Intersexe, Trans: limites et risques d'une transition*, Alexandra Brazzainville, *Média en 4-4-2*, 17 septembre 2024.

6. Quoted by Gaël Tchakaloff in *Tant qu'on est tous les deux*, Gaël Tchakaloff, Flammarion, 2021.

16

"BRIGITTE" BEFORE MACRON (I)

"An easygoing midinette"

When "Brigitte" was introduced to the French, and the story of her past had to be told, the mainstream press unanimously insisted that she had been a very beautiful and very attractive woman, "because she's pretty and sexy, young Brigitte Trogneux"[1].

"Around the age of 14 or 15, Brigitte gets bolder. She swaps her navy blue uniform from the austere Sacré-Cœur school in Amiens - pleated skirt, sweater and tights – for small shorts and mini-skirt. For a while, she can forget about her schooling, constrained by Catholic discipline."[2] "She loves to dance at the surprise parties of the time, wears tight miniskirts and, between two glasses of whisky-and-coke and wild rock'n'roll songs, dares to flirt behind the curtains"[3]. An "inveterate party girl in an ultra-small kilt, who was into rock dancing to the music of John Lee Hooker until dawn. [...] A rather hectic adolescence, the opposite of the quiet Emmanuel"[4]. "The youngest of the Trogneux family has always struck a chord with the public with her contagious good humor, her taste for partying and her often funny, down-to-earth way of speaking [...]. A shy midinette side... which led her, now in her sixties, to describe her appreciation for the "raw masculinity" of a Clint Eastwood. [...] In Le Touquet, as in "La Pro" or later in Paris, in Saint-Louis-de-Gonzague, the future Madame Macron is a unanimous favorite. At least among those who are willing to talk a little about it"[5].

"Among those who accept to say a bit more". The author's admission of this description reflects the weakness of the story, the scarcity of witnesses and, above all, the absence of pictures... In fact, it was necessary to create a continuity between the character sold to the French and her past, and make "Brigitte" desirable during her teaching years to normalize her affair with Emmanuel Macron. And so, in the hands of French journalists, "Brigitte" became an icon., almost a fictional character. Her biography took on the allure of a remake script for The *Dead Poets Society*, but with a sort of Claudia Schiffer in the lead role, that of John Keating, the charismatic professor of literature.

By seducing "Brigitte", "young Macron" had simply fulfilled the fantasy of all boys undergoing puberty who, one day, crossed paths with "Brigitte"... The press reported: "Young Renaud has indeed made friends with Sébastien and Laurence Auzière, but he is also very interested in their mother's conversation... "He must have been about twelve years old and he was captivated by her. She's pretty, you know". [...] "Her aim in class was not to dispense knowledge, but to create something passionate, exciting and participatory. She was someone you could discuss everything with" [...]. "She knew a lot about us: one would readily tell her of confidential matter." [...] The teacher's charm has an undeniable effect on her audience. "Especially on boys, I think!"[...] Teenagers are not indifferent to the elegance of a woman who would only write with a chalk holder. "At the start of her career, she was already very coquettish," continues her colleague. The students appreciated this effort." One of them remembers her fondly. "Several of us fell for her!" explains a former pupil of La Providence. The year I had her for French, I was very attentive, I must say!". "There was a particular exchange with the boys, a form of seduction [...]. There were good vibes in her class and many were charmed." Her daughter Tiphaine herself can testify to her enthusiasm, admitting that she was "jealous of all the students who wrote to her or called her at home". Some even came for dinner, with a bunch of flowers. For Brigitte, teaching is not limited to the classroom. [...] She is this cool teacher who invites her students for *aperitif* on Friday evenings, and tells them to address her with "tu" and her first name."[6]

"All the students were in love with her"

We were told that "A neighbor's son [who] has worshipped her ever since she asked him to say "tu" to her, a favor no adult outside his family had ever granted him. "He was a bit in love with her, I think," says the mother, whom I suspect is imagining her son at the Élysée Palace. [...] Brigitte's class can't believe that the French teacher is celebrating her fortieth birthday today. She looks so young in her short skirts and casual manner. [...] To capture the attention of the most dissipated, the teacher has another, less academic asset: her legs, showcased by tiny skirts. Brigitte didn't wait to become the First Lady to take great care of her appearance. "She was a pleasure to look at, not just to listen to. Always with perfect hairdressing, with make-up and perfumed one student recalls. The boys are seduced; the girls take her as a model"[7]. ""Ah! Brigitte… She was really very nice" says a former literature colleague who has been at the school for thirty years, though she avoids mentioning the risky affair with the young Macron. "All the high school students were in love with her" says Frédéric, from Emmanuel's class. "When I was a child, I was even jealous of all the students who wrote to her or called her at home," confides her youngest daughter Tiphaine[8]. "Another teacher goes further: "Brigitte arrived at La Providence wearing mini-tailleurs, beautiful, a pin-up." One student stresses: "We were all in love with her." So the protagonists are: a teenager who already looks like a grown-up, and a teacher who is approaching forty but does not look her age"[9].

As I read these descriptions, I was looking for the pictures of this "beautiful pin-up" in a "mini-tailleur" that didn't look her age. Unfortunately, there were no photographs of "Brigitte" at the time.

In January 2018 appeared the official biography of "Brigitte", *Brigitte Macron, L'Affranchie*, by Maëlle Brun[10], then head of the Celebrities department at the weekly magazine *Closer*. It was translated and distributed worldwide. It presented a synthesis of everything that had been told to the French in the two years leading up to Emmanuel Macron's access to power. But right from the introduction, the author made it clear that this story was nothing more than "sleek storytelling". And, as I am myself a biographer, I found there were several problematic elements. For instance, most of the witnesses interviewed and quoted in the acknowledgements were rather recent acquaintances of Brigitte Macron. The past was very succinctly evoked in a totally disembodied narrative. This lack of substance was obvious when examining the traditional glossy photographs featured in this type of book. Contrary to custom, there were no pictures of Brigitte Macron as a child, and none as a young mother. The earliest picture is a photograph taken in a professional setting, at the Lycée La Providence, in 1993.

It has the caption: "Brigitte Auzière is 40. Married, mother of three, quite appreciated at the high school where she teaches, she is about to make the encounter that will cause an upheaval of her life." As if her first 40 years had been erased…

Six months later, in June 2018, the biographical documentary *Brigitte Macron: un Roman français*[11] was broadcast on *France 3*. Virginie Linhart, a director whose favorite themes are the Second World War, the Holocaust and May '68, illustrated graphically the official biography. The film retraced "Brigitte's" teaching career through her class photographs, from her entry into the teaching profession in September 1986[12] in Strasbourg, at the Collège Lucie Berger (until 1991), then in Amiens, at La Providence (1991-2007)[13] and finally in Paris, at "Franklin" (2007-2015).

Where was the sexy gal in mini-tailleurs of the first storytelling? In *Brigitte Macron, Un Roman français*, we also find, for the first time, this picture of a weird-looking individual in a cardigan in the woods (undated, but this was logic dally in the period of the encounter), which definitively contradicts the attraction the teacher might have exerted on adolescent males in the pangs of puberty.

Total blackout

During the promotion of the film, Virginie Linhart mentioned the obstacles and pressures while making her documentary: "It's difficult to investigate Brigitte Macron. Much more than I imagined. On the substance. On the form. On... everything. As soon as I started making contacts, I was "summoned" (*convoquée*) by Pierre-Olivier Costa and Tristan Bromet [Brigitte's chiefs of staff]. It was almost like a police interrogation: What do I want to show? Who will I be interviewing? I made a list of people I wanted to meet, but could not apply it. The interviewees, apart from her former students, all had the authorization of the Élysée Palace and were very careful about what they said. There is a thick wall of silence. The level of control and checking is, well, quite astounding. [...] It's a 90-minute very personal portrait. For it, I needed photographs of young Brigitte Macron, small children... that would show an itinerary, not those approved by the Bestimage agency. What doesn't come out is anything to do with her former life. It's a total blackout"[14].

Yet she was provided with a few childhood photographs of Brigitte Trogneux, including one with a face already with an adult shape, therefore identifiable: the photograph taken at her First Communion.

Also shown is a photograph of the family shortly after Brigitte Trogneux's birth.

On the left of the photo stands a second brother who has never been mentioned before and does not appear, at the time, on the genealogical databases[15].

But there are no photographs of Brigitte Trogneux between her First Communion and her debut as a teacher in 1986. No photographs of her first marriage to André-Louis Auzière, no photographs of her as a young mother with her children, Sébastien (1975)[16], Laurence[17] (1977) and Tiphaine [18](1984). As in all the articles and reports about "Brigitte", Tiphaine Auzière is the only relative who agreed to answer Virginie Linhart's questions: "We did a very long interview, lasting over an hour, and at the end I said Cut!, and I saw her going..." she says, and mimick a long sigh of relief[19].

André-Louis Auzière

Banquier

Date de naissance : 28 février 1951

Date de décès : décembre 2019

Épouse : Brigitte Macron (m. 1974–2006)

And there is still no photograph of André-Louis Auzière. The director resorted to "evocations", i.e. illustrative images that do not represent the persons, especially where André-Louis Auzière or Brigitte Auzière's past as a young mother are mentioned[20].

At the time when the documentary was released, the only photograph of André-Louis Auzière available online at the time was debunked by politician François Ruffin, also an alumnus of La Providence: it was in fact the picture of a teacher of literature at the school, Mr Hugot.

That left blank the period of 1963-1986: almost 23 years with no pictures of Brigitte Trogneux alone or with her young children, or of her husband André-Louis Auzière was called by Virginie Linhart "the Republic's best-kept secret" [21]...

1. *Un jeune homme si parfait*, Anne Fulda, Plon, 2017.

2. *Les Macron du Touquet Élysée-Plage*, Renaud Dély and Marie Huret, Seuil, 2020

3. *Paris Match*, April 14, 2016.

4. *Brigitte Maron. L'Affranchie*, Maëlle Brun, L'Archipel, 2018.

5. *Les Macron*, Candice Nedelec and Caroline Derrien, Fayard, 2017.

6. *Brigitte Macron, L'Affranchie*, Maëlle Brun, L'Archipel, 2018.

7. *Il venait d'avoir 17 ans*, Sylvie Bommel, JCLattès, 2019.

8. *Les Macron*, Candice Nedelec and Caroline Derrien, Fayard, 2017.

9. *Deux Jeunesses françaises*, Hervé Algalarrondo, Grasset, 2021.

10. Reading *Brigitte Macron, L'Affranchie*, we learn that the book is "proposed" by Michel Taubmann, one of the main relays of American neoconservatives in France via *Le Cercle de l'Oratoire* and its magazine *Le Meilleur des mondes*. Michel Taubmann was notably the hagiographer of Dominique Strauss-Kahn, the author in 2012 of *Le Roman vrai de Dominique Strauss-Kahn* and then, after the Sofitel affair in New York, *Affaire DSK, la contre-enquête*, where her attempt at a reha-bilitation was deemed so based on a "conspiracy theory" that even the disgraced managing director of the IMF ended up distancing himself from her.

11. *Brigitte Macron: un roman français*, Virginie Linhardt, Siècle Productions (Georges-Marc Benamou), France 3, June 13, 2018.

12. "Brigitte"'s debut as a teacher is often dated 1984. In fact, like many other episodes in her life, her time in Alsace was the subject of numerous rewritings. We first heard about Alsace on May 8, 2017, through two local publications. The first, *France 3 Grand Est*, reported having found a leaflet from an election campaign in Truchtersheim, where "Brigitte" had been on the opposition list in the municipal elections of March 12, 1989. Meanwhile, *L'Alsace* reported that "Brigitte has lived in Alsace on at least two occasions. The first episode dates from the mid-1970s, when she followed her first husband, the banker André-Louis Auzière, who was based in Strasbourg for a time. She lived in Alsace again in the mid-1980s. In the meantime, she got a CAPES diploma in Literature. She teached at the college in Truchtersheim - where she lived with her children, who attended school there - then at the Lucie-Berger Protestant school in Strasbourg. She was an unsuccessful candidate in the 1989 municipal elec-tions in Truchtersheim. She returned to her native Amiens in 1991. In its definitive version, first in *Society* (May 26, 2017) and then in *Brigitte Macron. L'Affranchie*, "Brigitte" had lived in Truchtersheim between 1986 and 1991 and changed career to be a teacher at Strasbourg's Lycée Lucie-Berger. In fact, the confusion stems mainly from a wrong dating of her arrival at Lucie Berger, from an error in the *Bulletin des Anciens et des Amis de Lucie Berger*. In 2017, it says she taught there "in the 1990s". The following year, in the same publication, we learned that the association's former president, Lilly Guyonnet, had "personally sent her best wishes at the beginning of the year to our former colleague Brigitte Macron, now First Lady. To date, no reply has been received! In this regard, the association had been approached to take part

in the production of a documentary on Brigitte Macron. Lilly contributed six photographs to the film crew in December. A thank-you email has just been sent to us by the director with the following information: Virginie Linhart's documentary *Brigitte Macron, un Roman français* was broadcast on Wednesday June 13 at 8h55 pm on *France 3*". It was there that the first photograph of "Brigitte" as a teacher was dated 1984-1985. This date, 1984, can also be found in the directory of former Lucie Berger teachers published in 1995 for the school's 125th anniversary. But by cross-checking, using other editions of the *Bulletin des Anciens et des Amis de Lucie Berger* (2017), as well as student publications on the *Copains d'avant* website, and by contacting the current head of the association, Martine Douessin, we were able to establish that "Brigitte" had indeed started at Lucie Berger in 1986 and not in 1984 as is often stated. Along this track, we found the only record of a diploma obtained by "Brigitte": in the March 1992 issue of the *Bulletin des Anciennes Elèves et des Amis de Lucie Berger* (i.e. after "Brigitte" had left for Amiens), we read that "Mme Brigitte Auzière" had obtained a "*CAPES de Lettres modernes*", but this publication is by no means an official source. So we contacted Jean-Marc Uhrweiller, mentioned as Brigitte and André Auzière's neighbor in all the biographies. He refused to answer, and his wife remained evasive: "We haven't kept in touch. They left and that was that. The authenticity of the statement of intent (*profession de foi*) for the March 1989 municipal election in Truchtersheim, in which "Brigitte" stood as a candidate under the name "Brigitte Auzière", is sometimes questioned on social networks. All the cross-checks carried out show that this document is indeed authentic and represents "Brigitte" as we know her today, i.e. as she appeared in Alsace in September 1986. So there's a physical and biographical continuity from that date. It was at this time, on June 14 1988, that Jean and Simone Trogneux, along with Brigitte Trogneux, a French teacher born in Amiens on April 13 1953, residing in Truchtersheim (Bas Rhin), 4, rue des Coquelicots, wife of André Auzière, sold a property at 67, rue Saint-Louis in Le Touquet-Paris-Plage (Pas-de-Calais) to Bernard Lesselin and Nicole Dupuy. This transaction is mentioned in the deeds relating to the *Société civile immobilière* "SCI du 19, rue des Arts" filed at the Commercial Court of Lille Métropole on May 16, 2014.

13. Between "Brigitte"'s positions at La Providence and at Saint-Louis-de-Gonzague, journalist Sylvie Bommel (Il venait *d'avoir 17 ans*, JCLattès, 2019) mentioned a three-year gap between September 2004 and September 2007: "At the beginninng of the 2004 school year, La Providence informs the parents' associations that Ms. Auzière is taking training leave until March and will be replaced by Mr. Kazumba. This Mr. Kazumba obtained a permanent position, as Brigitte never returned to her job. She has now almost settled in Paris with Emmanuel, in a two-room apartment on Boulevard de Port-Royal so cramped that the sofa is abutted to the dining room table." This seems false: "Brigitte" actually worked at La Providence between 2004 and 2007, according to student's posts on Facebook , or the album *La Providence d'Amiens au fil du temps* published in 2018 by the school's archivist and former biology teacher Gérard Banc. Additionally, the substitute mentioned by Sylvie Bommel is in fact a woman: Mélanie Kazumba.

14. Quoted in *L'Obs*, June 7, 2018.

15. We have archived screenshots of genealogy databases in 2017-2018. They show

only five children in *Geneanet* (in addition to Brigitte Trogneux, two unidentified individuals born in 1932 and 1941, as well as Jean-Claude, born in 1933, and Monique, born in 1941) and four in *Roglo* (in addition to Brigitte Trogneux, Annie, Jean-Claude and Monique).

16. Sébastien, Jean-Louis Auzière was born on September 1st, 1975 in Amiens (Somme). At the time, her parents, Brigitte Trogneux and André Auzière, lived at 1 rue Claude-Matrat in Issy-les-Moulineaux (Hauts-de-Seine). After studying at the École Nationale de la Statistique et de l'Analyse de l'information (ENSAI) and graduating in 1999, he met Christelle Lorenzato, and they married on October 6, 2001 in Le Touquet (an announcement with a photograph was published in *Les Echos du Touquet*). The couple had three children: Nicolas, Camille and Paul. Christelle Lorenzato is an executive of the "Big Pharma" company Sanofi (Deputy Global Head for oncology biostatistics). After studying marketing at theFrench Fashion Institute (2000-2007), where he published a *Guide du textile et de l'habillement* (2002), Sébastien Auzière joined Kantar Healtha market research group specialized in the pharmaceutical industry, where he is Senior Vice-President for France. Presented as head of social networks for En Marche! in 2017, he remained relatively discreet during the campaign before appearing publicly since the big meeting in Bercy.

17. Laurence Christine Alexandra Auzière, born April 26, 1977 in Amiens (Somme). At the time, her parents, Brigitte Trogneux and André Auzière, lived at 91 rue Holden (résidence Flandre) in Croix (Nord). A contemporary of Emmanuel Macron (she was in his class), Laurence Auzière is the one who produced the formula "crazy guy who knows everything about everything" (thus referring Emmanuel Macron to "Brigitte"). She had been a member of the theater troupe through which "Brigitte" and her father-in-law met. A cardiologist based in Vincennes, she married Guillaume Jourdan, radiologist, on June 18, 2005 in Toulouse (Haute-Garonne). He was born on July 10, 1975 in Toulouse. They have three children: Emma, Thomas and Alice. She remarried Matthieu Gasser, known by his artist name "Graffenstaden". Although discreet, she made a public appearance at the electoral meeting in Bercy on April 17, 2017, then on the evening of the first round at Porte de Versailles and at the inauguration ceremony. Laurence's open *Facebook* friends list (78 members, mostly related to her family, with the notable presence of Michèle Marchand's paparazzo and right-hand man Sébastien Valiela) suggests that she plays a pivotal role between the communications teams and the various members of the family clan.

18. Tiphaine Monique Marie Auzière was born on January 30, 1984 in Amiens, when her parents were still living in Croix (Nord). While her elders kept a relatively low profile, Tiphaine Auzière became fully involved with her father-in-law at a very early stage, setting up a support committee in Saint-Josse (Pas-de-Calais) where she settled with Antoine Choteau, born on May 9, 1979 in Croix (Nord), a gastroenterologist and hepatologist, with whom she entered into a PACS [couple convention] on February 3, 2010 in Lille (two children, Élise and Aurèle). Antoine Choteau is a strange character, now the target of a complaint for "insult" lodged by the mayor of Le Touquet Daniel Fasquelle (member of Les Républicains). She has

been using Twitter/X almost exclusively to relay the paparazzo Sébastien Valiela, one of the main henchmen of Michèle Marchand, the celebrity press 'popess' working for the presidential couple. Tiphaine Auzière is a graduate of University of Paris I-Panthéon Sorbonnea, a jurist and legal counsellor for the trade union CFDT. She left the Opal'Juris practice in Pas-de-Calais and the Boulogne-sur-Mer bar (where she had been sworn in in 2009) to open an office forEn Marche! office in Le Touquet, then became secretary of the local section of the presidential party. A sign of the interest she was attracting from the top, Henri de Castries, former head of AXA and Chairman of the Bilderberg Group came to support her in the 2017 legislative elections, when she was only Thibaut Guilluy's deputy in the 4th constituency of Pas-de-Calais (defeated by Daniel Fasquelle). She vindicated "Brigitte" when mocked over her looks by Brazilian President Jair Bolsonaro, and took part in the communications operation designed to convince the French to accept the Covid-19 measures *(Europe 1*, October 16, 2020). Internationally, *The Times* and the *Daily* Mail covered her shift to teaching with the launch of the Lycée *Autrement*, which received considerable media coverage in France (cf. *Point de Vue*, August 19, 2020), although the experiment was short-lived; in April 2021 she stepped down as president of the association overseeing this private school.

19. *Europe 1*, June 13, 2018.

20. The family films supposed to represent the household formed by Brigitte and André Auzière in *Brigitte Macron: Un Roman français* are taken from *Les Mères au long cours*, a documentary about two women, Monique Godineau and Mireille Frotier, broadcast on *Antenne 2*'s *Aujourd'hui la vie* on May 7, 1984. Virginie Linhart used these images to fill the void.

21. *France Inter*, June 11, 2018.

22. *Un Jeune homme si parfait*, Anne Fulda, Plon, 2017.

23. *La Nouvelle République des Pyrénées*, April 11, 2017.

17

"BRIGITTE" BEFORE MACRON (II)

"You two got along quite well in Le Touquet"

As already noted, the false descriptions of "Brigitte's" youth were aimed at inventing from scratch a coherence, a continuity with the character presented to the French from 2015-2016 onwards; surgically reworked, wearing LVMH clothes, never going out without her miniskirt and stilettos... But from the start, "Brigitte" had created a way out, by explaining that she had been a "suffering teenager"[1]: "I didn't enjoy adolescence, and that's why I liked spending part of my professional life working with teenagers – because there are so many cracks in them. [...] They are never [mentally] where they are physically. I remember feeling that way"[2]. What inner bruises has "Brigitte" been trying to conceal by inventing a rebellious, flippant adolescence? This is a fictitious adolescence, impossible to substantiate by her benevolent biographers, or even by those who were supposed to have known her...

Anne Méaux is a key figure in business and politics. With Image 7, her PR company, she advises some of the biggest names in the CAC 40 [the top of the Paris stock exchange]. Like the Trogneux family[3], she is a regular at Le Touquet-Paris-Plage. She spent part of her childhood in the small seaside resort where her family has a second home. She later served as a local councilor between 1977 and

1983 with mayor Léonce Deprez, a close friend of "Brigitte"'s father Jean Trogneux[4], helping to launch in Le Touquet a literary prize, the *Grand Prix de la Biographie politique*. Additionally, Anne Méaux is an almost contemporary of Brigitte Trogneux (fifteen months apart). Necessarily, Anne Méaux has known "Brigitte"…

On March 8, 2015, to celebrate Women's Day, Anne Méaux attended a reception given by Emmanuel Macron at the Ministry of the Economy and Finance: "Emmanuel Macron discreetly holds a female guest by the arm. "Wait a moment, Anne, don't leave like that; Brigitte will come and kiss you. You two got along quite well in Le Touquet". […] Surprised by Emmanuel Macron's address, she waits for a moment. And here comes another blonde on stilts from the minister's private apartments, Brigitte Macron: "Hello Anne, how are you? It's been a while! All that time… […] The garage parties… do you remember?" asks Brigitte. "And L'Ascot Bar? And Le Chatham?", she insists. "And the Beep-Beep, did you go to the Beep-Beep too?" All the rich kids in town used to dance there." Anne approves tepidly: "Uh yes, yes, of course"[5]…

Anne Méaux wonders… In fact, as will be established in 2019[6], the two had never met before. "Brigitte" was bluffing. The great reunion played out that day was, again, theatrical…

In 2018, journalist Sylvie Bommel spent "two days hanging around the bars, boutiques, casinos and other pleasure spots in Le Touquet"[7] in search of people who knew "Brigitte" in her prime, in vain. Nor will she find any of "Brigitte's" classmates…

"When I was very young, death came into my life"

Sylvie Bommel[8] is one of the journalists who has worked most on the "Brigitte" story. In 2016, she wrote the first major biography, *Et Brigitte créa Macron*, published ahead of the presidential campaign[9]. She was the first to indicate the genuine date of birth of Brigitte Trogneux: April 13, 1953; until then, the mainstream press had written "at the end of the 50s"[10]. Sylvie Bommel continued her investigation until 2019, when she published her second biography of "Brigitte", falsely titled *He had just turned 17*[11]. This was a strange choice; its conclusion - *He was about to turn 15* - would have made for a less acceptable title. In writing this book, Sylvie Bommel – who cannot be suspected of hostility towards the presidential couple – came up against a wall of silence (an *omerta*) and had to look up telephone directories at the *Bibliothèque historique des Postes et des Télécommunications* (something no biographer would normally have to do) to find some traces of the couple of Brigitte Trogneux and André-Louis Auzière.

While scouring the regional daily press, she discovered a very strange "mistake" made by "Brigitte" in a long biographical interview in *Elle* in the summer of 2017[12] – and there is no reason to believe she did read the transcription, "Brigitte" mysteriously explained that "as a child, death came into my life": "My older sister was killed in a car accident, along with her husband and the child she was carrying. I was 8 years old. She's with me every day of my life. A year later, one of my 6-year-old nieces passed away".

Sylvie Bommel identified this sister, Maryvonne Trogneux, *épouse* Farcy[13] and established that she had indeed died in a car accident, but on February 24, 1960, when Brigitte Trogneux, born on April 13, 1953, was 6 years old, not 8. Mistake, or covering up? And what about the niece who died a year later? Since Sylvie Bommel had not identified her, I tried it myself... I was puzzled... All the more so since the biographies placed great emphasis on "Brigitte's" nieces, within the effort to paint as unsurprising the relationship with Emmanuel Macron: "Mme Macron is already experiencing these generational gaps before she falls in love with a man twenty-four years apart"[14]. "At age five, she is already an aunt. At family dinners, he is seated with Martine and Nathalie, her nieces. Very early on, the age markers were blurred for little Brigitte. Her older sister, Anne-Marie, was twenty-one when she was born. Maryvonne, the third of the siblings, passed her 8th-grade certificate (*brevet*) the same year her little sister received the anointing of baptism. Aged eight, when Brigitte plays with her doll, her brother

Jean-Claude cradles a real baby, Jean-Alexandre"[15]. "Such intergenerational crossovers explain why, for Brigitte, the age criterion is meaningless. This is an essential commonality with Emmanuel Macron" [16].

Talking about "Martine and Nathalie, her nieces", Sylvie Bommel explained that, when five years old, she was already an aunt. But I discovered that Brigitte Trogneux had become an aunt much earlier: at the age of 3, on March 26 1957, with the birth of Christine Boulogne, the daughter of her older sister, Anne-Marie. Was this yet another "mistake" or obfuscation? I had to identify this niece who died one year after" Maryvonne's death. I found that Sylvie Boulogne, the fourth child of Anne-Marie Trogneux and Gérard Boulogne, born on June 14, 1959 in Amiens, had in fact died, following a surgical operation, on August 31, 1966 almost six years after Maryvonne's death, not "one year after" as Brigitte had said. And Sylvie Boulogne had died when "Brigitte" was eight, not six as "Brigitte" herself had said.

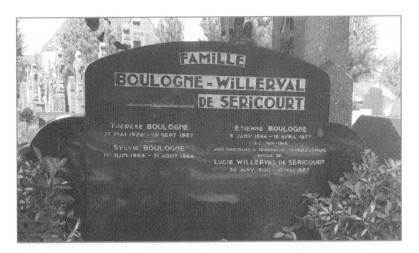

So this was not a succession of errors, but a strategy consisting in confusing the issue by shifting the dates of various events in "Brigitte's" life. Beyond the moral judgment and psychological analysis that can be made of this use of the death of two loved ones, there was the nagging question of the purpose and interest of such a move…

An episode of Black Mirror

For the most part, Sylvie Bommel's investigation consisted in tracking down André-Louis Auzière, Brigitte Trogneux's first husband, whom so many journalists had tried to find. But after months and even years, the cheated husband remained hopelessly unaccounted for, the father of the family who had had his wife (and three children) "stolen" by a teenager, and who ended up divorced twelve years afterwards (in effect in 2006; the divorce was backdated in the first version of the "official legend"[17]), even though he could have easily obtained the custody of the children under such conditions. What's more, in the face of pressure from the Élysée Palace, many journalists gave up looking for the "self-effacing man". In 2017, *Capital* magazine summed up the general impression: "A real ghost. Not a single photograph of him on the Web. Not a single image in the thick press agency catalogs. Biographies barely mention his career as a banker. Whatever happened to Brigitte Macron's ex-husband?"[18].

In her first biography of "Brigitte" Sylvie Bommel devoted a few lines to him: "He was never seen again in Amiens, and was supposed to have gone to Paris, but actually nobody knew anything about it. Wiped out, erased. As if he did not exist."[19]. In her second investigation on "Brigitte", Sylvie Bommel attempted to unravel the mystery and retrace his life. She evidenced that his name is André, Louis and not André-Louis as alleged everywhere, the "only" son (false too, as we shall see) of a colonial administrator, André Auzière met Brigitte Trogneux during a weekend at Le Touquet, and married her soon afterwards. After joining *Crédit du Nord* in Lille, he worked for *Banque Française du Commerce Extérieur* (BFCE), first in Strasbourg, then in Amiens. Concluding this intractable investigation, Sylvie Bommel writes: "The probability of André really having such a course is infinitesimal – he would be the single such case worldwide. In this bourgeois drama set in Picardy in 1994, he would be the only silent character throughout the show. The other two, the wife and the lover, are not averse, even if not admittedly, to evoking the beginnings of their story, but they always erase the husband. [...] How does this father and grandfather feel [...] when he hears someone else,

147

president though he may be, use possessive pronouns ("my children", "my grandchildren") to refer to his own progeny? As if himself, André, had never existed. [...] It is surprising that a man who worked as a senior executive in the banking sector should so drastically out of scope – unless a company specializing in deleting online information has been commissioned to do the housework. This is just a supposition… What can be proven in such a void? [...] "He was nice. Very kind." "A charming boy." "Adorable." "A man of exception." [...] What else? "Tall and slender." "Intelligent", with the variant "very intelligent". "Discreet" (I had noticed that). From a friend of the couple: "At dinner parties, he always let his wife talk; he never said a word." "A rigorous man, playing fair, always willing to do a colleague a favor", according to one of his former bosses. Fair, possibly, but awkward (which is not incompatible). Many acquaintances spontaneously told me how André got his fingers caught in the lawnmower and had to be taken to the emergency ward for stitches. It is probably one of only a few times when he has been noticed. The most critical qualified him as "a bit taciturn", even "not funny at all". A friend of Brigitte's summarizes it so: "Hm, how to tell you… it's hard to remember, he was so neutral. A bit like lukewarm water next to her, who is so bubbly." [...] In the archives of the banking industry, André Auzière has left even fewer traces than he is remembered for. Not a report, not a symposium, nothing to make him exist [...] Apart from the lawnmower episode mentioned above, the memories are blank. It is like an episode of *Black Mirror* where the President's offices have found a way to penetrate the brains of his former acquaintances and erase everything"[20].

Seven months after the publication of Sylvie Bommel's book, on October 8, 2020, André Auzière's death was announced in *Paris Match*. He died in the 15th arrondissement of Paris on December 24, 2019 and was cremated at the Père Lachaise cemetery crematorium on December 28, 2019[21]. By making her father's death official in *Paris Match*, Tiphaine Auzière created a new grey area: "My father died, I buried him on December 24, 2019 in the strictest privacy". Here are two "mistakes" in one sentence: one about the date, one about the funeral. Again, are these mere "mistakes" or just a way of covering their tracks?

148

Prior to the release of Sylvie Bommel's investigation, excerpts of the book were published in April 2019 in the magazine *Le Point* under the title *Sa vie d'avant*[22], with a new piece of evidence (described but not published in Sylvie Bommel's book) the photograph of the wedding of André Auzière and Brigitte Trogneux celebrated on June 22, 1974 at the town hall of Le Touquet-Paris-Plage.

Sylvie Bommel mentions a marriage certificate which "specifies that André is a *stagiaire hors cadre* (in banking jargon, a junior executive) and that his young wife is a student. A marriage contract was registered with a notary in Amiens, a decision probably dictated by the parents, but which ones? Is it André's father, an auditor, who likes clear-cut situations, or the Trogneux family, thinking of passing on their villa in Le Touquet to their daughter? The witnesses too seem to have been chosen by the parents. On the groom's side, the civil register bears the signatures of Georges Costes, aged 66, his maternal uncle, and Jacques Naudy, a colleague of his father's, head of a major accountancy firm. Brigitte is assisted by her two older brothers, Jean-Claude and Jean-Michel".

Jean-Michel Trogneux: the self-effacing brother

In the extensive media coverage of "Brigitte" and the Trogneux family since 2015, this is the very first time that the name Jean-Michel Trogneux was written out, even though merely mentioned, without further clarification, as the brother and best man in Brigitte Trogneux's first marriage. This brother, absent from genealogical databases so far[23] but her best man at her wedding (which implies a real closeness), had been completely erased from "Brigitte's" biography. This absence would have been anecdotal if the communication surrounding the couple had not made a fuss about the Trogneux family saga[24]. A family that not only justified the spurious false "age gap" issue, but also provided the presidential couple with a traditional, large, successful business family rooted in the "genuine country" [le pays réel].

As a result, biographies focused on the various members of the family, and television reports on the family confectionery business sprouted. When the Macrons arrived at the Elysée Palace, *Paris Match* headlined "*Brigitte et son clan*: "The gaiety of the clan gives the [inauguration] day a Kennedy-like atmosphere". Comparing the Trogneux[25] (confectioners), the Gueudet[26] (car dealers) from Amiens and the Boulogne (heating and sanitary) from Doullens[27] to the Kennedys, was daring... But soon, when the question of the real identity of "Brigitte" arises, the "clan" became totally silent...

150

1. Quoted by Philippe Besson, *VSD*, September 9, 2016.

2. *Elle*, August 18, 2017.

3. Again, "Brigitte" has maintained vagueness about the date when her family set up their vacationing spot in Le Touquet. Sylvie Bommel was told that the purchase of this second home occurred in 1950, while journalists Renaud Dély and Marie Huret were told it was "1958 or 1959, I would have to find the deed of ownership"... After due checking, I found that the Trogneux family, who had a holiday home in Berck, sold it in 1957 and bought the property in Le Touquet-Paris-Plage on September 5, 1957.

4. Regarding Léonce Deprez (1927-2017), UDF mayor of Le Touquet-Paris Plage for more than thirty years (1969-1995 and 2001-2008), we read that "the mayor, who played dozens of doubles tennis matches with Brigitte's father, knows the family well. But much less the youngest daughter"*(Les Macron*, Candice Nedelec and Caroline Derrin, Fayard, 2017). A daughter ("Brigitte") whom Léonce Deprez is supposed to have united twice, once in 1974 to André Auzière and a second time, in 2007, to Emmanuel Macron, with whom he became friends: "Manu plays tennis with the historical UDF mayor Léonce Deprez" (Libération, May 8, 2017).

5. *Les Macron du Touquet-Élysée-plage*, Renaud Dély and Marie Huret, Seuil, 2020.

6. In *Madame la Présidente* (Plon, 2019), Nathalie Schuck and Ava Djamshidi write that "Brigitte" and Anne Méaux "each have a house in Le Touquet. They met at Bercy on March 8, 2015.

7. *Il Venait d'avoir 17 ans*, Sylvie Bommel, JCLattès, 2019.

8. With a background in the business press, Sylvie Bommel specializes in intimate portraits of personalities, which she has published in the French edition of *Vanity Fair*, among others.

9. *Et Brigitte créa Macron*, Sylvie Bommel, *Pop story,* May-June 2016.

10. *L'Express*, October 28, 2015.

11. *Il venait d'avoir 17 ans*, Sylvie Bommel, JCLattès, 2019.

12. *Appelez-moi Brigitte, Elle*, August 18, 2017.

13. The third sibling, Maryvonne Raymonde Marguerite Louise Trogneux, born on January 17, 1937 in Amiens (Somme) died on February 24, 1960 as the result of a road accident in Orvillers-Sorel. *Le Courrier picard* (February 25, 1960) and Le Progrès de l'Oise (February 20, 1960) report on the tragedy that took place on February 17, 1960, claiming the life of her and her husband Paul Farcy, son of Alphonse Farcy, founding president of a powerful agricultural cooperative in the region, La Solidaire based in Albert, twenty kilometers from Amiens. The couple left behind a five-month-old daughter, Nathalie, Danielle, Simone Clotilde Farcy, born in Amiens on September 23, 1959 *Carnet* du *Courrier Picard* (May 9, 1982) in which the birth announcement of Ingrid Bataille, the elder of the two daughters of Nathalie Farcy and Richard Bataille (real estate developer, born November 23, 1954 and died May 11, 2015 in Lille) is presented as Jean-Claude Trogneux's

granddaughter. However, in the general population census of March 1968, Nathalie Farcy, then aged 10, did not appear in the household of Jean-Claude Trogneux, who that year declared himself, his wife, two children, Jean-Alexandre and Martine, and their maid, Jeanne-Marie Moreels.

14. *Les Macron*, Caroline Derrien and Candice Nedelec, Fayard, 2017.

15. *Il venait d'avoir 17 ans*, Sylvie Bommel, JCLattès, 2019.

16. *Les Macrons du Touquet-Elysée-Plage*, Renaud Dély and Marie Huret, Seuil, 2020.

17. Implying that the divorce had occurred at the start of the relationship with Emmanuel Macron, it was initially explained that "to live her crush freely, Brigitte Trogneux divorces" (cf. *Gala*, July 1, 2015, *VSD*, July 9, 2015, etc.). Sometimes it was reported that "Brigitte" did not want to divorce if her parents were alive; sometimes that the divorce had taken place before Emmanuel Macron entered Sciences-Po Paris. In both cases, the divorce could be dated at the turn of the 1990s and 2000s (cf. *L'Express*, April 13, 2016, for example). It was only later that the date now generally accepted was given, i.e. a decision of separate residence issued in May 2005 and a divorce pronounced on January 26, 2006.

18. *La Trognella, ses tenues Vuitton, Carla... découvrez ses petits secrets, capital.fr.*

19. *Et Brigitte créa Macron*, Sylvie Bommel, *Pop story*, May-June 2016.

20. Testimonials quoted by Sylvie Bommel in *Il venait d'avoir 17 ans*, Sylvie Bommel, JCLattès, 2019.

21. Before *Paris Match* (October 8, 2020) André Auzière's death had first been very discreetly listed on December 31, 2019 by Philippe Prové on the *Roglo* genealogy forum.

22. *Sa vie d'avant*, *Le Point*, April 25, 2019.

23. See *Chapter 16*.

24. This legend of "Trogneux confectioners [*confiseurs*] for 6 generations" was largely forged by the father, Jean Trogneux, until then a pastry maker rather than a confectioner (*pâtissier* vs *confiseur*) (as the 1931 census shows), who built up his business mainly by buying *La Maison des Baptêmes* from the Danjou family (sold in 1947 to the Amiens trade association collecting war damages, and acquired by Jean Trogneux in 1949), then by taking over, in 1963, the actual historical confectioner in Amiens, Magniez-Baussart, founded in 1859 (through the purchase of the production facilities and integration of the staff).

25. The history of the Trogneux family is well documented. Originally from the village of Vaulx (Pas-de-Calais), In the *ancien régime* they were *fermiers propriétaires* ("farmer-owners"), suggesting some affluence. But for some unknown reason, this social status collapsed under Louis XV, with several generations of *manouvriers* (farm hands). In 1834, in the space of two weeks, the death certificates of André Trogneux, his wife and their nineteen-year-old son were recorded, the decimated family leaving behind an orphan, Horeillie Trogneux. She became a spinner and gave birth to Marc Étienne Xavier Trogneux (1952-1911). Born of an unknown father, this pastry-boy from Amiens is considered the founder of the line in the family's mythology. There is even a Wikipedia page dedicated to the

152

Trogneux family, which is quite unusual for a family with no ties to the nobility (of any kind) or to the great dynasties of the bourgeoisie and the business world. The Trogneux family are in fact successful shopkeepers (large SMEs), initially with low social standing. In short, the Trogneux family belongs to the "*nouveau riche*" category (not pejoratively; a way to says small recently affluent bourgeoisie), and are fully integrated in this milieu. Brigitte's father, Jean Georges Trogneux, born on April 26, 1909 in Amiens and died on January 15, 1994, married Simone Pujol on September 26, 1931 in Amiens. Simone Pujol was born on August 18, 1913 and died on February 18, 1998 in Amiens, the daughter of a wine and spirits merchant from Ariège. Jean Trogneux's success was crowned by his presidency of the Rotary Club of Amiens, founded in 1938 (District 1520, located at 2, rue de Noyon in the Grand Hôtel de l'Univers), with some 70 members of the local bourgeoisie, including such families as Yvert (Yvert & Tellier catalogs), Désérable (Mr Bricolage hardware stores), Gueudet (Gueudet car dealers), Boulogne (Ets Boulogne – heating and sanitary wholesalers) and other families. Closely linked to the Trogneux family, the Couineau (Robert Ledoux Diffusion Bureautique) father (Henri) and son (Philippe) also belong to this ecosystem. Jean Trogneux married his daughters within the Rotary network, thus moving up the social ladder. In Amiens, where they pride themselves on their influence on local politics, the Trogneux now support the UDI mayor Brigitte Fouré and are credited with playing a key role when, in 1989, Gilles de Robien ousted the Communist mayor René Lamps, who had held the town hall since 1971. Jean-Claude Marie Joseph Trogneux was born in Amiens on August 14, 1933. In the early 1970s, the eldest son took over from his father at the head of the Maison Trogneux as president of Jean Trogneux la Maison des Baptêmes but also in sports, as president of the Amiens Tennis Club and the organization of the "Promenade", an annual cycling tour between Amiens and Le Touquet. On June 14, 1960, Jean-Claude Trogneux married Danièle Courbot in Amiens, the youngest child of Henri Courbot, owner of the Courbot construction company and at the time president of the *Syndicat professionnel des entrepreneurs travaux publics France et Outre-Mer*, member of the CNPF (today's MEDEF), Chairman of the Paris Chamber of Commerce and Industry and of the Assembly of Chambers of Commerce of the European Economic Community. The couple had four children, including Jean-Alexandre Trogneux, born on April 26, 1961 in Amiens, who in turn took over the family business in July 2016, never hesitating to show his support for the presidential couple. After graduating from the *École supérieure de commerce de Paris* (ESCP), he launched a new boutique on rue Saint-Jean in Le Touquet in April 2019. From his marriage to Véronique Catteau on June 10, 1989 in Montigny-sur-l'Hallue (Somme), came Jean-Baptiste Trogneux (1993), married to a Hong Kong Chinese woman (they had a son, Sin Yin), and a daughter Margaux (1996). When, in 2023, three drop-outs are tried for molesting Jean-Baptiste Trogneux during a brawl near a demonstration, the Prime Minister intervenes before the judgment, declaring: "They went after him because a Trogneux, like some people went after the Jews because they were Jews." (Radio J, May 28, 2023). Jean-Claude Trogneux's second daughter, Martine Trogneux, born on April 12, 1964, a general practitioner in Longjumeau, married Hacene Abbar, a maxillo-facial surgeon and stomatologist in Arpajon (with four children: Maxime, Baptiste, Jules and Tom). When asked whether the Macrons and Trogneux were meeting regularly before, Sylvie Bommel was told that, despite their geographical proximity, they did not belong to the same world: "On one side, doctors and notaries, and on the other, successful shopkeepers." (*Il Venait d'avoir 17 ans*, JCLattès, 2019). But the Trogneux side also boasts a substantial number of medical doctors, including Laurence Auzière (cardiologist), Antoine Choteau (gastroenterologist), Martine Trogneux (general practitioner) and Hacene Abbar (maxillo-facial surgeon). On September 26, 1990 in Amiens, Jean-Claude Trogneux married Brigitte Poillion, and there were two Brigitte Trogneux in the family – but it is Brigitte Poillion who appears in the articles of association of the Trogneux companies. From her first marriage to Alain-Georges Deledicque, a doctor born on January 17, 1944 in Roubaix (Nord), director of thalassotherapy centers successively in Oléron, Carnac, Quiberon, Dinard, Deauville and Siouville-Hague, former municipal councillor in Saint-Trojan (1976), member of the Rotary and treasurer of the French Society of Thalassotherapy. Brigitte Trogneux is the mother of the film director Robin Deledicque, now a member of LREM. Jean-Claude Trogneux, who initially waged a bitter war against "Brigitte and Emmanuel" before accepting his brother-in-law after he entered the *École Nationale d'Administration* (ENA) (which, in this thoroughly milieu à la Claude Chabrol, seems quite credible) died on November 9, 2018. Surprisingly, it was Emmanuel Macron, usually so skittish about traveling to Amiens in his capacity as head of State, who delivered his brother-in-law's eulogy on November 13, 2018 at Saint-Martin church in the Henriville district, completely cordoned off from public and press alike (see *"Un discours émouvant d'Emmanuel Macron"*, *Le Courrier picard*, November 14, 2018). Although Trogneux is a very common name in Amiens, most of the people bearing this surname are not related to the "Brigitte" family. The only remaining branch was that of Jean Trogneux's uncle, Ernest Trogneux. The latter's daughter Renée Trogneux died in 1993, and her only son Bernard Philippe (born of her union with Maurice Philippe) died in Amiens on September 16, 2017. Although this ranch was into producing marble elements for funeral monuments, Bernard Philippe's name strangely does not appear on his parents' family vault.

26. The Trogneux connected to the Gueudets through the marriage, in 1963, of the fourth sibling, Monique Trogneux, born in Amiens on August 7, 1940, to Jean-Claude Gueudet, who, like Gérard Boulogne, came from the paternal network in the Rotary Club of Amiens. Jean-Claude Gueudet heads France's second-largest automotive distributor, with 158 dealerships. The Gueudet Group, based in Amiens, generated sales of € 1.2 billion in 2016. The Gueudet family ranked 395th in *Challenges* magazine's list of France's largest professional fortunes, with 200 million euros. The new rich Gueudet brothers have been operating garages from father to son since 1880. They seized a unique opportunity when Jean-Claude's father, Robert Gueudet, signed a distribution contract with Louis Renault in 1920, soon becoming the main dealer for the brand with the diamond-shaped logo. Patrick Gueudet, Jean-Claude Gueudet's younger brother, was married to Florence Hersant-Boneat (1948- 2013), daughter-in-law of Robert Hersant and former PR director of *Le Figaro Magazine* (1978-88) and then *Le Figaro* group (1988-2004). From a previous marriage, his son Édouard Gueudet, based in Geneva, was a vice-president of

Banque Hottinger & Cie and is currently managing the development of CISA Trust Company, a company setting up trusts (for tax avoidance) in the British Virgin Islands for a wealthy international clientele. A member of the Automobile club de France (ACF), Travellers Paris, Polo de Paris and the [caritative] *Service hospitalier de l'Ordre de Malte en Suisse* (SHOMS), in 2014 he reactivated the Swiss edition of the *Who's Who* (700 entries). Monique Gueudet is the organizer of the *President's Cup* at the Amiens Golf Club in Querrieu, and a director of Gueudet Frères. Her son, Cyril Gueudet, born in Amiens on November 24 1966, is the Managing Director of Gueudet Sarva and Palais de l'Automobile in Abbeville. Jean-Claude and Monique Gueudet have two other children: Anne-Catherine Gueudet, and Arnaud Gueudet, born on December 13, 1972 in Amiens, who also joined the Gueudet Group. Baptiste Pecriaux, son of Caroll Gueudet and nephew of Monique Gueudet, has been running since 2018 Impact Campus, a subsidiary of Groupe SOS, the behemoth of the "social and solidary" economy headed by Jean-Marc Borello (see Chapter 10), after starting his career in 2008 at Lysias Partners, the law firm of Jean-Pierre Mignard (François Hollande's closest friend) and then joining Transparency International France, where he was in charge of Private Sector & Higher Education programs.

27. The Trogneux connected to the Boulognes through the marriage of the eldest sibling, Anne-Marie Gisèle Marguerite, known as "Annie" Trogneux, born in Amiens on July 9, 1932, to Gérard Boulogne (1930-2022), a member of the Amiens Rotary Club, who like his future wife came from a family of downtown shopkeepers. He is proud to have made Établissements Boulogne "a key player in the sanitation/heating sector in northern France". With annual sales of some 15 million euros and some 40 employees, it is now run by his son Thierry Boulogne, born on February 28, 1968 in Amiens. His elder sister, Christine Boulogne, born in Amiens on March 26, 1957, married Benoît Haquin in 1983. Born on May 4, 1954 in Brégy (Oise), owner of a large farm (GAEC Haquin Rémi et Benoît), mayor of his native village since 1989 and president of the Pays de Valois community of communes from 2014 to 2020. Through the marriage of one of the couple's four children to a Reynal de Saint-Michel, the Trogneux family is now connected to this famous Martinique "*béké*" (White in the tropics) family, itself allied to the Hayot family, among others. Despite being her first known niece and belonging to the same generation, Annie Trogneux's eldest daughter Christine Haquin was not inserted into the storytelling, and the death of her younger sister Sylvie was used by "Brigitte" to muddle her past.

155

PART IV

THE JEAN-MICHEL TROGNEUX AFFAIR

"She didn't believe in feelings. She judged low, she judged just."
Louis-Ferdinand Céline, *Mort à crédit*, Denoël, 1936.

"If not you, then your brother."
Jean de la Fontaine, *The Wolf and the Lamb*, 1668.

"Only puny secrets need protection. Big discoveries are protected by public incredulity."
Marshall McLuhan, *Take Today. The Executive as Dropout*, 1972.

"Journalism is a profession where you spend half your life talking about what you don't know, and the other half keeping quiet about what you do know."
Henri Béraud.

18

NATACHA REY

"Sitting naturally with legs apart"

June 12, 2021. My phone rings. On the other end of the line, one of my contacts whispered that he "might have something about Brigitte Macron". The day before, he had dinner with a former *France 3* news anchor who told him he had met a woman who could prove that Brigitte Macron is… a man! Name: Natacha Rey.

For years I've known there was something wrong with Brigitte Macron. Her biography, rewritten over and over, is shrouded in mystery. A senior civil servant, with a look of innuendo, once said to me: "In fact, it's a man". A man? But then, who?

In Parisian editorial offices, the subject is taboo and the instruction is that "Brigitte is untouchable". However, in a few anonymous confidences reported by journalists, we find here and there traces of these rumors in low intensity and anonymously: "She didn't always have this physique, she built it up", says someone who used to work at the Élysée palace, with a sting; "She's made every effort, every effort…", laments another familiar of the halls of power, with heavy innuendo, reiterating this cruel maxim: "To be present, you have to be presentable"[1]. There were whispers in the gay *Tout-Paris*, of which we find a public trace on television, in 2018, in a skit by the

159

homosexual comedian Vincent Dedienne: "The circumstances of their encounter, their love at first sight, their very intimate album, the glorification of the couple... Okay, we get it. And your story is so banal... We had a little hope at one point, but you're not a fag and she's not a trans. So it's terribly boring"[2].

What was the true nature of "Brigitte's" "wasp's nest" referred to by journalists Caroline Derrien and Candice Nedelec, who pointed out that Emmanuel Macron "likes to refer to 'families' and not the [typical] family in the singular, because he "recognizes himself in these different tribes, homoparental families in particular"[3]? And what about this portrait by journalists Nathalie Schuck and Ava Djamshidi describing "Brigitte" as the "heroine of a play she partly wrote, an actress in the comedy of power, where she has an off-center role, perched on her vertiginous heels that make her suffer, with a stilted smile, she puts on her costume: "I put on my stilettos, my tights, my dress and I step into my role, I'm there. In my head, I'm in the role of first lady." Her favorite role?"[4] Why did comedian Jérôme Commandeur imitate "Brigitte" with the voice range of Amanda Lear, a singer who gained worldwide notoriety by cleverly maintaining ambiguity about her transsexuality through a biography that has been reworked many times?

From a purely biographical point of view, in the most technical sense of the term, the "Brigitte's" biographers had stumbled over pitfalls very similar to those faced by the biographers of Amanda Lear, Salvador Dali's transsexual muse turned pop muse for Silvio Berlusconi's TV channels[5]. This is the result of a complex psychological mechanism that could be described as suspension of disbelief applied to one's own story. The result is a fictional life (hence "Brigitte's" recurring reference to Gustave Flaubert's Madame Bovary), lived as if it were reality[6]. All this while regularly sending signals to the outside world to claim, at least subliminally, the deception. A more or less conscious tug-of-war that pushes the subject to unceasingly deny his birth identity, and in so doing, to always put another coin into the slot machine by nurtufing doubt... A complex mechanism, touching at the deepest level of what characterizes, as categories, the masculine, the feminine and their corollary, the relationship to truth, according to the Austrian philosopher Otto Weininger[7]. This concealment mechanism is an inner labyrinth that the subject projects onto the outside world. A labyrinth which disorients the public and in which the biographer loses his bearings…

What kind of unease did press cartoonist Xavier Delucq feel when drawing "Brigitte"? He reflected on this "very special, very unique face. Starting with a very particular nose… very flat, very wide, with very visible nostrils… Just because she's a woman doesn't mean we shouldn't caricature the features… as for a man"[8]? Why is it that the most popular memes exchanged between friends and family on e-mail always find similarity between "Brigitte" and singers Iggy Pop and Patrick Juvet, as if everyone were unconsciously wondering: *What if she were a man?*

In June 2021, I called Natacha Rey to find out more about this woman who had claimed to be "able to demonstrate that Brigitte Macron is a man". On the other end of the line, I hear a voice as frail as it is determined, with an accent that makes me think of Bordeaux. She is actually from Charente and lives in the backcountry of La Rochelle. In the course of our discussions, I understood that, while I had been interested in "Brigitte" by combining off-the-record testimonies with the findings of other journalists' investigations, Natacha Rey had taken an interest in the character via the Internet, essentially by observing the photographic material published daily on celebrity sites aimed at a female readership. Every day, the Internet has a lavish of "Brigitte" content supplied jointly by 6Médias and Bestimage to the websites of magazines of Prisma group *(Gala, Femme Actuelle, Voici, Télé Loisirs*, etc.)[9]. Based on the brand content model, there are every day one or two text pieces relayed on all the group's media sites: a short article, taking an anecdote from one of the hagiographies devoted to the presidential couple, reworked according to current events by 6Médias and accompanied by an sleek photographs of "Brigitte" from the photographic database of Bestimage, Michèle Marchand's agency[10]. This process designed for search engine optimization (exploiting Google) is unprecedented in the history of the Internet, as journalist Maëlle Brun points out: "Typing Brigitte Macron's name into Google brings up over ten million hits. That's twice as much as David Beckham" [11]. From time to time, this content insists on "Brigitte's" "look", sometimes emphasizing her "androgynous" style...

While talking with Natacha Rey, I realize that she is not a journalist and has not investigated with the usual methodology. She is an ordinary, self-taught citizen who, on her Facebook page, wonders about Brigitte's "extraordinary" physique, her the "width of her neck, her shoulders, the length of her ribcage compared to her narrow, waistless lower body. Hence this unbalanced silhouette, this virile gait always with long strides, this way of sitting naturally with legs apart".

The Rey thesis

Assuming that Brigitte Macron is a man, Natacha Rey set out to find her birth identity. When she came across the family photo in Virginie Linhart's documentary, she was struck by the face of the child on the left. Then, as she studied the Trogneux family, she realized that this brother,

Jean-Michel Trogneux, never appeared, and that there was virtually no trace of him on the Internet, so presumably there was an effort to hide him. Natacha Rey had developed the following conviction: "Brigitte Macron is Jean-Michel Trogneux".

But how could one explain the three children: Sébastien, Laurence and Tiphaine Auzière? Assuming that Brigitte Macron was a man born Jean-Michel Trogneux, Natacha Rey deduced that "Brigitte" was not their mother, but their father. So they needed a mother, whose name would have to be Auzière. As the sister's name is  Catherine, Natacha Rey had typed "Catherine Auzière" on *Facebook* and come across a Catherine Audoy-Auzière.

 Surprise! Catherine Audoy was in a relationship with a man named Jean-Louis Auzière, a friend of Laurence Auzière's on *Facebook*, who bears a striking resemblance to the André Auzière in Sylvie Bommel's 2019 photograph of Brigitte Trogneux's first wedding.

From her find, Natacha Rey deduced the following thesis: "Brigitte" was born a man under the name Jean-Michel Trogneux; he had had a relationship with Catherine Audoy, and they had had three children: Sébastien, Laurence and Tiphaine, who were adopted by Jean-Louis Auzière after his marriage to Catherine Audoy, hence their name "Auzière" and not "Trogneux"; and Brigitte Trogneux and André Auzière are fictitious characters invented to disguise the real life of "Brigitte".

163

A disproportionate police custody

I was immediately interested in any physical correspondence between "Brigitte" and Jean-Michel Trogneux, and between André and Jean-Louis Auzière. I did some research and found Catherine Audoy's cell phone number, which I passed on to Natacha Rey, explaining that we would contact her in due time… But Natacha Rey took the initiative and, on June 22, 2021, ten days after our first exchanges, sent Catherine Audoy via *WhatsApp* the two sets of photos (Brigitte = Jean-Michel / Jean-Louis = André), with the message: "I know everything. I know all about you, Jean-Michel, Sébastien, Laurence and Tiphaine!"

The reaction was prompt. On July 13, 2021, Natacha Rey saw the *gendarmerie* arrive at her home. She was taken into custody (without being summoned) on the pretext of a complaint lodged by Catherine Audoy with the public prosecutor of Lisieux. She was released after five hours of harsh interrogation, which included a moralizing sermon, humiliations and threats of all kinds. She was asked for the list of journalists she had been in contact with, and her phone was seized. In 2024, this episode, which marks the real beginning of the Trogneux affair, was narrated by journalist Emmanuelle Anizon: "July 13, 2021, Natacha has almost not slept durint the night as she finishes packing her moving boxes. […]. She hasn't seen time go by - it's 1:30 p.m., she hasn't dressed yet, hasn't had breakfast, she's fully occupied with completing her task, when the doorbell rings. She doesn't open the door, it rings again, longer. She finally asks who is there and hears in return: "It's the gendarmerie. Open the door!" There are three of them and they ask her to follow them: "They said to me: You're under arrest." I asked them if they had a warrant, and they replied: "This isn't an American movie." They wouldn't tell me what I was being arrested for. […] When I arrived at the police station, they told me I was in custody, searched me, confiscated my cell phone and interrogated me. They were misogynistic, scoffing, sometimes threatening. The adjutant yelled at me: "What do you care if she's a man? It's her private life! It's none of your business." "Natacha asks for a lawyer. "They told me it would delay the interrogation and that I might have to spend the night at the police station. It was the first time in my life I had been in police custody, and I didn't know what to do. I was obsessed with the fact that I had to finish packing and move home two days later. I was so stressed that I foolishly agreed to answer without a lawyer. After five hours, the prosecutor, with whom they were in constant contact on the phone, finally authorized my release. I left without any means of communication, as they had refused to return my phone. I have not got it back since, despite several requests"[12]. Had Natacha Rey touched a sensitive nerve?

As I have been based in Italy since 2018, it is *Faits & Documents*'s webmaster who is paying the price for my interest in "Brigitte's" biography. On August 19, 2021, a month after Natacha Rey's police custody during which she revealed my name, he was arrested and placed under judicial supervision, under the pretext of his activity on an ultra-confidential *Telegram* feed (with several hundred subscribers). He underwent three home searches, was placed under judicial supervision, and his two computers and his telephone were seized.

Continuing the investigation in connection with Natacha Rey, I sent my team to carry out extensive research in the National Archives at the *Bibliothèque nationale de France*. But when I present Natacha Rey with documents that contradict her thesis, she always gives the same answer: "It's a fake!" The two birth announcements for Brigitte Trogneux that I have fished out from the *Courrier Picard*'s archives: "Fake!" What about the announcements published in *Le Courrier Picard* for the births of Sébastien, Laurence and Tiphaine Auzière, which include the names of their parents, Brigitte and André Auzière? "Fake!" Forged documents and modified facsimiles of newspapers deposited in the National Archives? While an operation on this scale seems unlikely, the methods employed by the people who manage "Brigitte's" image mean that, for the time being, we can legitimately ask the question, without falling into the realm of defamation.

And the photograph of Brigitte Trogneux's communion? "An edited photograph", Natacha Rey continues: "You can tell it's Tiphaine and not Brigitte. And the wedding photo: "Another fake one. Clearly, they have inserted Laurence's face!" In effect, the first evaluations I am getting with *Face++*, a world leading software in visual artificial intelligence (facial recognition) developed by the Chinese company Megvii, show that the communicant and the bride, i.e. the two usable photos of "Brigitte" in her "former life", tend not to represent "Brigitte". But if it is not "Brigitte" on these two photographs, who is it?

For her part, Natacha Rey twice requested Jean-Michel Trogneux's birth certificate from the Amiens registry office. Twice she was told: "We regret that we are unable to send you the birth certificate of Jean-Michel Trogneux. This deed is not in our possession. We invite you to contact Jean-Michel Trogneux's birthplace". However, I quickly discovered that Jean-Michel Trogneux was born in Amiens on February 11, 1945…

Suite à votre demande du 24 mars 2021, nous regrettons de ne pouvoir vous adresser votre extrait sans filiation concernant l'acte de naissance de Jean-Michel TROGNEUX.

Cet acte ne se trouvant pas en notre possession.

Nous vous invitons à vous mettre en rapport avec la Mairie de naissance de Jean-Michel TROGNEUX qui détient cet acte.

Nous vous prions d'agréer, Madame, l'expression de nos salutations distinguées.

Amiens, le 15 avril 2021
L'Officier de l'Etat Civil délégué
Marie URBANIAK

Suite à votre demande du 12 avril 2021, nous regrettons de ne pouvoir vous adresser votre extrait sans filiation concernant l'acte de naissance de Jean-Michel TROGNEUX.

Cet acte ne se trouvant pas en notre possession.

Nous vous invitons à vous mettre en rapport avec la Mairie de naissance de Jean-Michel TROGNEUX qui détient cet acte.

Nous vous prions d'agréer, Madame, l'expression de nos salutations distinguées.

Amiens, le 5 mai 2021
L'Officier de l'Etat Civil délégué
Marie URBANIAK

166

For my first open-source research on Jean-Michel Trogneux on the Internet, I typed his name into *Google Book* and found a mention in the *Bulletin officiel des annonces civiles et commerciales* dated June 12, 1973. There, "Jean-Michel, Henri Trogneux purchased the Gallice jewelry store at 25, rue des Boucheries in Toulon (Var), an address he used as his home address". I relayed this information in *Faits & Documents*, before realizing, a few months later, that it was a reading error due to the partial display of the document on *Google Book* (two superimposed columns). Strangely enough, instead of pointing out this flaw when the story broke, the Trogneux entourage preferred to send me in the wrong direction...

"Brigitte", a shareholder of the family company?

Continuing my investigation on legal and financial information websites, I found a trace of Jean-Michel Trogneux in one of the Trogneux family companies. These are the minutes of the Extraordinary General Meeting of *Société d'exploitation des établissements Arrasse* held on May 25, 2007. Jean-Michel Trogneux is a shareholder and company teller, alongside his nephew Jean-Alexandre Trogneux (Managing Director) and his brother Jean-Claude Trogneux (Chairman of the Board). The document formalizes the transition of *Société d'exploitation des établissements Arrasse* from a *société anonyme* (limited liability company) to a *société par actions simplifiée* (simplified joint stock company). Nothing unusual so far. But when we consulted the copy of the document ratifying the modification filed with the Amiens Commercial Court on October 17, 2007, three days before the wedding between "Brigitte" and Emmanuel Macron, Jean-Michel Trogneux disappeared from the articles of association. He never reappeared there. However, according to her official biography, "Brigitte" remained a shareholder in the family company until 2007... like Jean-Michel: "A business in which Brigitte could have become involved once she had packed her *baccalauréat* (A-level exam). Of course, her name is not Jean, and she is not part of the "father to son" tradition boasted on a poster at the Trogneux's company. Her brother Jean-Claude, who took over the business, would have found a role for her, but she dreaded this lifestyle.

Being a director of the family company - a position she held until 2007 - was more than enough for her"[13]. But the only Brigitte Trogneux who appears in the articles of association of the family companies over the years is in fact the other Brigitte Trogneux, *née* Poillion, the second wife of Jean-Claude Trogneux. Even stranger still, when we ask the *Institut national de la propriété industrielle* (INPI) for the original document registered with the Amiens commercial court on October 17, 2007 (and not a duplicate), we discover an additional signature clearly reading "BTrogneux", whereas no Brigitte Trogneux appears in the document[14]. I asked two court-licensed graphology experts in (in Italy and in France) to examine the handwriting; they concluded that this is not the signature of Brigitte Trogneux épouse Auzière, nor that of Brigitte Poillion épouse Trogneux... Finally, on September 29, 2017, in the wake of Emmanuel Macron's election, the *Société d'exploitation des établissements Arrasse* was renamed *SAS Les Spécialités picardes* and moved from 14, rue des Vergeaux in Amiens to 1, rue Delambre, the address of the Trogneux fiefdom...

Certified by Amanda Lear

In the meantime, Natacha Rey's police custody provided a factual anchor to relay her description as a hypothesis, but forced us to stick to this thesis. For Natacha Rey, the counterpart for the publicity given to her case would obviously be the publication of all the documents and information[15] that contradicted the conclusions of what was so far an interesting but purely intuitive thesis. I used this aberrant and disproportionate period of police custody (Natacha Rey had only sent a few messages to a collateral relative of "Brigitte's") to relay her thesis in a conclusion leading to a series of articles published between late summer and early autumn 2021 in *Faits & Documents*, the confidential information newsletter I was editing at the time, under the title *Le Mystère Brigitte Macron*. This included this question about to the presidential couple: "Why is "Brigitte" reluctant to speak openly about her past? Is she afraid that Jean-Michel, the boy with fine limbs and the troubled heart will resurface? The suffering teenager who won't let it slip into his head that, without forgery, he's just a boy? "

A few days after the publication of the "Rey thesis", a very strange interview with Amanda Lear appeared in *Gala*, titled *Brigitte Macron, le féminisme et moi*. In it, "Amanda" said she had introduced "Brigitte" to a photo editing application. A few months later, on the occasion of Emmanuel Macron's re-election, "Amanda" published a photo of "Brigitte" on X, with the comment: "Brigitte" "I'm in for another 5 years".

Thereafter, "Amanda" was much less teasing towards the presidential couple. It is worth noting that she received a large check, estimated at half a million euros, for the use of her song *Follow Me* in a Chanel advertising campaign... At the end of October 2021, the first review of my investigation was published. The author, Lionel Labosse, a teacher and writer, is a homosexual activist opposed to the LGBT agenda. His article, featured on the profession-gendarme. com website, soon attracted hundreds of thousands of hits.

In the weeks following the publication of the "Rey thesis" *Le Monde* ran an article which revealed that "the Élysée is monitoring online conversations, whether on *Facebook*, on *Telegram*, or on popular forums such as *jeuxvideos.com*"[16]. The mention of the *jeuxvidéos.com*, a gamers' forum, seemed strange to me. So I looked it up, and discovered dozens and dozens of pages of discussion about my investigation, scanned versions of which were being passed around...

In the wake of the publication of Le *Mystère Brigitte Macron*, a tax audit was launched on November 19, 2021 on EDP SAS, the parent company of *Faits & Documents*, as well as on all the companies in the portfolio of *Faits & Documents*' majority shareholder. When the tax reassessment was completed in 2024, the shareholder notified me of an "end of collaboration", judging that this investigation was costing him too much. And yet, as the sole editor and publication director of the newspaper that was the primary source in the Trogneux affair, I have never been sued for defamation...

In this month of November 2021, I continue my research and take an interest in the only friend common to the *Facebook* accounts "Brigitte Auzière Macron" and "Jean-Michel Trogneux". This is about a Jean-Jacques Trogneux, who has completely escaped the radar. Her name never appears in biographies of "Brigitte" or in articles about the Trogneux family. He does not appear in any genealogical database, but has a *Facebook* account, which allows me to establish that he was born in November 1982. Natacha Rey is convinced that he is a hidden son of "Brigitte", i.e. Jean-Michel Trogneux, and Catherine Audoy. I went to the National Archives and found, in *Le Courrier Picard*, the birth announcement published by her parents Jean-Michel Trogneux and... Véronique Dreux – not Catherine Audoy, who, according to my research, probably never had children...

When I presented the results of my new research to Natacha Rey, I assured her that I would continue the investigation, but advised her not to express herself publicly, as it was still too early, and her original thesis had already been partly invalidated. But feeling that the case was slipping away from her, Natacha Rey cut her ties with the firm intention of publicizing her thesis on her own…

1. Quoted by Ava Djamshidi, and Nathalie Schuck in *Madame la présidente*, Plon 2019.

2. *Quotidien*, TMC, June 6, 2018.

3. *Les Macron*, Candice Nedelec and Caroline Derrien, Fayard, 2017.

4. *Madame la présidente*, Ava Djamshidi, and Nathalie Schuck, Plon 2019

5. About Amanda Lear, born Alain Maurice Louis René Tap, male, on June 18, 1939 in Saigon (French Indochina), watch Patrick Jeudy's documentary *Amanda Lear : Appelez-moi mademoiselle* broacasted onr *Arte* in 2023. The French version of the Wikipedia *page* gives a fairly accurate idea of the mechanism described here.

6. The character of Diane Selwyn in David Lynch's *Mulholland Drive* is an example of total "bovarianism".

7. *Sex and Character: A Fundamental Investigation*, Otto Weininger, Wilhelm Braumüller, 1903.

8. Xavier Delucq, cartoonist at *L'Écho-Le Régional*, on his *Youtube* channel @ pdelucq, January 29, 2020.

9. Long owned by Germany's Bertelsmann, Prisma Media was taken over in 2021 by Vincent Bolloré (Vivendi).

10. See *Chapter 12*.

11. *Brigitte Macron. L'Affranchie*, Maëlle Brun, L'Archipel, 2018.

12. *L'Affaire Madame*, Emmanuelle Anizon, StudioFact Éditions, 2024.

13. *Brigitte Macron. L'Affranchie*, Maëlle Brun, L'Archipel, 2018.

14. The documents were published on the *Telegram* feed "L'Affaire Jean-Michel Trogneux".

15. We mention André Auzière's death certificate and publish Brigitte Trogneux's birth announcement, which appeared in *Le Courrier Picard* at the time. We add the precision that Jean-Louis Auzière was married to Susan Spray when Brigitte Trogneux married André Auzière. But at the time, some press articles devoted to the untraceable "André-Louis" Auzière called him Jean-Louis. What's more, both were born on February 28: February 28, 1943 for Jean-Louis, André; February 28, 1951 for André, Louis. This is fairly complex… But Jean-Louis, André Auzière is indeed André-Louis's uncle, as we will evidence later. Born on February 28, 1943

in Meudon (Hauts-de-Seine), he studied law and foreign languages, before embarking on a career in the luxury goods industry, where he held successive positions as sales and marketing director at Fabergé (1972-1978) and Revlon (1978-1981), before joining Parfums Grès as the general manager (1981-1987). Still in the same sector, he launched and chaired Indipar in Jouy-en-Josas (Yvelines), while also joining various professional organizations, having been the General Secretary of the *Fédération des cristalleries et verreries à la main et mixtes* and of the *Comité des Arts de la Table*. A French foreign trade advisor (1983 and 1996), chevalier de l'ordre du Mérite (2012), he was sworn in before the Caen Court of Appeal in February 2021, becoming *conciliateur de justice* (ombudsman) in the Lisieux (Calvados) jurisdiction. Before settling near Honfleur, Jean-Louis Auzière had, according to the Who's Who in the 1980s, a second home in Cannes, the villa "Les Aquarelles" on avenue de Vallauris. On May 7, 1966, he married Susan Spray, an interpreter who now does volunteer work with the *Meudon 7ᵉ art* cultural association in Meudon (Hauts-de-Seine). From this first union, he is the father of Pascal Auzière, Director of Sales Strategy at Laboratoires Urgo, and Vice-Chairman of the Burgundy-Franche-Comté region's healthcare cluster (BFCare). He is listed in the *Bottin mondain* with his wife Isabelle de Sury d'Aspremont and their four children. Much more discreet, his other son, Marc Auzière, is a business manager at L'Argus in Versailles. On June 21, 2003, he married Catherine Audoy, a civil aviation executive born on April 2, 1944 in Bazas (Gironde).

16. *Les macronistes à l'affût des mouvements de la société française*, Le Monde, November 8, 2021.

17. Quoted by Philippe Besson, *VSD*, September 9, 2016.

18. *Elle*, August 18, 2017.

19. Again, "Brigitte" has maintained the vagueness about the date when her family set up their vacationing spot in Le Touquet. Sylvie Bommel was told that the purchase of this second home occurred in 1950, while journalists Renaud Dély and Marie Huret were told it was "1958 or 1959, I would have to find the deed of ownership"... After due checking, I found that the Trogneux family, who had a holiday home in Berck, sold it in 1957 and bought the property in Le Touquet-Paris-Plage on September 5, 1957.

19

A "CHUBBY GUY"

Friday, December 10, 2021

It has been a month since I cut ties with Natacha Rey. I receive an alert on my cell phone: Natacha Rey will appear live on December 10, 2021 on an obscure *Youtube* channel hosted by a psychic: Amandine Roy. Without any hedging, Natacha Rey unfolded her thesis on "Brigitte", very affirmatively, for almost 4.5 hours, insisting on the "strangeness of her physique", her "rhinoplasties", her "gestures" which "are not those of a woman"… "There's absolutely no grace, there's no femininity in her gestures, and I'm surprised [...] her gait is a catastrophe. Even in an evening gown, even in heels, even on the day of the inauguration, she's always walking in long strides; I've never seen a feminine woman in her, and from that social class, because it's someone who comes from the high bourgeoisie, someone who's the First Lady of France, so she should have a modicum of attitude. You can see her walking… I often posted videos on my *Facebook* page. I often posted photographs of her walking. In fact, in the comments on *Youtube* videos, some people would say "No! That's not possible! It's a man!". [...] She's always being compared to men anyway, whether it's Amanda Lear, Patrick Juvet, Iggy Pop, I don't know. [...] No waist, there are no hips, there are no… There are broad, square shoulders… look at a woman in a suit jacket and look at Brigitte in a suit jacket, and you'll see the difference right away. [...] There are rather large feet."

She explains the origin of her thesis: "The family photograph… I looked at this photo since she's supposed to be on her mother's lap. I wasted time.,. No way. And then one day I enlarged this photograph, I enlarged Jean-Michel, I looked at Jean-Michel a lot and I took a photograph of Brigitte, I put the two together and then eureka! eureka! I had just found the answer to the question I had been asking myself for weeks and weeks: who the heck was she? And then I understood, then everything became clear, everything became clear, I understood. And you see, Jean-Michel's hair implantation is Brigitte's – if you remove the fringe, if you remove it, it's the same. So it's the same nose, exactly the same mouth, the same smile, the same chin, the same face shape and yet in the photo he must be 10, 12 years old at the most, it's a photo where he's still very young, that's all. As for the gaze, you should know that Brigitte wears blue contact lenses."

She tells of "the impossibility of obtaining a copy of my birth certificate. [...] Oh yes, I was told that Jean- Michel, and even when I got the exact date of birth, I was told that Jean-Michel was not born in… Jean-Michel Trogneux was not born in Amiens and to check with the town hall of his place of birth. But Jean-Michel was born in Amiens, as were all the children in the Trogneux family; all the siblings were born in Amiens, and the parents never left the city. So why shouldn't there be… Would we have made this birth certificate disappear? Transsexuals have the right to have their birth certificate amended. So… It's legal, so as soon as the birth certificate has been modified, of course there's no longer a birth certificate in the name of Jean-Michel Trogneux, but of Brigitte Trogneux". Natacha Rey was later convicted of defamation on this specific point.

"So this just confirms my doubts: either Brigitte didn't marry an André-Louis Auzière, and I thought: "Well, if my hypothesis is right and she's Jean-Michel, then she's obviously not the children's mother, but the father… If she's the children's father, there's necessarily a mother, hidden somewhere…" And then, you'll see… So I said to myself: "I have to look for her, yes, but what's her name since I don't have her maiden name and she can't be called Madame

174

Auzière, considering that if she had married Jean-Michel, she would have become Madame Trogneux; so it's not Madame..." And I said to myself: "well I'm going to look anyway", I don't know, a hunch, I said to myself: ""I'm still going to get the Madame Auzière", and yet it didn't hold water, it didn't hold water..." And then I typed random names, several first names, and I ended up typing Catherine, which is also my sister's first name. And then I saw a Catherine, a Catherine Auzière, a Catherine Audoy-Auzière, I saw her photo appear on Google, I was on Google, I saw a painter, see... So that's her, but twenty or twenty-five years ago, so she was much younger at the time, so there you go, a woman who is rather... Maybe we'll show you later... Yes, well, it's as she is now, she's much older because she's someone who was born in 1944"...

A mutual friend

The next morning the video began to rank up on *Youtube*, despite the censorship algorithms running full blast during the COVID-19 period. The friend who came to visit me at the office that day spotted Jean-Jacques Trogneux's *Facebook* page on my computer screen: "Who's that?" When I explain the situation, my friend reaches for his smartphone and says: "Look, in my *Facebook* contacts I see that he's "friends" with one of my best friends, A de C. If you want, I can connect you."

Late in the morning of December 13, 2021, I contact A de C. He tells me that he has shared a flat with Jean-Jacques Trogneux for several years in the early 2000s, at the home of her mother Véronique Dreux, and her new husband Alain L'Eleu de la Simone, a major insurer from Amiens. If he was Jean-Jacques Trogneux's roommate and very close friend, then he must have met his father Jean-Michel. But A de C certifies that he has never physically seen Jean-Jacques Trogneux's father, has never seen any photographs of him and that Jean-Jacques Trogneux has never spoken to him about his father. When we present Natacha Rey's hypothesis to him (that his former roommate might be "Brigitte's" son), he starts pondering and suddenly remembers that, at the time, Jean-Jacques Trogneux often talked to him about a young politician who was going to make a big splash, and that he now understands that it was Emmanuel Macron...

Three hours after the end of our exchange, in the early afternoon, A de C calls me back. His calm, cooperative tone has disappeared. This time his voice is jerky. He seems to be hastily reciting words whispered by others. He tells me that Jean-Michel Trogneux's current existence is confirmed, that he used to be a jeweller in Toulon [Author's note: this is false, as we shall see later], that he lives at 14, rue des Vergeaux and that Jean-Jacques Trogneux used to organize parties at the home of this father who simply didn't want to appear because of a poor curriculum and an unattractive physique, because, says A de C, "he's a chubby guy"[1]...

Debunking

Natacha Rey's video continued to climb during the following weekend. It quickly reached 400,000 views, and the hashtag *#jeanmicheltrogneux* was now solidly established in *Twitter France*'s general top trends. During this initial buzz, the *Wikipedia* page "Famille Trogneux", which mentioned five children (omitting Jean-Michel), was amended to list six, then squarely deleted! Now that the matter is on the table, I reflect that, without even resorting to their relays in the celebrity press, the Presidency's PR unit is going to leak on social media photos of Brigitte Trogneux with her brother Jean-Michel in their youth, photos of Brigitte Trogneux as a young mother with her children and her first husband. I also reflect that if "Brigitte" was indeed born Jean-Michel Trogneux, then a witness will spontaneously show up on social networks...

None of this happened. Instead, the "Brigitte Auzière Macron" *Facebook* account was closed and the "Jean-Michel Trogneux" account deactivated the display of its "friends" list[2]. Stranger still, we norice some mysterious disappearances of some Trogneux-related references from the Amiens city and urban community archives, such as 366W392 concerning "damage claims files" relating to "Trogneux JM" in 1986.

BEFORE

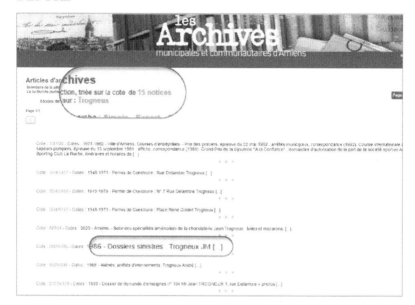

AFTER

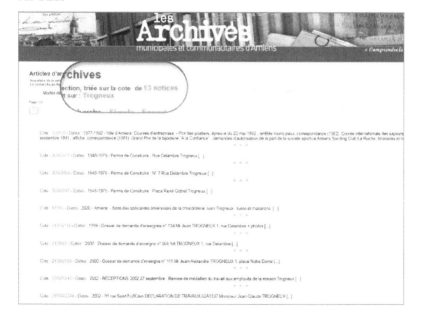

As soon as the hashtag *#jeanmicheltrogneux* appeared, a journalist set about debunking the affair: Jonathan Moadab[3]. Between December 16, 2021 and January 19, 2022, he conducted a counter-investigation on *Twitter*, relayed a few months later by the *Blast*news site[4]. He published Jean-Michel Trogneux's birth certificate (the document refused twice to Natacha Rey, and which will be eventually delivered to her on December 31, 2021 by the city of Amiens) and the marriage certificate of Jean-Michel Trogneux and Véronique Dreux, featuring Brigitte Trogneux, *épouse* Auzière, as her brother's best man. Apart from having a proof that Brigitte Trogneux and Jean-Michel Trogneux were witnesses in their respective weddings, and therefore key figures in their respective biographies, I was surprised to receive this document, legally unavailable to third parties. This implied that Jonathan Moadab had operated in more or less direct connection with the interested parties[5]. But the crux of this debunking was to explain that Jean-Michel Trogneux was a "chubby guy" who could be spotted at Emmanuel Macron's inauguration ceremony at the Elysée in 2017. To conclude his investigation, Jonathan Moadab traveled to Amiens to meet this "chubby guy" who was designated to him as Jean-Michel Trogneux at 14, rue des Vergeaux – which is both Jean-Michel Trogneux's official address and the address of L'Atelier Jean Trogneux, one of the Trogneux boutiques[6]. But the said "chubby guy" refused to meet him inside and closed the door on him. Later, Jonathan Moadab sent him a letter requesting an interview, which went unanswered[7].From then on, the presentation of the "chubby guy" as the individual born Jean-Michel Trogneux will be the only counter-argument to our investigation. At the time, we were not ruling out this possibility. It was simply a new piece of data. So we accumulated as much information as we could[8], including available photographs of the "chubby guy". Here is a compilation of the individual's public or social media appearances between 2017 and 2024.

In response to Jonathan Moadab's debunking effort, Natacha Rey posted on social networks this array of pictures showing that by the shape of his ears (a reliable feature), the young boy in the family photograph looks much more like "Brigitte" than like the "chubby guy".

In any case, now that the subject was on the table, I had to work methodically, tracing the lives of Brigitte Trogneux and Jean-Michel Trogneux from the beginning. Was "Brigitte" born Brigitte Trogneux and was the "chubby guy" born Jean-Michel Trogncux, as the presidency claimed? Or, as a large number of the French public, now thought, had Natacha Rey made a crucial point?

1. Interviews with the author, recorded on December 13, 2021 at 11 a.m. and again at 2 p.m.

2. These accounts were archived before being deleted.

3. Describing himself as a "practicing anti-Zionist Jew", Jonathan Moadab is a photojournalist. In France, he was a pioneer of street mini-interviews on *Youtube* (*Le Cercle des Volontaires, Agence Info Libre*) before joining *RT France*, then *Valeurs actuelles* in 2021. He has announced that he will retire from journalism in December 2023.

4. *Brigitte Macron: if not her then her brother, Blast*, April 1 and 3, 2022.

5. As journalist Pierre Jovanovic stated in a *Youtube* interview with Mike Borowski on January 27, 2022.

6. In the 1980s, L'Atelier Jean Trogneux at 14, rue des Vergeaux in Amiens was the store of another confectionery family, the Arrasse family, which the Trogneux family bought out in 1989 under the name "Les Spécialités amiénoises" until 2016. The name Trogneux appears nowhere; the packaging is neutral, with no inscription. In 1991, the Trogneux family opened a "miniboutique" at 4, rue Duméril. L'Atelier Jean Trogneux, at 14, rue des Vergeaux, opens after 2019. Meanwhile, in October 2007, Jean-Michel Trogneux disappeared from the articles of association of *Société d'exploitation des établissements Arrasse*, renamed in 2017 SAS "Les Spécialités picardes" and statutorily moved from 14, rue des Vergeaux to 1, rue Delambre (see *Chapter 18*). If the individual born Jean-Michel Trogneux is "retired" as we are told, he cannot be involved in ithe launching of the boutique, contrary to what the common address at 14, rue des Vergeaux implies.

7. Interview with Jonathan Moadab on the *Youtube* channel "*Nicolas Faure - Sunrise*", March 12, 2024.

8. Even though, at the time of writing, no identity document including a photo (passport, identity card, driving license) has been shown to attest that the "chubby guy" is currently living under the identity of Jean-Michel Trogneux, the person does reside at 14, rue des Vergeaux in Amiens, is registered in that name at a polling station in that city, has a social security number in that name and drives a vehicle listed for that name in the official SIV register.

20

#JEANMICHELTROGNEUX

"Nobody's perfect!"

On Sunday, December 12, 2021, the hashtag *#JeanMichelTrogneux* caught on like wildfire on *Twitter* and rocketed up the general trends in France. In addition to the success of Natacha Rey's video, which reached 500,000 views (it was removed from *Youtube* after five days, following pressure from the Elysée), there was an outcry of Éric Zemmour's supporters after Antoine Choteau, "Brigitte's" son-in-law, said he "hoped for a crash" of the plane in which the presidential candidate was traveling with Philippe de Villiers[1]…

The hashtag *#JeanMichelTrogneux*, which has been in the top trends for four solid days, is generating a tremendous (if somewhat anarchic) flow of information, and soon groups of investigators were set up all over France to contribute[2]. Various de-posted photos of "Brigitte" reappeared, tagged with *#JeanMichelTrogneux*. Another reappearing piece of evidence is an interview from 2017 in which, reacting to a blunder by Emmanuel Macron, "Brigitte" spontaneously said: "Personne n'est parfait, Nobody's perfect [NB: reiterated in English]. – It's one of my best films: *Certains l'aiment chaud*. [Some like it hot]. I recommend it"[3]. This was a surprising reference to the last scene of Billy Wilder's film, Daphne reveals to Osgood that she is in fact a man: "- Daphne: I cannot have children; - Osgood: We'll adopt some; - Daphne (taking off the wig): You don't understand, Osgood!... I'm a man!; - Osgood: Well... nobody's perfect!".

Parisian editorial teams feign indignation. The celebrity magazine *Ici Paris*, for example, writes: "Nor does anyone point out that even if this were true, what would be wrong with a man wanting to become a woman, even if she were to become the First Lady in France? We are speechless". While *Le Monde* sees it as an attempt to "Trumpize political debates in France[4]", *Marianne* magazine compares the affair to the pre-revolutionary libels of the 18th century...[5]

After four days, on December 16, 2021, the *#JeanMichelTrogneux* hashtag was removed from trends by the moderation service of *Twitter France*[6]. The day before, Jean Ennochi, "Brigitte's" lawyer, announced his client's intention to take legal action[7]. While it would have been sufficient to publish a few photos of the family's past to extinguish the affair, the choice of legal action provoked a "Streisand effect" of international amplification, first with the *Daily Mail*[8], followed two days later by *Reuters*[9], whose dispatch was relayed worldwide. For example, Turkey's leading news channel *a Haber*[10] runs a feature on Jean-Michel Trogneux, as does Dmitri Kisselev's news program on *Rossiya-1*[11] as part of a long-format special feature on transsexualism in the West.

While the buzz was in full swing, Gérald Darmanin, then Emmanuel Macron's Minister of the Interior, perfidiously referred to Emmanuel Macron's "husband" and explained that "given the violence of the personal attacks, the President is not yet sure of running for office again" in the 2022 presidential election[12]...

"Minors are my fight"

It was against this turbulent backdrop that "Brigitte" embarked on her traditional media tour at the beginning of January to launch the annual *Pièces jaunes* [yellow coins] operation, the First Ladies's charity founded by Bernadette Chirac to help hospitalized children[13]. On *TF1*'s 1 p.m. news show on January 12, 2022, "Brigitte" appeared feverish, not knowing what to do with her hands, mixing up "he" and "she" and producing numerous slips of the tongue. Asked to comment on Emmanuel Macron's provocative statement about the no-jab people "I really want to piss them off" ["*J'ai très envie de les emmerder.*"][14], "Brigitte" explains that she cannot "order what the President says [a striking lapsus substituting "commander" for "commenter"; in English, command for comment]". Then, commenting on the violence of public debate, she says she hopes, "if there is an election campaign…" before changing her mind "when there is an election campaign, that it will be an exemplary campaign". Asked about the "conspiracy theory that [she was] born a man", "Brigitte" replies: "obviously it's a lie, butk, hey… Take from it what you will." [*Une fois que j'ai dit ça, je n'ai rien dit*]. This has made me realize, since I've been on it for four years, that I'm asking for minors. […] Minors are my fight."

There is another strange sequence in the media tour two days later on *RTL*[15], for an interview recorded the day before, with numerous cuts done in the editing process: "- It was said that you were a man on social media. First, did that hurt you? - Well, first I looked at it with some distance. I had heard about it, but, bah… And then, at some point, I realized that they were turning my genealogy upside down. That is, they had changed my family tree. In other words, for three quarters of the family, it was correct, and then suddenly it's about my brother, and… [according to them] I am my brother! Here, this is about my parents' genealogy. That's just impossible." Even the most skeptical will be astonished by this utterance, with its self-centered arguments and its total lack of consideration and empathy for Jean-Michel Trogneux, the brother who is undoubtedly attached to his anonymity and whose name is fed to the bloothirsty mob…

Since then, like a groundswell, the Jean-Michel Trogneux affair has never stopped its undermining effect. Implicitly, "Brigitte's" political weight was constantly scrutinized in the light of this new situation. Someone familiar with the corridors of power told me: "It's circulating a lot… Copies of *The Brigitte Macron Mystery* are circulating everywhere…

That explains everything. Everything…". It was as if we had found the key or tuning frequency that had produced such a strange feeling, so difficult to express with words, that for years had left the couple's interlocutors speechless. All in all, this broke the spell of collective hypnosis, but was only reported in undertones in the media-political field.

"Brigitte's" absence from the 2022 presidential campaign was conspicuous, as *Blast* notes, four months after the affair rocked the media: "As part of the transparency charter relating to the status of the spouse of the Head of State, the Elysée website publishes Brigitte Macron's agenda every month. However, the program has not been updated since December[1,] 2021. What did Brigitte Macron do for two months? Have Natacha Rey's revelations shaken the top echelons of government? It is hard to say, especially as neither the presidential spokesman, Emmanuel Macron's wife's office nor her lawyer have responded to our requests."

Meanwhile, *Le Point*'s website[16] asks: *Where is Brigitte Macron?* "Unlike 2017, the First Lady has kept a low profile during the 2022 campaign. Brigitte Macron remains a key figure. [...] This time, no *Paris Match* cover, no cleverly distilled quips of confidences, no interviews except in her First Lady agenda. [...] "Five years ago, the mood was light. Now that's a burning topic!" says a close friend". Later, *L'Express* wrote about "Brigitte's" obsession for "rumors that swell, flow, ebb, smear and, as an oil slick, constantly return. [...] Evil corrodes, exhausts and stuns"[17].

Since then, "Brigitte" has been fighting the relays of the Jean-Michel Trogneux affair with the pretext of… opposing school bullying: "Brigitte leads a relentless fight against cyberbullying, and she says she has been a victim of it herself. [...] In particular, she wants the harassed children to be able to obtain the deletion of content that targets them. [...] The French heads of *Facebook*, *Twitter*, *TikTok*, *Youtube* and *Instagram* all visited in turn his office at the Elysée Palace, vowing to do their best and moderate their content. But she will judge this by the results: "I won't let go"[18]. But, in addition to the censorship on social media, "Brigitte" is taking the case to court…

1. Natacha Rey's video was notably propelled by Isabelle Smadja-Balkany, a close associate of Éric Zemmour, in a tweet (dated December 13, 2021) hypocritically supporting "Brigitte". It turns out that her husband, Patrick Balkany, a colorful figure in French politics, had been included in "Brigitte's" official biography, probably against his will. We were told that Patrick Balkany had formed a "gang" (of friends) with "Brigitte" and singer Michel Sardou in Le Touquet during his childhood. There is a problem: with respect to the Trogneux siblings, Patrick Balkany and Michel Sardou, born respectively in 1948 and 1947, do not belong to Brigitte Trogneux's generation, born in 1953, but to Jean-Michel's, born in 1945… In the same vein, Le Touquet beach attendant Jean-Luc Van Godtsenhoven referred to "Brigitte" as his childhood friend, as she is allegedly two years older than him *(Les Macron du Touquet-Elysée-Plage*, Seuil, 2021). In fact he was born on March 27, 1951, and is therefore two years older than Brigitte Trogneux.

2. These include Alain Beyrand's *Pressibus*group and the *Telegram* group "L'Affaire Jean-Michel Trogneux".

3. *Quotidien, TMC*, June 13, 2017.

4. *Le Monde*, December 20, 2021.

5. Emmanuel de Waresquiel, *Marianne*, May 18, 2023.

6. This information was revealed by journalist Daniel Schneidermann in *Rumeur et communication: Tango infernal à l'Elysée, Arrêt sur images*, December 16, 2021. At the time, the "public policy manager" at *Twitter France* was Alice Garza, a former employee of Emmanuel Macron's group at the National Assembly.

7. *#JeanMichelTrogneux: what is the origin of the transphobic fake news targeting Brigitte Macron?", libération.fr*, December 15, 2021.

8. *Brigitte Macron says she will sue after absurd rumour that she was born male and is really named Jean-Michel Trogneux trends on French Twitter, Mail Online,* December 20, 2021.

9. *Brigitte Macron takes legal action against false rumours she was born a man,* Reuters, December 22, 2021.

10. *Macron'un eşî hakkindakî iddîalar Fransa'yi çalkaladi, Haber Global*, December 21, 2021.

11. Россия-1, Вести недели December 26, 2021.

12. Interview on *CNews*, December 14, 2021.

13. Since 2020, the *Pièces Jaunes* fund-raising campaign has been run in partnership with Coinstar France, whose Managing Director, Patrick de Baecque, is one of the few Frenchmen whose contact details appear in Jeffrey Epstein's *Black Book*. Previously, Patrick de Baecque, born in 1972, began his career at *Le Figaro* as director of development for the *France-Amérique* newspaper in New York, then ran the *lefigaro.fr* website (1998-2003), before being appointed head of Derivative products (2004-2006). He subsequently held similar positions at *Le Monde* (2006-2008), where he became Sales Director (2008-2012) before running the *www.quotatis.fr* website (2012-2017).

14. Quoted in *Le Parisien*, January 5, 2022.

15. RTL, January 14, 2022.

16. *Lepoint.fr*, April 26, 2022.

17. *L'aile Madame, le couloir des intrigues* April 13, 2023.

18. *Brigitte Macron, educational advisor, L'Obs,* December 8, 2022.

21

THE AUZIÈRES AND THE BALD MAN IN A SWIMSUIT

A strange obituary

The legal proceedings promised in mid-December 2021 by Jean Ennochi, "Brigitte's" lawyer, became clearer two months later. The first wave (three lawsuits) only targets Natacha Rey's very long video on the *YouTube* channel of the medium Amandine Roy on December 10, 2021. In the three summonses, the plaintiffs were careful not to go to the heart of the matter, i.e. the real identity of "Brigitte"…

For my part, I don't receive any summons. However, in addition to the tax inspection of the parent company of *Faits & Documents* and the searches of my webmaster's office[1], my personal and professional accounts were closed by my bank[2]. I have also been summoned to 'Le Bastion', the headquarters of the Paris judicial police, on the pretext of an unrelated PHAROS[3] breach report. The police wants to interrogate me about an excerpt from a radio broadcast I did in the summer of 2021, in which I list media owners and editors in France; according to the *Parquet national de lutte contre la haine en ligne* (National Prosecutor's Office for Combating Online Hate), this might qualify as incitement to hatred on the grounds of race or religion… When I suggest a webcam session from the French consulate in Milan, where I live, the Paris Judicial Police does not follow up…

The first writ of summons sent to Natacha Rey and Amandine Roy on February 15, 2022, is astounding. Jean-Michel and Brigitte Trogneux, as well as Sébastien, Laurence and Tiphaine Auzière, are suing them before the Paris Court of Justice, not for defamation but for… "violation of the right to privacy" and "violation of image rights". This is a surprising choice of motives, given the seriousness of Natacha Rey's accusations. For this reason, on March 7, 2023, the Paris Court of First Instance declared the summons null and void, ruling that the facts invoked constituted a case not of public defamation, but of breach of privacy[4].

The second summons is not directly related to Brigitte and Jean-Michel Trogneux. Dated March 3, 2022, the document is a direct summons for the offense of defamation of Jean-Louis Auzière and Catherine Audoy. The incriminating utterances are those made by Natacha Rey on medium Amandine Roy's *YouTube* channel on December 10, 2021, and later on her *Facebook* page. Once again, the trial is not about the core topic, and is based solely on Natacha Rey's sweeping conclusions.

In the run-up to the trial, the plaintiffs provided interesting documentation on the Auzière family in order to characterize the defamation. To invalidate the Rey thesis that she was the mother of Sébastien, Laurence and Tiphaine Auzière, Catherine Audoy-Auzière provided her resume and an employment contract dated October 3, 1983, when she was hired by Japan Airlines, stating that she was not pregnant (with Tiphaine Auzière, born

on January 30, 1984) when she joined the airline's passenger sales department. She enclosed several letters from colleagues certifying that she had never had a child, as well as copies of her passports proving that she was not in France when Sébastien and Laurence Auzière were born. As for Catherine Audoy's husband, Jean-Louis, André Auzière, the characterization of defamation is based on the evidence provided to prove that he is not André, Louis, Auzière.

These items include a family photo of Jean-Louis and André Auzière as children, a photo of Jean-Louis Auzière at his wedding in 1966 and especially two photos of Jean-Louis Auzière in 1974, the year in which the wedding photo of André Auzière and Brigitte Trogneux was taken.

In the case of André Auzière, the family record book of his parents, Louis Auzière and Renée Costes, was provided at the trial. We discover that André Auzière was not a single child as previously reported, but that he came from a large family well-established at a high level of the French public administration[5]...

Next comes the 1974 wedding photo. It's not captioned by Jean-Louis Auzière or "Brigitte", but by one of André Auzière's cousins at the wedding, a certain Gérard Anrep.

189

Finally comes the most important and intriguing piece: André Auzière's death notice. The death announcement, which aims to prove the existence of Brigitte Trogneux's first ghost husband, features him has a bald man, strolling on a beach in an odd swimsuit.

André AUZIERE

Cérémonie 28 décembre 2019

A notre ami, notre frère, notre compagnon, notre grand père, notre papa

Confirmation via visual Artificial Intelligence

To feature a deceased person in a swimsuit on an obituary is very rare, if not unique. And it's true that, at first glance, the André Auzière in the 1974 wedding photo looks more like Jean-Louis Auzière than the "bald man in a swimsuit"... I remember that, as I was unsure of how to use this new material, while studying the Trogneux family I was struck by "Brigitte's" strategy of creating gray areas and keeping almost every member of the clan in the dark, whether siblings or nephews and nieces. This begs the question: what if this intriguing death announcement was just a decoy to provide a bone to chew on? What if the "bald man in a bathing suit" was in fact the same person as André Auzière in the 1974 wedding photo? The hypothesis was worth exploring...

As my investigation progressed, in order to speed up the processing of photographic data, I had familiarized myself with the "face comparison" function technology of *Face++*, a software solution developed by Megvii, the Chinese giant in visual artificial intelligence, presented by the World Economic Forum (WEF) as the world leader in the sector. The *Face++* technology is used by the authorities of the People's Republic of China, notably for the famous "social credit" program. Technically, this tool "verifies the probability that two faces belong to the same person" by "producing a confidence score and thresholds for assessing similarity". It is therefore a case-by-case assessment in the form of a probability percentage. This was an ideal tool for our investigation, which at this stage was taking the form of an identity check. Just like when you are about to board a plane and are asked to scan your passport, a visual AI program (facial recognition) evaluates in real time whether the face captured by the camera is the same as the one scanned on the passport. It never answers as "yes" or "no", but provides a percentage. The specialists agree overall that at 70 % and above, the result is positive and that, in general, the match is established. But errors are possible. To reduce the error margin, it is recommended to remove eyeglasses for example when taking new photographs for analysis.

The results we present must therefore be read, not "in themselves", but in relation to reference values. Before getting started, let's consider two relevant examples.

Example 1. Let's find out if Françoise Noguès, who attended the Lycée Mixte d'Amiens at the age of 15 (1965-66) (in the front row, fourth from the right on the map), is the same individual as the Dr François Noguès-Macron[6] we know today.

Despite the 52 years that separate these two photos, we obtain,

High - 72,669%

72, 669 % (high) a score that suggests that between Françoise Noguès at age 15 (1965) and Françoise Noguès at age 67 (2017) we are indeed dealing with the same individual.

Example 2. Is Catherine Audoy, here in her March 1977 passport (a document presented as part of her case against Natacha Rey) the same person as Catherine Audoy, shown here in 2022 with her husband Jean-Louis Auzière?

With an estimate of 70.475 % (high), we have every reason to believe that Catherine Audoy, aged 33 (left), is the same individual as Catherine Auzière, aged 78 (right).

High - 70,475 %

After this warm-up exercise, we could attempt to answer the central question: did the evidence provided by the plaintiffs definitively rule out that Jean-Louis = André Auzière?

Very high - 92,568 %

Firstly, we could check that the two photos taken by Jean-Louis Auzière in 1974 were pictures of the same individual. With a match rate of 92.568 % (very high), *Face++* had no doubt that the two photos of Jean-Louis Auzière in 1974 represented the same individual. But was this individual the Jean-Louis Auzière we were dealing with now?

Very high - 79,269 %

Very high - 75,651 %

With ratings still in the "very high" bracket (79.269 % and 75.651 % respectively) *Face++* considers that the individual presented as Jean-Louis Auzière in 1974 is indeed the same as the individual who sued Natacha Rey in 2022-23. But was this individual in the wedding photo of Brigitte Trogneux and André Auzière in 1974, as Natacha Rey thought?

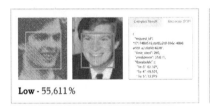

Low - 55,611 %

Normal - 62,959 %

Low - 52,219 %

With results of 55.611 % (low) and 62.959 % (normal) for Jean-Louis Auzière in 1974, and a score of 52.219 % (low) for Jean-Louis Auzière in 2022, *Face++* clearly believes that Jean-Louis Auzière is definitely not the André Auzière in the 1974 wedding photograph. But was this individual the "bald man in a swimsuit" presented as André Auzière in the obituary?

With a score of 81.161 % (very high), facial recognition gives as

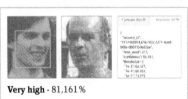

Very high - 81,161 %

counter-intuitive as it is clear a match between André Auzière, married in 1974, and the "bald man in a swimsuit". These items, and their analysis by facial recognition, confirm that

André Auzière and Jean-Louis Auzière are indeed two distinct individuals: Jean-Louis Auzière is André Auzière's uncle. And Catherine Audoy's late arrival in the family makes her a secondary character.

On this point - which does not concern "Brigitte" - Natacha Rey and Amandine Roy were fined €2,000 each on February 14, 2023 by the Court of Lisieux (Calvados), a sentence reduced on June 28, 2023 by the Caen Court of Appeal[7].

Were the Auzières manipulated by "Brigitte"?

The trial was covered by Emmanuelle Anizon, a journalist and senior reporter at *Le Nouvel Obs*[8], in her book *L'Affaire Madame, le jour où la première dame est devenue un homme: anatomie d'une fake news*[9]. Emmanuelle Anizon entered the case in June 2022, six months after the buzz triggered by Natacha Rey's video, whom she will follow in her travels until December 2023. This is why Emmanuelle Anizon's book is essentially about the Auzière trial, allowing her to shield herself by writing that those are "fake news" while in fact revealing a sizable amount of strategic information that is deeply disturbing for the presidential couple. Perhaps the most important piece of information is the origin of Natacha Rey's police custody. On the face of it, we would say that "Brigitte" is too far removed from Catherine Audoy to have played any role whatsoever in the run-up to the police custody that triggered the affair. Including from the media's point of view, since it was this event which, factually, enabled the Rey thesis to be relayed in *Faits & Documents*…

However, Emmanuelle Anizon will establish that without "Brigitte's" ambiguous intervention, Natacha Rey's police custody would probably never have occurred: "On this June 21, 2021, [Catherine Audoy] picks up her cell phone and discovers that a message has been sent to her on *WhatsApp* at 3 a.m.: "I know everything. Absolutely everything. For you, for Jean-Louis, for Jean-Michel." Catherine is stunned with surprise. She does not know the calling number, but the profile picture shows a pretty, smiling blonde [Author's note: upon a call from a number not listed in the address book, WhatsApp, automatically suggests blocking it...]. She shows the message to her husband Jean-Louis. [...] After Natacha's messages, Jean-Louis prefers to consult [Laurence Auzière], who is also his cardiologist. "Laurence told us right away: Call Mom; she's thinking of filing a complaint too." He calls, Brigitte answers immediately: "She tells me she's sorry, that it's all her fault, that we need to press charges, and that she agress to have a joint action. I hear Emmanuel Macron's voice in the background, asking him to hurry up because they nust leave. Before hanging up, she promises to send me a copy of her family record book, which she did. I also ask her to certify in writing that it was her in the 1974 wedding photo with André, which she didn't. I did not speak to her directly on the subject after that." Catherine and Jean-Louis lodge a complaint against Natacha Rey at the police station. They also contact Brigitte's lawyer and send him their documents. Some time later, Brigitte calls Jean-Louis back. "She told me that the Élysée preferred to launch two separate actions. She was walking out on me. It clearly meant: 'If you want to continue, you're on your own; get a lawyer of your own.' We had already filed a complaint: there was no turning back, so we went ahead on our own. Since then, when I try to call Brigitte back, I don't get through to her but to her secretary, who has become unreachable." He shrugs. "Well, that's not very important." The Auzières are obviously bitter. The are collateral victims of this crazy story, and they find themselves isolated, even abandoned."

Let us recap

1– The first custody would not have taken place without the intervention of the Élysée. 2– The Auzières would not have pursued the case without "Brigitte's" promise of joint action. 3– The Élysée dropped the Auzières along the way; they were manipulated and betrayed by the presidential couple. 4– In the course of the proceedings, "Brigitte" failed to fulfill her promise commitment to caption the wedding photo between Brigitte Trogneux and André Auzière. 5– Despite her promise to do so, "Brigitte" never certified in writing that it was indeed her in the 1974 wedding photo. 6– At the trial between Natacha Rey and the Auzières, Gérard Anrep, a first-degree cousin of André Auzière, took it upon himself to certify in writing that "Brigitte" was indeed the person in the 1974 wedding photo. 7– Gérard Anrep refused to answer Emmanuelle Anizon's questions.

"All other photos have been destroyed"

At the time, the "Jean-Michel Trogneux rumor" became quite a social phenomenon. The affair went global, and is now an integral part of "Brigitte's" biography, with a dedicated section on the "Brigitte Macron" page of French *Wikipedia*. This was the motivation behind Emmanuelle Anizon's approach, with whom I communicated via the encrypted *Signal* messaging system, sharing our discoveries. In her book, she tells of her surprise to see the "bald man in a bathing suit" on André Auzière's obituary: "Jean-Louis Auzière, nevertheless, has found a few photos of himself as a young man, proving to the courts that he is not the groom in the 1974 wedding photo with Brigitte [Trogneux]. And he provides a photo of André, a black and white photo that the biographers would have loved to find: A thin, bald man in a bathing suit is posing in front of the sea and a wooden pontoon. He has a serious gaze. At the top there is the mention: "André Auzière / Ceremony December 28, 2019", and immediately below: "To our friend, our brother, our companion, our grandfather, our dad". "This photograph was taken from a booklet distributed at the funeral," Jean-Louis explains. It was associated with prayer texts." I ask Jean-Louis about this strange choice. "I understand that it may surprise you," he replies, "but it's really a photo of André, and I recognize the location: it was taken at Mouré Rouge, the beach near their house in Cannes. I think this was the only photo that turned up when they went looking for one for the funeral, because all the others had been destroyed." Destroyed? I am not Natacha Rey, but I still am a bit puzzled. What, so all that's left of a man's life in pictures (apart from his wedding photo) is a photo in a swimsuit to illustrate his final departure? "

In response to Emmanuelle Anizon's doubts, I assure her that, contrary to Sylvie Bommel's assertion, we have traced him in the banking archives[10] (but he never was a banker at Crédit du Nord as initially reported) and that, in addition to facial recognition analyses, the two handwriting expert reports we commissioned (one from a certified French expert, the other from Italy) agree that Jean-Louis and André Auzière are indeed two different persons. As Emmanuel Anizon seems dubious, we suggest that she contact André Auzière's former work colleagues, who should be to be found on *Facebook* in the group *Les Joyeux rémanents de la BFCE*, which one of my correspondents has identified. The rest is Emmanuelle Anizon's story: "His sisters wouldn't talk to me, nor his children, so I called a few former colleagues, via Facebook groups of former bankers. They all speak enthusiastically of "Dédé", "kind, cult, polite", who talked a lot about his children, whom he adored. Dédé, who "smoked too much", whom they felt was "lonely", "devastated" [...]. One of them sent me a professional collection of portraits from the mid-2000s, where André poses, serious, in a suit and tie, among his colleagues at the Amiens bank branch. The 1974 groom is clearly recognizable, even if he has started to lose his hair. These colleagues kept in touch with each other after retirement. Not him, who cut all ties. With them too. André Auzière has disappeared from the radar's scope." For my part, I tried to contact members of the Auzière family, but no one wanted to reply. Susan Spray, Jean-Louis Auzière's first wife, even hurriedly hung up on me when I told her I was interested in Brigitte Macron: "Ah yes – no, no thank you sir! *Ohlala*, no. Goodbye!"[11]. I thought that with her reassuring label as a left-wing journalist, Emmanuelle Anizon would be more successful than me, especially with André Auzière's sisters: "They refused to testify, claiming they wanted nothing to do with the story. Maybe they were afraid. [...] "I don't talk about family matters," Hélène replied, before closing the door of her Paris apartment[12].

"Reality sometimes surpasses imagination"

As for André Auzière's cremation, and despite the shadows surrounding the event, a source confirmed that the Pascal Leclerc funeral company would be organizing a cremation at the Père Lachaise crematorium on December 28, 2019, with a 30-minute secular ceremony officiated by Tiphaine Auzière. Emmanuelle Anizon follows this track, Jean-Louis Auzière describes the ceremony: "Jean-Louis, informed by André's sisters, went to the funeral, which took place at the Père-Lachaise crematorium "just four days after the death. No information had leaked to the newspapers, the Élysée wanted it to happen quickly, and it seems that Emmanuel Macron was personally involved in making sure it did," he says. The express funeral, organized on the sly and in a hurry, early in the morning (at 8:30 a.m.), "before opening time to avoid journalists. The booklet with the photo was placed on the chairs. A dozen people were present, seated in separate clans. On one side André's sisters, on the other Brigitte's three children, Tiphaine, Laurence and Sébastien [...]. Brigitte didn't come. André's companion, unknown to all, was also there, as some distance. Each side read a text. After twenty minutes, the ceremony was over and everyone walked out immediately. Afterwards, I went with the Auzière children and André's sisters for a coffee and croissant. Members of security staff stood on guard outside. We ended up letting them in because it was cold. The atmosphere was heavy, and everyone left quickly afterwards. The death would not be revealed publicly until a year later, by Tiphaine, on October 8, 2020, in *Paris Match*, the family's decidedly recurrent communication channel: "My father died, and I buried him on December 24 in the strictest privacy. I adored him, he was a very special person, a non-conformist who insisted on his anonymity more than anything else. You must respect him. "It should be noted that the "December 24" date is undoubtedly an error, since it would be that of the death, and not of the funeral, which would have taken place on the 28[th13]. [...] In an article in *Paris Match* on March 3, 2022, journalist Sophie des Déserts wrote that he would in fact have ended his days in a psychiatric clinic, with a guard at his door supervised by Alexandre Benalla, the Elysée's notorious and controversial *"Monsieur Sécurité"*. The information was denied the same day on Twitter by Tiphaine, who wrote that she "cannot accept that my father's memory be damaged. The information in *Paris Match* on this day is wrong. My father was never confined to a psychiatric clinic with a security arrangement [...]". André Auzière, according to his death certificate, died on December 24, 2019 at Georges-Pompidou Hospital, in the 15th arrondissement of Paris, aged sixty-eight. According to Jean-Louis, his companion found tickets to Africa in his jacket pocket, and a bag with a large amount of money in it. "He had emptied his accounts, organized his departure on the sly. He dreamed so much of going there again". If what Jean-Louis has been told is true, reality sometimes exceeds imagination".

---

1. See *Chapter 19*.

2. On the political mechanisms of bank account closures, see *Fermeture de comptes en banque: le casse du siècle contre les dissidents, Éléments*, n° 206.

3. PHAROS (acronym for *Plateforme d'harmonisation, d'analyse, de recoupement et d'orientation des signalements*) is a website created in 2009 by the French government to report illegal online content and behavior. PHAROS is implemented by the Office central de Lutte contre la criminalité liée aux technologies de l'information et de la communication, a branch of the *Direction centrale de la police judiciaire*.

4. On the media side, the cannulment of this first procedure was the subject of an *AFP* dispatch (Rumeurs transphobes: la justice annule une procédure intentée par Brigitte Macron, March 8, 2023).

5. André, Louis Auzière was born on February 28, 1951 in Eseka (Cameroon). Far from being an only child, as reported and written everywhere, he was in fact the fifth of six children born of the marriage, on December 7, 1939, in Montpellier (Hérault), of Renée Costes, born in La Tour-du-Crieu (Ariège) on April 2, 1920 and who died in Cannes (Alpes-Maritimes) on February 23, 2014, and Louis, Alexandre Auzière, born on May 18, 1917 in Paris XIe and who died on April 29, 1985 in Paris Ve. André Auzière was the brother of Line Auzière, born on March 6, 1941 in Ségou (Sudan) (Mrs Laurent Lucchini, three children: Jérôme, Anne and Laurent) of Renée Auzière, born May 6, 1942 in Tananarive (Madagascar) (Madame François Ribard), of Hélène Auzière, born November 19, 1945 in Port Gueydon (French Algeria) (Madame Jean Pellefigue, three children: Marie, Julien and Nicolas) of Pierre Auzière, born on September 20, 1947 in Brazzaville (Congo) and died October 30, 2014 in Cannes (Alpes-Maritimes) and Laure Auzière, born 1955 (Mrs. Yves Gheebrant, three children: Rémi, Antoine, Cécile). His father, Louis Auzière, was not a mere "colonial administrator". Graduating as first of his class from the colonial school in 1935, Louis Auzière began his career in Sudan, in the general service of the *cercle de Segou* (1940), where he was promoted to deputy commander (1942), before being transferred to Algeria, where he was successively administrator of the civil services of Algeria and secretary to the prefect of Algiers at the time when General de Gaulle's Provisional Government of the French Republic was set up in Algiers, and moved to Paris a few weeks later on August 31, 1944. Remaining in Algeria, Louis Auzière was again stationed in Kabylia (Djurjura, then Azeffoun), before being promoted to head of the private secretariat of the High Commissioner for French Equatorial Africa (AEF). He continued his

career in the Congo (head of the Madingo-Kayes district), Cameroon (head of the Eseka, then Sanaga-Maritime, then Moungo subdivisions) and Madagascar (inspector of provincial services in Fianarantsoa, head of the Ambatondrazaka district, general Secretary of the Government Council, Director of Personnel and Civil Service, State Inspector), before ending his career under General de Gaulle, as Chief Administrator of Overseas France, then General Secretary of the Government Council at the end of decolonization.

6. See *Chapter 15*.

7. Amandine Roy was fined €1,000 and Natacha Rey €2,000, of which 1,600 were suspended. As the information does not directly concern "Brigitte", this conviction was only covered by the local press *(Ouest-France, Le Pays d'Auge, Le Courrier Picard, Paris-Normandie)*.

8. Emmanuelle Anizon spent most of her career at *Télérama*, where she headed the media department. In 2015 she joined *Le Nouvel Observateur*, a weekly newspaper within the Le Monde Group, where she specialized in covering social movements *(Gilets jaunes)* and trends *(#MeToo)*.

9. *L'Affaire Madame, le jour où la première dame est devenue un homme: anatomie d'une fake news*, Emmanuelle Anizon, StudioFact Éditions, 2024.

10. Chronologically, we first trace him back to December 10, 1992, in a certificate of deposit. Alongside his colleague Xavier Delrue, he represents the Amiens branch of Banque Française du Commerce Extérieur, the custodian of funds for a société civile immobilière, under the name SCI Somme-Habitat-Service; - On March 21, 2000, he appears as a representative, alongside Henri Rigaud, of Natixis Banque in a transfer of funds to SCI Campagne and SARL Campadis; - On June 20, 2001, his name appears on a deposit receipt, alongside Jean-Pierre Vittu, acting on behalf of Natixis Banques Populaires, certifying receipt of funds on behalf of Envimat; - On January 23, 2004, André Auzière represented, alongside Grégory Querel, Natixis Banque Populaire, custodian of funds for SAS Information Pour les Professionnels de Santé; - On April 12, 2005, he represented, alongside François Mark, Natexis-Banque Populaire, in Paris, on the occasion of a capital increase for Amedeus, a company chaired by Gérard Dautresme. It should be noted that, after Strasbourg, his was into wrapping up his career in Amiens and then in Paris, which contradicts Tiphaine Auzière's statement: "My dad was working in Lille and came back on weekends. During the week, I was with my mom, and on weekends with my dad, and mom visited Emmanuel" *(Brigitte Macron, a French novel*, Virginie Linhart, France 3, 2018).

11. Interview with the author by Susan Spray, December 7, 2021.

12. *L'Affaire Madame, le jour où la première dame est devenue un homme: anatomie d'une fake news*, Emmanuelle Anizon, StudioFact Éditions.

13. In this cover story devoted to "Brigitte" and Tiphaine Auzière *Paris Match* (October 9, 2020) reported extensively on the Lycée *Autrement*, in which Tiphaine Auzière had recently teamed up with Christophe Cadet, a history teacher who was expelled in 2011 from *Institution Saint-Jean* in Douai, where he was in charge of preparatory classes for the *Grandes Écoles*. *Paris Match* (October 9, 2020) reported

on how this "self-confessed homosexual, still living with his mother", organized "red hot parties" during which he "danced with the students", before evoking "the polemics about his style, his closeness to certain boys, this tendency to often talk about homosexuality - in 2003, he gathered his troops in the chapel to get them thinking about the subject". In 2019, following "new rumors", Christophe Cadet was also dismissed from his next position in the private preparatory school *Intégrale*.

22

THE DISAPPEARANCE OF BRIGITTE TROGNEUX (1 – THE COMMUNICANT)

The communicant

Once André Auzière had been found and physically identified, we had to look into "Brigitte's" past, retrace her life and above all identify whether or not she was indeed the individual born Brigitte Trogneux, female, on April 13, 1953 in Amiens (Somme)[1].

Brigitte Trogneux's childhood photos have long remained a mystery. In June 2018, after three years of intensive "Brigitte" media coverage, documentary filmmaker Virginie Linhart was finally able to view and publish some photographs of young Brigitte Trogneux[2]. Only one of them is fully exploitable by facial recognition: her picture as a communicant[3].

This photo meets all the requirements for exploitation and analysis. The face of the little girl, aged 10-12, already has personal features and can therefore be identified, either by third parties (with the naked eye) or by visual AI, i.e. facial recognition. This shot also clearly shows the whole face (both eyes open, nose, mouth closed, chin, etc.).

But there are still several issues that need to be resolved before it can be used. relating to the use of photographic equipment.

The first is authenticity. This problem has largely increased through the diffusion of digital technology, and even more so with the emergence of artificial intelligence. The second problem is that of captioning, which includes the identity of the individual(s) featured in a photograph, as well as the dating of the photograph.

The picture with its caption must therefore be authenticated before it can be used. As it stands, the caption stating that the individual is indeed Brigitte Trogneux comes from a single source: the Élysée Palace. Under Emmanuel Macron, it is an understatement to say that the Élysée is not a reliable source. Left-leaning news website *Mediapart* went so far as to describe the presidential palace as a "fake news factory"[4].

How can we confirm or deny 1- the authenticity of the photograph, 2- the identification provided by the Élysée, 3- the dating of the document? Through classic cross-checking. For this, we had to find more photographs of Brigitte Trogneux from the same period.

Photos with indisputable captions (identity of the individual, dating of the document). Photos that immediately settle the caption question are those taken in an institutional (as opposed to private) context. It is the institutional framework that certifies the identity of the individual and provides an indisputable date. As far as the photo of Brigitte Trogneux as a communicant is concerned, the traces left by her school curriculum were the shortest route to cross-checking.

In search of class photographs

At the time of her communion, Brigitte Trogneux was, according to the official "Brigitte" biography, attending school in downtown Amiens, with the nuns of *Sacré-Cœur de Jésus*. The school's *Wikipedia* page says "Brigitte Macron, wife of French President

Emmanuel Macron" as one of the "personalities associated with the school", in the Student category.

Despite this pride, the school seems unwilling to provide more information. None of Brigitte Trogneux's class photos were supplied to the press when it came to recounting "Brigitte's" life on glossy paper. Following the media coverage of suspicions about "Brigitte's" real identity, a team from *France Dimanche*[5] traveled to Amiens and knocked on the school's door to obtain the documents that would have immediately put an end to the Jean-Michel Trogneux affair. Unfortunately, the establishment denied this, explaining that they had not kept the photos in their archives: "At *Sacré-Cour*, we are told they got rid of their archives[6]. We were hoping to find some class photos, but we didn't! Even in the Heritage section of the Amiens library, there's not much more to get your teeth into".

As the *Sacré-Cœur* never responded to my requests, I decided to reconstruct Brigitte Trogneux's schooling from the lists of classes to which she had belonged. The aim is to compile a list of former classmates, in order to contact them and gather testimonials, information and hopefully class photos.

So I proceeded to reconstruct Brigitte Trogneux's schooling. My team's research on class lists in the Amiens departmental and municipal archives has enabled us to reconstruct her elementary school career, and to cross-check the information that Brigitte Trogneux did indeed attend *Sacré-Coeur*. A relatively late entry, its name only appears from 1960-1961, called *neuvième* at the time, now CE2 (3th grade in the USA). As a result, she repeated the *septième* year, now CM2 (5th grade).

Then we need to find the class lists for middle school and high school. At the Bibliothèque nationale de France, we check that Brigitte Trogneux obtained her *baccalauréat* A at Sacré-Cœur in 1972. However, only one list is available: that of her *troisième* year class, i.e. 9th grade (1968-1969), produced as part of the process of obtaining the BEPC (Brevet d'Études du Premier Cycle). 1968 was the year of a general population census. On the census residency sheet, Jean Trogneux, the father, declares his wife Simone Pujol, his youngest daughter Brigitte Trogneux (the older children have already left), his mother-in-law Marie-Louise Pujol-Bertin and the family's faithful maid, Liliane Depoilly. Brigitte Trogneux's individual report card mentions her attendance at the Collège Sainte-Clotilde in Amiens…

This information enables us to complete the description of Brigitte Trogneux's schooling. In fact, this period coincided with the temporary twinning of Sacré-Cœur with another of the town's private Catholic establishments, now the Sainte-Clotilde school complex, as part of the process of bringing both establishments into line with the "Debré law" of 1959 on the relations between the State and private schools. However, Sainte-Clotilde depends on another religious congregation: the Order of Sainte-Ursule, also known as the Ursulines of the Roman Union.

While we begin the preparatory work of contacting Brigitte Trogneux's former comrades on the basis of the lists at our disposal, one of my correspondents contacts the archive center of the Ursulines' France, Belgium, Spain province in Beaugency (Loiret). The Ursuline archivist is very professional and available. After reconstructing and providing my correspondent with Brigitte Trogneux's class lists for *sixième* through *terminale* (grades 6 to 12), she proposes to search for the corresponding class photos.

Problem: for the years we're interested in, the documents have disappeared. In his first e-mail message, the archivist answers: "Unfortunately, we don't hold any photographs of classes or anything close to them between 1958 and 1968. [...] I'll soon be investigating why class photos for Amiens no longer exist (or don't exist) for this period. If I get around any photographs from the 1960s, I'll let you know." Later, the archivist confirms: "After extensive research, no photographs of classes between 1949 and 1980 have been found. Either the photographs were not kept locally, or there simply weren't any. The photographs I've been able to find are either albums of photos sent in by some alumni (wedding photos, photographs of the first child, souvenirs…) or individual photos. I'm sending you an example of what was being done in 1957"[7]. According to the document sent, these are not class photos as such, but annual school albums featuring, for each class, individual photos of pupils set against a black background on the right-hand page, while first and last names are written in the corresponding space on the left-hand page.

We move upstairs and contact the Ursuline Generalate's archives in Rome. They do not hold the requested documents. If the province doesn't have the class photos, the archivist explains, we will have to contact the school directly…

In the meantime, class lists from middle school and high school have already enabled us to complete our file, now made up of 111 women now in their 70s, all of whom have been in the same class as Brigitte Trogneux. The compilation process is tedious. By definition, we need to delve into the life of each one to determine their current identity (married name). Some are dead, others untraceable or unaccounted for. This first step provides an initial skimming and reduces the file to 58 persons, whom we will contact once we have found their address, telephone number or e-mail address. Often, you have to proceed through a relative who is an independent professional, and whose personal data, as such, are freely accessible online.

Then we classify them into several categories that correspond more or less to their status as day students or half-boarders at the time. We proceed by concentric circles, to give priority to those who were just passing through (because of their parents' careers for example). After this, we look at those who have left Amiens. Finally, we focus on those that were part of the Amiens bourgeoisie ecosystem, a small milieu of large families, largely connected by marriage or otherwise. In addition to the Trogneuxs, there were the families Jenlis, Guillebon, Leleu de la Simone, Lepage, Lafarge, Yvert, Simencourt, Gueudet, Decaudaveine and others. It was a world of (very) large families (this was the baby boom), where the girls went to school at Sacré-Cœur, while the boys went to La Providence…

"I didn't even recognize her"

Of the 58 former classmates of Brigitte Trogneux contacted in May and June 2023, only 18 responded to our requests, most of them to tell us they didn't want to talk, as if there were some secret.

"I don't want to say anything", declares one of them, even though she spent all her high school years in the same class as Brigitte Trogneux. "I'm not interested. I know what I have to do. Thank you. Goodbye!" exclaims another (in the classes of 7ème and 6ème with Brigitte Trogneux). Another, who was in the class of 3ème with Brigitte Trogneux, claims to have kept photos, but no longer responds to our requests. "I have class photos", says another, "but I don't want to take part in this about Brigitte, who was a classmate. She was a good friend, I can't tell you anything else. [...] As I said, even if I'm not a Macronist, I won't harm my classmate in any way. I have so many fond memories of her, and used to say hello to her mother on family trips to Amiens. Here, let all this mud be washed away! Best regards." I point out that supplying the photos is the best way to "wash away the mud", but this goes unheeded.

Only one of them (7^e, 2^e, 1^e, *terminale*) is very positive: "I swear on the heads of my children and my husband, that it is Brigitte Trogneux, I swear [...]. These girls are crazy, they're nuts [NDA: Natacha Rey and Amandine Roy]; I can say that loud and clear. [...] We were friends. She was a hard-working, wonderful girl who loved life, a good girl, a great girl. Then we taught in the same place, in Paris, together, at Franklin. She had the same hairdressing and the same legs, I can tell you". Unfortunately, she didn't keep any class photos, and was not asked by "Brigitte" to take part in the Trogneux affair. None of Brigitte Trogneux's classmates have been contacted by the Public prosecutor, as we established step by step…

But, surprisingly, many of Brigitte Trogneux's former friends apparently never really crossed paths with "Brigitte". One of them, for example, maintains that Brigitte Trogneux was not in her class because she "was a year above or a year below". When we point out that they were together for two years in primary school, she replies with surprise: "I don't remember at all", repeating "Brigitte Trogneux wasn't in my class", before asserting, without much conviction: "I haven't seen her for ages. [...] There was a Brigitte Trogneux when I was there, it's totally obvious. I wasn't friends with her, she was much wilder than I was", she says, no doubt thinking back to high school. An even more surprising testimony is that of a former student of Sacré-Cœur, who was in *7ème* with Brigitte Trogneux, and who, after telling us that she "remembers her very well", goes on to explain: "When the president was elected, one of my best friends, who lives in the Somme [department], told me: "but you know, it's Brigitte Trogneux", I hadn't made the connection". Another was similarly confused: "I didn't know Brigitte Trogneux, I didn't go to school with Brigitte Trogneux. I spent a year with Brigitte Trogneux in my final year. [...] I... Brigitte Trogneux... I'm beginning to remember... I'm sure I attended *terminale* at the Sacré-Coeur with her. When I saw her name as Macron was elected, when I saw her name – I didn't even recognize her – when I saw her name, I said... Ah!.. Brigitte Trogneux must be the one I was with in *terminale*". When we point out that she was in *troisième* and *quatrième* with Brigitte Trogneux, she exclaims: "I remember her very well in terminale, but I have no memory of her in *troisième* and *quatrième*; but frankly that doesn't ring a bell... I'm not sure... [...] I have no memory of her before [...] It's true that in the photos, I didn't recognize her at all". We look at the lists. Our interlocutor was in *terminale* C and Brigitte Trogneux in *terminale* A [scientific vs literary track]: "Well, then it's not the same person [...]. My sister said to me: "She's got the Trogneux face with that chin a bit forward – physically she looks like them", eh. [...] As for me, I have no memory of her, but my sister, who has remained in Amiens, says "Well, yes, she's got the Trogneux face, with that chin that's quite distinctive". Another, in *septième* with Brigitte Trogneux, simply has no memory of "Brigitte": "Really? Was she there? [...] I have no memory of her, she didn't make any impression on me, We were at least 20-25 girls in that class. She didn't make any impression on me". Yet another (*quatrième* and *troisième* with Brigitte Trogneux) says: "Quite frankly, I'll tell you quite frankly, we're the same age, we're a few months apart – but I don't even remember. I don't even remember. Besides, I'm not even sure we went in the same classes. [...] I can't remember. [...] Actually, when her husband was elected, I said to myself: "It's funny, she attended the Sacré-Coeur, I remember Trogneux well", [...] but I don't remember her at school". Another, who spent two years in primary school in her class, certifies that she has never been in class with Brigitte Macron: "Not at all, no, no, no"... A sincerity that somehow expresses the ineffable feeling that this was another person, as if the Brigitte Trogneux they had known was not "Brigitte"...

The Anizon file

At this stage, the research and telephone canvassing had taken me a month and a half (a parallel search was carried out on Brigitte Trogneux's brother, Jean-Michel Trogneux), fruitlessly. Although I could not be satisfied with testimonies - and contradictory ones at that - I was convinced that something was wrong. By gathering biographical information and making calls, we were able to further streamline the file into a small contact list of those likely to have class photos - those who had been close to Brigitte Trogneux and who had probably shared a long common past with her.

On June 14, 2023, I provide this skimmed list to Emmanuelle Anizon, a journalist at *Nouvel Obs*, the weekly magazine of the Parisian left-wing intelligentsia. Emmanuelle Anizon is genuinely intrigued by the Jean-Michel Trogneux affair. She is acutely aware that the biography of "Brigitte" is a "cursed dossier". When I contacted her in June 2022, I decided to lay my cards on the table. At the time, I had just been summoned again by the police as part of a legal action launched by Emmanuel Macron for *"faux et usage de faux"* ("forgery and use of forgery") in the so-called Dar Olfa palace affair[8]. When I tried to contact my source, a well known facilitator of French-Moroccan networks, I learned that he had died a few months earlier in murky circumstances... "Forgery and use of forgery"? I had a feeling that this argument would be used if I supplied evidence in the Jean-Michel Trogneux case. So I had no choice but to adopt a strategy of total transparency with Emmanuelle Anizon: she will be, *de facto*, a sort of "guarantor" of my probity and ethics in the event of accusations of "forgery"...

While Emmanuelle Anizon is a consummate professional, at that moment I have no illusions about her intentions: this has to be fake news. Let's not forget that its revenues come from press subsidies (Ministry of Culture), the *Nouvel Obs* shareholder (Xavier Niel, supporter of Emmanuel Macron and son-in-law of Bernard Arnault), advertisers (LVMH, controlled by Bernard Arnault, France's leading advertiser and costume designer for "Brigitte"), money from GAFAM (neighboring rights) – plus the press card which, in France, is essentially a tax niche.

Let us be clear. Her probity is not in question. Like a history teacher speaking about World War II to her class of 8rd graders, she is required to follow the program set by her employer, who thinks that the Jean-Michel Trogneux affair is spurious.

During our discussions, I stress that the problem lies mostly in the transition to an image-based mode or presentation – that testimonials must be supported by photographs. At this stage, I don't know what the result will be. But spurious or not, at least Emmanuelle Anizon will be writing with full knowledge of the facts.

And so, after two months of intensive work, I sent her my slim list, comprising five "privileged" contacts for Jean-Michel Trogneux and six "privileged" contacts for Brigitte Trogneux. Emmanuelle Anizon might have chosen not to use it, but she followed my advice to collect some documents during her trips to Amiens[9]. This is why I call this roadmap sent to Emmanuelle Anizon the "Anizon File".

The first on the list, Anne-Marie Bouchez, supplied Emmanuelle Anizon with the document enabling her to cross-check the communicant's photograph (identification of the person, and caption).

This is a photo of the group of communicant girls to which Anne-Marie Bouchez and Brigitte Trogneux belonged. They form a choir.

Although the lower part of her face is hidden by the song sheet, the same little girl is clearly recognizable as in the communion photo published by Virginie Linhart in 2018. The two photos seem to have been taken on the same day. And the clothes of the people in the audience in the photo leave no doubt: the photo was taken in the early 1960s.

After hesitating, I consider that the information has been cross-checked: the photo of a communicant genuinely represent Brigitte Trogneux at her First Communion in the early 1960s – the same Brigitte Trogneux her classmates didn't recognize when they saw Brigitte Macron on every TV screen from 2015-2016…

Once the conditions for exploiting this photograph had been met (captioning, dating, authentication), we could move on to analysis using visual artificial intelligence. With a simple question: was "Brigitte" the same person as Brigitte Trogneux, born on April 13, 1953 in Amiens, pictured here at her First Communion?

To make it easier to read the results given on Brigitte Trogneux's communion photo by *Face+++*, the facial recognition software used by the authorities of the People's Republic of China, here are a few reference values, corresponding to the results expected in the "Brigitte" case. Here, Lady Diana (11 vs 36), Bernadette Chirac (12 vs 70), Elizabeth II (10 vs 70), Jodie Foster (10 vs 61), Madeleine Albright (10 vs 70), Shirley Temple (10 vs 70), Marine Le Pen (8 vs 56) and Hillary Clinton (11 vs 62).

High - 72,253%

Very high - 77,503%

Very high - 77,001%

Normal - 68,128%

Very high - 75,381%

High - 71,72%

Normal - 66,418%

very high - 78,053%

Our results range from 66.4% (normal) to 78% (very high). The results of comparing Brigitte Trogneux's communion photo with "Brigitte" between 1986 and today should therefore fall into this bracket.

Significantly lower than expected, the scores, ranging from 44.332 % (low) to 65 % (normal) – with an average of 57.529 % (low) over 60 photos – mean that facial recognition clearly estimates, beyond any margin of error, that "Brigitte" is not the individual born Brigitte Trogneux, female, on April 13, 1953 in Amiens.

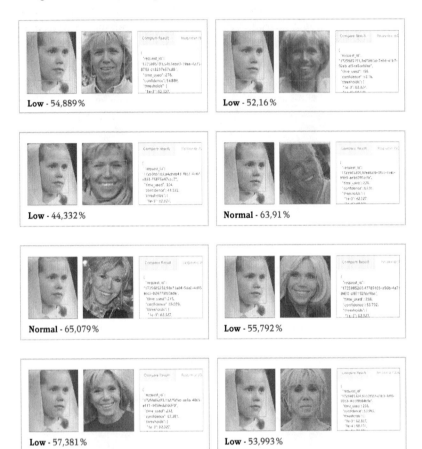

Technical testing

To claim that "Brigitte" is not the individual Brigitte Trogneux, born on April 13, 1953 in Amiens (Somme), female, is an accusation with consequences, so we did everything we could to get hold of Brigitte

Trogneux's class photos, so we could cross-check the information 100 %. After all, isn't publication the easiest way to put an end to the "rumor"? The Sacré-Coeur d'Amiens and the Congregation's Generalate in Rome never got back to us, but we were able to contact the *Union française des Anciens et Anciennes du Sacré-Coeur* (UFASC). The president of the association has assured us that she did not keep these photos. Some of Brigitte Trogneux's classmates, who seemed prepared to photocopies of the documents, questioned the interest of doing so, invoking the "respect for privacy". However, in parallel with our research, we were able to establish that, from a legal point of view, Brigitte Trogneux's class photos have in fact been in the public domain and accessible to any citizen requesting them since 2022. Faced with the establishments' refusal to provide me with the requested documents, I referred the matter to the relevant authority, the *Commission d'accès aux documents administratifs* (CADA), which is responsible for settling disputes between the French and their administrations. In its Opinion n° 20243660 issued on July 18, 2024, the CADA noted that "Mr. Xavier POUSSARD [..] contacted the *Commission d'accès aux documents administratifs*, by letter registered with its secretariat on May 24, 2024, following the refusal by the headmaster of the Sainte Clotilde - Amiens school complex of his request to consult digitized reproductions of class photos and portrait tables [trombinoscopes] of the following classes, from the current "Sainte Clotilde school complex", at the time associated with the current "Lycées & Campus Sacré-Coeur" under the name "Sainte Clotilde - Sacré Coeur":

1- 1967/68 : 4e 1 ;
2- 1968/69 : 3e 1 (CL) ;
3- 1969/70 : 2de A-2-5 ;
4- 1970/71 : 1re A ;
5- 1971/72 : *terminale* A.

Having taken note of the reply from the head of the Sainte-Clotilde school, the commission recalls that, as a matter of principle, public archive documents are communicable by right, under article L213-1 of the French Heritage Code. However, through derogation, certain categories of documents, considering the information they contain, are not immediately communicable and only become so after the deadlines and under the conditions set out in article L213-2 of the same code. [...] In the present case, the commission notes that, although the class photographs and portrait tables from the classes of 1967-1968 to 1971-1972 necessarily contain information covered by the secrecy of the private lives of the pupils concerned, the aforementioned fifty-year period has expired. The documents requested, if they exist, are now freely available to anyone who asks for them. [...] The commission then issues a favorable opinion for the communication of the documents requested, according to the method chosen by the applicant, if these documents exist in an electronic version."

The *Commission d'accès aux documents administratifs* (CADA) has sent its opinion to me and to the administration concerned, i.e. the Sainte-Clotilde school complex in Amiens, which has tacitly refused to follow the CADA's opinion and provide me with the requested documents, despite a formal notice sent by my lawyer Fabrice Delinde. These documents could be requested by courts in order to judge in conscience, or by a journalist who would like to perform cross-checking before branding as misleading any questioning of "Brigitte's" identity...

The CADA's opinion also applies to the Lycées et Campus Sacré-Cœur d'Amiens and the archive center of the Belgium, France, Netherlands province of the Religious of the Sacred Heart of Jesus (RSCJ) in Lyon (Rhône). When I contacted him on May 24, 2023, the archivist at this center was initially surprised that I was asking openly, for Brigitte Trogneux's class photographs. He explains that I am not the first to ask. When I asked him if he has ever been contacted by "other journalists", the cheerful archivist said: "No, it's not journalists; it's private individuals who make requests. So I know, they don't ask me directly about Mrs Macron, obviously, because they know very well that I'm not going to satisfy their request [...]. Actually, we get requests that are indirect and then, when you dig a little deeper, the person doesn't want to spill the beans because they're still looking for Brigitte Trogneux." As the

Sacré-Cœur d'Amiens did not reply, I invoked the authority of his position as archivist of the congregation overseeing the establishment: "I would prefer if you do it yourself, I'll tell you what, because I've already sent a lot of requests… I would prefer that they take responsibility afterwards for answering you, see? Because I don't know if they'll want to answer you. I know because if that's the Brigitte Macron case, I don't know if they will be willing to answer you. I'm washing my hands of the whole affair, I'll tell you that much"…

---

1. It's absurd to say, as sometimes alleged on social media, that Brigitte Trogneux didn't exist or that she was born a man. Brigitte Trogneux was born a female on April 13, 1953 in Amiens (Somme). Traces of her birth can be found in the 10-year table of the city of Amiens (1953-1962), in *Le Courrier picard* (April 14 and 15, 1953) and in the *Bulletin de La Providence* (Vacances 1953). Her baptism was announced in *Picardie Dimanche* (April 19, 1953).

2. Photo first published in *Brigitte Macron, un roman français*, Virginie Linhart, *France 3,* June 13, 2018.

3. See Chapter 16.

4. *Comment une nébuleuse LREM instrumentalise les réseaux sociaux*, *Médiapart*, April 9, 2019.

5. *France Dimanche*, February 4, 2022.

6. The policy for the conservation of archives received and produced by services and schools involved in the French education system has been fully clarified, with a history of the official texts, in a 52-page circular issued on February 22, 2005 by François Fillon, Minister of Education, and Renaud Donnedieu de Vabres, Minister of Culture. The text can be consulted on FranceArchives under the code SIAF DPACI/RES/2005/003.

7. All e-mails messages sent and telephone calls made in the course of the survey were recorded and archived.

8. The *Dar Olfa* palace lease affair originates in the publication in *Faits & Documents* of a rental lease issued by the Marrakech commercial court registry, listing Emmanuel Macron as co-owner with financier Guillaume Rambourg of the *Dar Olfa* palace in Marrakech's palm grove.

9. In *L'Affaire Madame, le jour où la première dame est devenue un homme, anatomie d'une fake news* (StudioFact Éditions, 2024), the episode is recounted by Emmanuelle Anizon: "Xavier Poussard would even like me to pull a few threads myself, hoping that with the prestige of *L'Obs*, it will be easier than with *Faits & Docs*. […] As we have seen, Brigittologists are obsessed with finding traces of Brigitte as a teenager or young woman, before her supposed transformation. So, somewhat as a game, I collected some evidence as I traveled and met new people."

23

THE DISAPPEARANCE OF BRIGITTE TROGNEUX (2 – THE BRIDE)

Sylvie Bommel's description

Once all possible steps had been taken to find out about Brigitte Trogneux's school curriculum, I continued to retrace her life. Brigitte Trogneux obtained her *baccalauréat* A in 1972, and married André Auzière in Le Touquet-Paris-Plage (Pas-de-Calais) on June 22, 1974. This episode corresponds to the second known photograph of Brigitte Trogneux's youth, the wedding photograph. A decade separates her from communion photography. This photograph does not appear in the official biography *Brigitte Macron, l'affranchie*[1], which devotes only one line to the wedding of Brigitte Trogneux and André Auzière: "On June 22 1974, at the tender age of 21, Mlle Trogneux became Mme Auzière in the town hall of Le Touquet. Things happened quickly, and some of her friends were quite surprised. But she has a good reason for wanting to get married: her strong desire to be a mother."

The circumstances of this wedding were long unclear, but were only brought to light by Sylvie Bommel in 2019. In *Il venait d'avoir 17 ans*[2], she describes the day of June 22, 1974 in great detail. As this episode is the focal point of her investigation, Sylvie Bommel mentions it several times. Here is a compilation of excerpts from the book in which the 1974 wedding is described:

"The father of the bride is radiant, the sun of Le Touquet much less so. To accompany his youngest daughter to the altar of the Jeanne-d'Arc church, Jean Trogneux bought a tuxedo as white as the hair is still has. Brigitte looks lovely in her long dress with a lace bustier. A floor-length veil flows from her bun, and her gloved hand holds a bouquet of roses, or maybe buttercups. She turned twenty-one in April, just in time to help elect Valéry Giscard d'Estaing to the presidency of the Republic, at least if she followed her family's instructions. She is one of the last young French women to have had to wait until that age to vote; and, more embarrassingly, to have access to the pill without asking for parental permission. On July 5, the age of majority will be lowered to eighteen. Brigitte has tucked her arm under her new husband's, which may comfort her but doesn't solve his problem of not knowing what to do with his hands. He holds them slightly apart as if he wanted to catch a ball. His outfit, a frock coat, does little to relax him, yet he wears it well. André Auzière – this is his name – is dark-haired, tall, and slim, and has fine features. Yet, in the photo, he winces; like a premonition of his misfortune. The photographer must not be that good: he failed to capture Brigitte's gaze, which goes sideway. Only the parents of the bride and groom smile openly for the camera. André's mother Renée is giving up her only son to another woman, but she doesn't seem to take it too badly. She wears a silk dress printed with large flowers. Brigitte's mom, Simone, has chosen a cream suit with navy blue polka dots and a floral floppy hat. She holds her kid gloves in her hand, as ladies do on Sundays in a provincial town after mass, just before buying a cake; except Simone, because she runs the pastry. [...] Here he is at last, Brigitte's first husband, the man whose face the French have never seen. The man whose friends can't or won't tell him anything except that he's alive and well. I had a hard time, but I finally found an old photo of him. As I write this book, none have ever circulated. André Auzière looks handsome in this 1974 photo, but I must admit I wasn't expecting him. [...] On June 22 1974, the two young people got married in Le Touquet. André's parents, Louis and Renée Auzière, are a bit confuded. Unlike the Trogneux family, who know everyone in this small seaside resort, they have never laid down their bathing sheet on a North Sea strand – Africa has accustomed them to warmer waters. The mayor, Léonce Deprez, who is a friend and tennis partner of the bride's father, acknowledges this in his speech: "I wish happiness to the bride and groom; and I am particularly delighted to see two families from Amiens and Paris choose our city as the setting for their union. I salute the young wife as the daughter of the Tennis Club president and vice-president of the *Union des propriétaires, résidents et amis du Touquet.*" The marriage certificate states that André is a *stagiaire hors cadre* (which, in banking jargon, means a junior executive) and that his young wife is a student. A marriage contract was registered with a notary in Amiens, a decision undoubtedly dictated by the parents, but which ones? Is it André's father, an auditor, who prefers squared out situations, or the Trogneux family, who are already thinking of passing on their Touquet villa to their daughter? Witnesses, too, seem to have be chosen by the parents. On the groom's side, the civil status register bears the signatures of his maternal uncle, Georges Costes[3], aged sixty-six, and Jacques Naudy, a colleague of his father's, head of a major accountancy firm. Brigitte is assisted by her two older brothers, Jean-Claude and Jean-Michel. The first has an annoying tendency to think of himself as his father. He could be."

April 25, 2019: a first release

The photograph of Brigitte Trogneux's wedding found by Sylvie Bommel is not published in her investigation book, but is the basis for a long description. The photo is being released for the first time to coincide with the publication of the excerpts published in *Le Point*[4], a week before the book's release on May 2, 2019... The photo is captioned as follows: "Her life before. [...] Sylvie Bommel recounts Brigitte Trogneux's youth".

At first glance, one is astonished by the discrepancy between the precision of the information gathered by Sylvie Bommel (marriage certificate, mayor's speech, etc.) and the poor quality of a photograph, that seems completely anachronistic in its composition. As if something wasn't right. Before delivering a definitive analysis, we had to understand this document, and to do so, we had to unravel, reconstitute and cross-check everything…

The origins of the document

Contrary to what Sylvie Bommel's account suggests, the photo does not come from a private collection. It is openly available – which does not detract from her merit. At the time, the photograph was used in two announcements published by the family in the local press. One appeared in two editions of *La Voix du Nord* (Boulogne-sur-Mer and Montreuil-sur-Mer, June 30-July 1, 1974), the other in *Les Echos du Touquet* (June 28, 1974).

When we read the texts accompanying the two announcements, we realize that Sylvie Bommel has constructed her story by describing

the photo, then copying *Les Echos du Touquet* for the speech by the mayor, Léonce Deprez, and *La Voix du Nord* for the marriage certificate. The journalist did not have a look at the marriage certificate, which is normal. By law, a town hall can only issue a copy of a full marriage record to a third party after a period of 75 years has elapsed (2049 in this case), or 25 years from the date of death of one of the spouses, whichever is shorter (2044 in this case, i.e. 25 years after André Auzière's death in 2019). Before this period expires, a third party can consult the alphabetical table of weddings celebrated annually in a municipality.

TABLE ALPHABETIQUE DES ACTES DE MARIAGES CELEBRES AU TOUQUET-PARIS-PLAGE
POUR L'ANNEE MIL NEUF CENT SOIXANTE-QUATORZE.

N° des ACTES	DATES DES ACTES	NOMS & PRENOMS DES EPOUX
40	7 Septembre	ALLARD Christian Albert & JULLIER Dominique Berthe Palmyre
54	22 Novembre	ANDRE Françoise Michèle & VANOVERSCHELDE Didier Michel Gérard
25	22 Juin	AUZIERE André Louis & TROGNEUX Brigitte Marie Claude
22	1 Juin	BAILLET Dominique Marie-Noëlle & BOULANGER Guy Jacques Henri
31	3 Août	BELPALME Dominique Marcelle Fernande & LAZELL Geoffrey Kenneth Michael
56	7 Décembre	BERSOUNIOUX Jean Louis & DEBYSER Christine Suzanne Alice
22	1 Juin	BOULANGER Guy Jacques Henri & BAILLET Dominique Marie-Noëlle
58	7 Décembre	BOULLY Bernard Léon Albert & VARLET Martine Lucile Fernande

Found then quickly erased

Puzzled by the untraceable André Auzière, Sylvie Bommel had been looking for traces of his wedding to Brigitte Trogneux. Then she put together the documents she had found - two announcements with photos - to piece together a story. This in itself poses no ethical problem, even if the content of an announcement in the press cannot be assimilated to a civil status document. But the mention of the wedding in the alphabetical tables of weddings celebrated annually in Le Touquet-Paris-Plage establish that it occurred. But this photograph of Brigitte Trogneux at the age of 21 never really made it into "Brigitte's" "personal album". In the documentary *Brigitte Macron l'influente* broadcast on *BFMTV* in September 2019[5], it is very briefly shown, with a transparency effect that makes the bride and groom physically unidentifiable.

At best, the photo is reproduced in very low quality, as here on *Closer*'s website on October 13, 2020, in the wake of the announcement of André Auzière's death ten months earlier.

From then on, we had to figure out what was wrong with this photo and try to find it in the best possible quality. And why not find other photos of the event or other photos of Brigitte Trogneux at the same time?

Is "Brigitte" Brigitte Trogneux?

This is the best quality photo available to date. This is a high-definition scan based on the copy of Les *Echos du Touquet* available at the Bibliothèque nationale de France.

For this survey, we have made the editorial choice to use only original documents and not to use photo restoration software, to avoid distorting the analysis by visual AI, i.e. facial recognition used to support the analysis of photographic material. For your information, we reproduce Brigitte Trogneux's face obtained by restoring the photo above. One does not really recognize the "Brigitte" we know today – this is an understatement.

Once we had obtained the best quality photo available (that of the wedding photo digitized in HD), we were able to verify whether the individual shown on the 1974 wedding

High - 71,08 %

225

announcement was indeed Brigitte Trogneux, as we had identified her at her first communion. With a result of 71.08 % (high), *Face++* believed it was most likely the same individual.

To be able to analyze the photo of Brigitte Trogneux's wedding to André Auzière in 1974, I had to be sure of the authenticity of the image and of the caption provided on the invitation, and verify that Brigitte Trogneux was indeed the woman in the photo. We therefore consulted these wedding invitations wherever they were available, whether at the BNF or in various municipal or departmental archives. If it was a fake, as Natacha Rey thought, there would be some flaw. But copies of wedding invitations are always identical. These two versions are the same wherever we have consulted them, including on microfilm at the Lille municipal library. The wedding was announced the same day in *Le Courrier picard* (June 22-23, 1974): "Mr. and Mrs. Jean Trogneux, Mr. and Mrs· Louis Auzière, are pleased to announce the wedding of their children Brigitte and André, which will be celebrated on Saturday June 22, 1974, in the church of Sainte-Jeanne-d'Arc in Le Touquet. 1, rue Delambre, Amiens. 174 rue de Courcelles, Paris". As it is highly improbable, not to say impossible, to produce modified facsimiles of several newspapers, in several local editions, and to dispose of these forgeries, including on microfilm, in archive centers all over France, we had to conclude that the wedding announcements between Brigitte Trogneux and André Auzière published in the regional daily or weekly press in June 1974 were genuine, and that the photograph accompanying them depicted Brigitte Trogneux and André Auzière.

The final cross-check was to be made possible by the roadmap I had sent on June 14 2023, to Emmanuelle Anizon, a journalist and senior reporter at *L'Obs* covering the Jean-Michel Trogneux affair[6]. We were right to place Anne-Marie Bouchez at the top of the list of people Emmanuelle Anizon could contact in Amiens. Indeed, the woman who had validated the communion photo had remained close to Brigitte Trogneux after their school days. So much so that, when she married in 1976, Anne-Marie Bouchez made Brigitte Trogneux her maid of honor. To Emmanuelle Anizon, Anne-Marie Bouchez will provide a photo of her wedding, featuring her alongside her husband and her maid of honor, Brigitte Trogneux[7]. In this photo, which Emmanuelle Anizon has in her possession, we can clearly see the same woman as in the 1974 photo: Brigitte Trogneux[8]. Once the conditions for exploiting this photograph had been met (captioning, dating, authentication), we could move on to the analysis using visual artificial intelligence. This revolved around a simple question: was "Brigitte" the same person as Brigitte Trogneux, born April 13, 1953 in Amiens, pictured here at her wedding to André Auzière in 1974?

To make it easier to read the results given for Brigitte Trogneux's wedding photo by *Face++,* the facial recognition software used by the authorities of the People's Republic of China, here are the reference values established from tests on eight women born, like Brigitte Trogneux, in 1953. Regarding dates, we have chosen configurations as close as possible to those confronting Brigitte Trogneux in 1974 to "Brigitte". From left to right and top to bottom: former Pakistani Prime Minister Benazir Bhutto (1972 vs 2007), former Argentine President Cristina Kirchner (1974 vs 2024), American singer Cyndi Lauper (1970 vs 2019), American politician Elaine Chao (1979 vs 2019), actress Isabelle Huppert (1974 vs 2018), American actress Kim Basinger (1978 vs 2023), French politician Ségolène Royal (1980 vs 2017) and TV host Dorothée (1978 vs 2010).

Very high - 79,47 %   Very high - 80,759 %

Very high - 79,243 %   High - 69,936 %

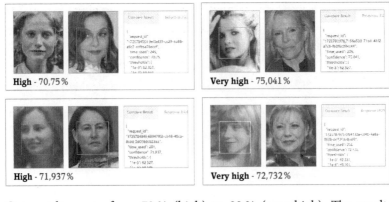

High - 70,75 %   **Very high** - 75,041 %

High - 71,937 %   **Very high** - 72,732 %

Our results range from 70 % (high) to 80 % (very high). The results obtained by comparing Brigitte Trogneux's 1974 wedding photo with "Brigitte" between 1986 and today should therefore fall into this bracket…

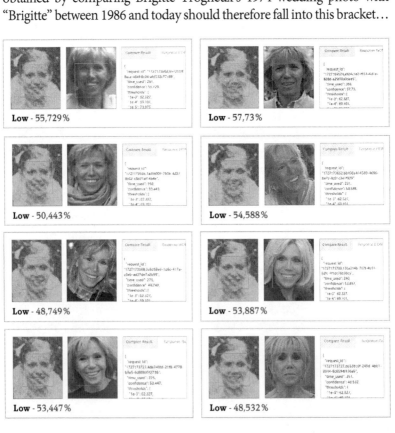

Low - 55,729 %   **Low** - 57,73 %

Low - 50,443 %   **Low** - 54,588 %

Low - 48,749 %   **Low** - 53,887 %

Low - 53,447 %   **Low** - 48,532 %

The scores are significantly lower than expected, ranging from 48.5 % (low) to 57.7 % (normal) - with an average of 53.816 % (low) over 60 pictures. This means that the facial recognition system clearly estimates, beyond any reasonable margin of error, that "Brigitte" is not the individual born Brigitte Trogneux, female, on April 13, 1953 in Amiens.

As established by the cross-checking, by the photographic material collected during our investigation, and by the analysis of the photographic material: yes, the communicant and the bride were indeed Brigitte Trogneux, wife of Auzière. But it wasn't "Brigitte", who since at least September 1986 had lived under this identity to become Brigitte Auzière *épouse* Macron. Therefore this seems to be a case of identity theft.

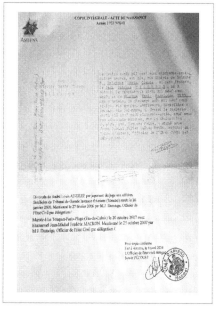

The main witness in the case was now deceased: André Auzière. It was he who, on the civil status certificate, acted as the bridge between his wife's life and the life of the individual who, in the mid-1980s, had taken her place and her identity... At this point, we noted three facts.

"Brigitte" is an individual who has been living, since at least September 1986, under the birth identity of another individual, namely Brigitte Trogneux, born April 13, 1953 in Amiens, who became madame Auzière on June 22, 1974 in Le Touquet. Despite this identity theft (as in the case of statutory rape, consent has no value in identity theft), the family nucleus remains unchanged (Brigitte and André Auzière and their three children), which points the case in the

229

direction of the worst obstacle in investigation: family secrecy. A family secret that explains the silence of the Trogneux and Auzière families, against us and all other journalists and biographers. Following the trail of family secrets, the candidate who emerged as the individual who had lived under Brigitte Trogneux's identity since 1986 was this hidden brother: Jean-Michel Trogneux.

This is why it was necessary to retrace his life from the very beginning, to consult photos of her other than the one in the family photo, in order to carry out a simple fact-check: Had Jean-Michel Trogneux, born on February 11, 1945, become a "chubby guy" as the Élysée suggested, or had he become "Brigitte"?

By contacting Jean-Michel Trogneux's classmates, I identified a few who had remained close to the Trogneux family. I passed on the list of these privileged contacts to Emmanuelle Anizon along with those about Brigitte Trogneux's past. From the first person on the list, Alexis Brunet, Emmanuelle Anizon recovered two class photographs of Jean-Michel Trogneux, one from 9ᵉ (1952, age 7) and one from 7ᵉ (1954, age 9). These photographs suggested so strongly that "Brigitte" was indeed the individual born Jean-Michel Trogneux that I wondered: maybe whoever had given these photos to Emmanuelle Anizon had tried to manipulate her. So I went on looking for another source of class photographs to cross-check. If so, new copies of these and other documents confirmed that Natacha Rey was right: "Brigitte" was born a man under the name Jean-Michel Trogneux, and this individual now called "Madame la

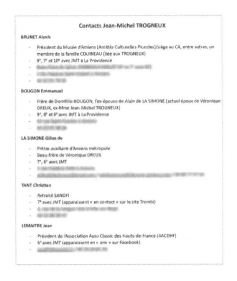

230

Présidente" became known under the civil birth identity of his sister, Brigitte Trogneux. Hence it was by presenting himself to the general public as his younger sister, Brigitte, that Jean-Michel Trogneux moved into the Élysée Palace and rose to the top of the Republic... This is how I concluded my investigation in *Faits & Documents* in February 2024, a month before the publication of Emmanuelle Anizon's book, *L'Affaire Madame, le jour où la première dame est devenue un homme, anatomie d'une fake news...*

---

1. *Brigitte Macron, l'affranchie*, Maëlle Brun, L'Archipel, 2018.

2. *Il venait d'avoir 17 ans*, Sylvie Bommel, JCLattès, 2019.

3. A portrait of Georges Costes can be found in Yves Courrière's *La guerre d'Algérie*, published in four volumes by Fayard: "The Renseignements Généraux police force, all-powerful in Algeria, is headed by a remarkable man, M. Costes. A great cop. He knows Algeria like the back of his hand. Certainly better than many *pieds-noirs*. He has close ties with Mr. Borgeaud, the Algerian potentate whose immense power reaches across the Mediterranean. Costes played a very important role on November 1st 1954, and due to his unwavering friendship with the Borgeaud group, he was eviced by the Mendès-France government. Costes is tall, slim and muscular. He impresses, yet he knows how to put himself within reach of his interlocutor. The intelligent, hollowed, bony, slightly equine face is topped by a long, light-brown hairbrush. He's got charm. A colt, not a tired horse, despite his already long experience of Algeria. His lucid and passionate intelligence spared him the blunders so easily made by an important civil servant in Algeria well before 1940! He has been in Algeria since 1932. This is rare for a valuable metropolitan civil servant. Usually a job in Algeria is a chore, an internship that you complete - as quickly as possible - before moving up the ladder. But Costes is of a different caliber, with much more ambition. He is originally from Pamiers (Ariège), and has kept a hint of his accent. His parents are not rich. Through sacrifice and deprivation, he pushed on until a law degree. There are two career paths: legal professions, or public administration. To be a lawyer, you need money. It will be the administration. But in the administration, he chose the less static, less "sleepy" branch, because Costes is a thoroughbred. So it will be the police. He quickly makes his mark. But he ambitiously targets the summits. In Algeria, where there is not much competition for jobs, things will go faster. In 1937, five years after his arrival, he is deputy head of the *Renseignements Généraux* (secret services) in Algiers. From 1938 to 1940, he is Controller General of *Sécurité du territoire* (Homeland Security). He loves his job and wants to do everything in it. And he is already hooked on Algeria. But then come 1940 and Pétain. He "crashes". He is nowhere to be seen. And it naturally returned in the luggage of the landing Allies. Appointed Commissaire Divisionnaire in 1943,

he takes charge of the Algiers P.R.G., which he knows well, and starts to build his empire. Borgeaud, who knows his way around clever men, prefers to have him in his clan. He will stay there until the end. Costes is a specialist in Muslim "opposition". It is he who, on the orders of General Catroux, arrested Ferhat Abbas in 1943. He is the first to add Sergeant Ouamrane's name to the list of "hardliners". He knows the Arab-Kabylian antagonism. He plays with subtlety. His links with the all-powerful Aït Ali family are notorious. The 1946 amnesty law, which freed all political prisoners except those convicted of murder, has no fiercer opponent than him. It is a sign of weakness towards the Arabs," he says. "That's the kind of language that appeals to Algiers. He made no mistake when he spoke of the 1946 amnesties. He followed them out of the corner of his eye. They all belong to the underground O.A.S. Movement. Costes keeps an eye on them. It's not yet time to dismantle the organization. By chance, the opportunity arises in 1950."

4. *Sa vie d'avant, Le Point*, April 25, 2019.

5. *Brigitte Macron l'influente, BFMTV*, September 16, 2019.

6. See Chapter 22.

7. To cross-check the caption provided for this photo of Brigitte Trogneux, witness at Anne-Marie Bouchez's wedding in 1976, I first consulted her civil status, which tells me that, born on May 27, 1953 in Paris XIVe, Anne-Marie Bouchez did indeed marry, on July 1, 1976 in Amiens, Édouard Delarue, who is incidentally the brother of lawyer Hubert Delarue, former vice-president of Amiens Métropole, in charge of urban policy (2014-2020), who was made Chevalier de la Légion d'Honneur by Éric Dupond-Moretti, then Minister of Justice, alongside whom he had pleaded, among others, in the child-crime cases of Outreau and Mannechez (See *Chapter 2*). Anne-Marie Bouchez and Édouard Delarue divorced soon, on September 17, 1982. By definition, we couldn't confirm that Brigitte Trogneux had indeed been the witness at this wedding, since the marriage certificate can only be legally communicated to a third party after a period of 75 years has expired (2051 in this case). However, we had no reason to disbelieve Anne-Marie Bouchez's testimony, at least on this point. All the more so since a photo of the wedding was published in the wedding announcement in *Courrier Picard*. In the car, the bride and groom are wearing the same clothes as in the photograph sent to Emmanuelle Anizon, and in the background we see the maid of honor dressed in black and white. We therefore had a photograph of Brigitte Trogneux from the front at her wedding in 1974, cross-referenced with a photograph of Brigitte Trogneux seen from the side at Anne-Marie Bouchez's wedding in 1976. It should be pointed out that, like many of the witnesses we met in the Trogneux affair, Anne-Marie Bouchez seems to have tried to mislead Emmanuelle Anizon after giving her the photo of the group of communicant girls and the photo of her wedding, by implying that in 1976, Brigitte Trogneux was not married to André Auzière. Perhaps (but this is less likely) it was a simple mistake on the part of Anne-Marie Bouchez? In any case, here is how Emmanuelle Anizon describes the episode in *L'Affaire Madame* (StudioFact Éditions, 2024): "I also had lunch with one of Brigitte's best friends, who knew her as an adult, a young mother and in a couple. In her pretty house with a vegetable garden, this friend took great pains not to tell me anything, and swore she had not kept a single photo of these

years of friendship. A few weeks later, she called me back to tell me that, at Brigitte's express request, I must reveal "nothing" of what she had told me, even though it was so harmless. I thought with empathy about her biographers. It canno t have been easy. Then one day, another of Brigitte's chatty, funny classmates tells me after an hour on the phone that Brigitte Trogneux was the maid of honor at her wedding in 1976. However, she was astonished to learn that her witness was not married at the time, and in any case had no children, whereas she was supposed to have married two years earlier and given birth to Sébastien [Auzière]. I was not able to get to the bottom of this, as the friend cut short our exchanges afterwards. But she assured me it was Brigitte and sent me a photo of the ceremony. A pretty couple in a church, in front of the altar, and next to the bride in a white dress, sideways, the witness's broad shoulders, a haircut à la *Stone et Charden* with a short fringe, jacket and bell-bottom pants". I later learn that Brigitte Trogneux was also the maid of honor at the wedding of Benoît Lafarge and Sophie Bernard on June 26, 1973 in Amiens.

8. In the Friday August 23, 1974 issue of *Lynn News & Advertisers*, a publication based in King's Lynn (Norfolk, Great Britain), Brigitte Trogneux's name appears among those thanking the town's inhabitants for accomodating them during their one-month language course. This information contradicts "Brigitte's" official biography, which says that she learned English five years earlier in the United States, in the summer of 1969, where she stayed with a family of morticians.

24

"THOSE WHO END UP BELIEVING IT"

"My worst memory as a President of the Republic"

March 8, 2024. Women's Day. On the sidelines of the ceremony he organized to constitutionalize the right to abortion, Emmanuel Macron was interviewed on *TF1* by journalist Paul Larrouturou. With a tense face, he refers to "those who say that my wife would be a man" and "people who end up believing it and who push you around in your private life" as his "worst memory as a President of the Republic".

This episode is the culmination of a crazy media sequence that began with the publication between December 2023 and February 2024 in *Faits & Documents* of four previously unpublished childhood photos of Jean-Michel Trogneux (officially "Brigitte's" brother), copiously relayed on *X France*, notably by the *@zoesagan* account hosted by the writer Aurélien Poirson-Atlan[1].

Emmanuelle Anizon, author of *L'Affaire Madame, le jour où la première dame est devenue un homme, anatomie d'une fake news*[2], felt she had been targeted by Emmanuel Macron's statement. She made this public in a radio interview[3]: "And then there's this response from Emmanuel Macron that's very surprising and quite hard to explain...

235

Maybe he knew the book was about to be published? Maybe it was a way of reacting to it automatically?" During this interview, Emmanuelle Anizon also ponders about a "potential" tail operation by the "Élysée security services" in the lobby of a hotel where she had made an appointment with Natacha Rey to gather information for her book... The interviewer then expresses surprise at the Élysée's failure to produce "a few very simple documents": "A photograph of Brigitte Macron pregnant with her children? Did the defense, may I say, run out of archives from this rather rocky family?" When you know what Emmanuelle Anizon had seen, it's easy to understand why she included herself among the "people who end up believing it and who push you around in your intimacy", despite a book whose title promised to reveal "the anatomy of fake news"...

"Ahead of Trump"

After the first buzz in December 2021/January 2022, this statement by Emmanuel Macron on his "worst memory as a President of the Republic" paves the way for a second "Streisand effect". After Turkey and Russia, the case lands in the United States. On March 11, 2024, the conservative influencer Candace Owens described the affair as "one of the greatest political scandals in the history of mankind". This exposure, as well as the fact that the affair was picked up by the cream of American influencers[4], fueled paranoia in Paris, at the Elysée Palace and in Parisian editorial offices. When the FBI raided Donald Trump's Mar-a-Lago estate in the summer of 2022, they discovered a classified file titled "*1A Info re: president of France*" that could relate to Emmanuel Macron's private life. Asked about this, he complained on *CNN* of a "not very pleasant" situation, while explaining that he was "trying not to be paranoid[5]". In Russia, Olga Skabeyeva, a star of public broadcasting, had directly linked the two cases in the opening of her program *60 Minutes:* "Ahead of Trump, many French people were certain that their First Lady - and this was even published in the newspapers - named Brigitte Macron, would actually be transgender. Overall, according to the press, she was born a man under the name Jean-Michel Trogneux"[6].

236

Fearing the opening of a Pandora's box, the Élysée decided, in the spring of 2024, to accelerate the judicial agenda on the third procedure initiated by Jean-Michel and Brigitte Trogneux against Natacha Rey and Amandine Roy following their video of December 10, 2021. Obtained on April 3, 2024 by Jean Ennochi "Brigitte"'s lawyer, during a surreal hearing interrupting the statute of limitations, the advancement of this trial from March 6, 2025 to June 19, 2024 (unprecedented in French judicial history) is obviously aimed at securing a rapid conviction, were reflected in the media by the publication of the AFP dispatch "*Intox transphobe contre Brigitte Macron: deux femmes condamnées pour diffamation*" ("Transphobic intox against Brigitte Macron: two women convicted of defamation"). In fact, these proceedings are in no way aimed at the heart of the case (Brigitte's birth identity), but at Natacha Rey's accusation of "falsifying civil status documents", based on two letters from the Amiens town hall refusing to issue a copy of Jean-Michel Trogneux's birth certificate, even though it had been established that he had indeed been born in this city, as confirmed by the issuing by the same administration of the birth certificate on December 31, 2021[7].

The full copy of this birth certificate, as well as that of Brigitte Trogneux, Jean-Michel Trogneux's voter's card and the divorce decree between Brigitte and André Auzière, will be used to convict Natacha Rey and Amandine Roy. We note that, unlike the Auzières' lawsuit, the Trogneux family did not provide any photographic material. Prior to this, the civil party goes through the senior investigating judges to sue anonymously. Downstream, the Trogneux's lawyers requested that the minutes of the judgment not be made public[8], refusing to provide the defendants' lawyers with copies of their client's identity papers. As the excuse of "good faith" was not accepted by the court (in fact, Natacha Rey pleaded her initial thesis), Natacha Rey therefore received a suspended fine for defamation of Jean-Michel and Brigitte Trogneux. While a wave of repression and censorship had preceded the judgement handed down on September 12, 2024[9], Jean Ennochi, leaving the court, announced that he had launched systematic legal proceedings in France and abroad. As a result, Aurélien Poirson-Atlan(*@zoesagan*), a relayer of the case on X, was prosecuted (along with Bertrand Scholler) for "cyberharassment"[10], an offence instituted by the Schiappa law of 2018 under the heading of adolescent protection. Then Candace Owens received a summons in Nashville (Tennessee) on December 2, 2024, in which "Brigitte's" local lawyers had Emmanuelle Anizon and her book *L'Affaire Madame* identify the "chubby guy" as the individual born Jean-Michel Trogneux on February 11, 1945 in Amiens.

"Eaten up by this story"

On this precise point, Emmanuelle Anizon is much more evasive in her book, in which she merely recounts a (very) brief interview, on a sidewalk, in front of a bar in Amiens *(Le Nemrod)*, with the person which the Presidency, noncommittally, let suppose and hint to be the individual born Jean-Michel Trogneux, on February 11, 1945 in Amiens, i.e. the "chubby guy". The latter explains to Emmanuelle Anizon that "the whole *#JeanMichelTrogneux* affair hasn't really had any impact on his life" apart from the fact that he had to "close his *Facebook* account because of the troll messages[11]". However, in Emmanuelle Anizon's book, this statement is contradicted a few lines up by Jean-Alexandre Trogneux, the current boss of the family confectionery. Like all the other members of the clan, writes Emmanuelle Anizon, Jean-Alexandre "declined my request for an interview, dropping just, after a long sigh: "You know, we're being eaten up by this story", i.e. the Jean-Michel Trogneux affair, as Emmanuelle Anizon confirmed to me over the phone. In a family whose members are "eaten up" by an *a priori* preposterous story ("a sister = her brother") that anyone would ignore or silence in two minutes, how do you explain that for the main interested party the affair has "not really had any impact on his life"?

"A requirement for exemplarity and democratic transparency"

In promotional interviews, Emmanuelle Anizon never mentioned this meeting with "Jean-Michel Trogneux" described at the end of her book, but she discussed at length the reality libel suit against

Natacha Rey, explaining quite rightly: "Natacha Rey has requested civil records from the town hall of Amiens, particularly on Jean-Michel Trogneux, and did not obtain them. Here lies a problem. Normally, in a republic, in a democracy such as ours, one has the right to receive such documents upon request. And this is where we have a demand for exemplarity, for democratic transparency which would already make it possible to reduce this mistrust, which today is at such a level that we can no longer say anything"[12]...

What's more, in her book, in which she paints rather laudatory portraits of the relayers of the Jean-Michel Trogneux affair (Natacha Rey[13], Xavier Poussard[14] and Aurélien Poirson-Atlan[15]), Emmanuelle Anizon never expresses her feminist sensibility, which would have been a natural angle had she been convinced that Brigitte Macron was a woman. What could be worse than insinuating that a woman could be a man? Why is it that Emmanuelle Anizon's feminist sensibility, so committed to covering the #MeToo movement, comes out so little in L'Affaire Madame? Logically, this angle should have been highlighted in his investigation had it been *fake news*. Aside from the book's subtitle, there is no instance of fake news in Emmanuelle Anizon's book, except once, when the notion is ridiculed by Natacha Rey: "So I would have the – supernatural – ability to convince all those serious people with intellectual baggage of some ridiculous, even grotesque fake news, without the slightest ground, the slightest rational argument, coming from the dregs of the Internet, as reported in all the press and media. Ah! I'm so smart!"

Not a single instance of what Emmanuelle Anizon should have treated, had it been *fake news*, as odiously symptomatic of "ambient machismo" against women in power, a mark of the failure of fifty years of feminist struggles. Stranger still, in L'Affaire Madame, the question of "misogyny" is only raised to describe the police officers' behavior towards Natacha Rey during her first police custody, in the summer of 2021: "When I arrived at the police station, they told me I was in custody, searched me, confiscated my cell phone and interrogated me. They were misogynistic, mocking, sometimes threatening, the adjutant yelled at me: "What do you care if it's a man? It's his private life! It's none of your business." In this case, which logically should have been treated as a paroxysm of machismo and violence against women in society, the victim of misogyny was not "Brigitte" but Natacha Rey?

More than a paradox, it's a cognitive disjunction. The failure of feminists, who should have been on the front line, to denounce the *fake news* had already been maliciously pointed out by Roselyne Bachelot, a "gay-friendly" former minister, who explained that she "had a grudge against certain feminists. If you don't share President Macron's ideas, that's part of democracy. [...] But to attack your wife or someone close to you, and in such a low, trivial, trashy way, and for a number of my fellow feminist fighters not to have said: "Here we stop[16]". An observation not contradicted by the reaction of feminist activist Sandrine Rousseau, who, when asked to comment on the Trogneux affair by Jean-Jacques Bourdin, supported "Brigitte" desperately: "Me, I would just like to tell LGBTQIA+ people, trans people, that they are included in society"[17].

"A family photograph in the pages of Paris-Match?"

In fact, as she recounts in her book, Emmanuelle Anizon found some previously unpublished photos of Jean-Michel and Brigitte Trogneux; all of which suggest that "Brigitte" is not the individual born Brigitte Trogneux, but her brother Jean-Michel thus pretending to be her, since the mid-1980s... In her book, Emmanuelle Anizon wonders: "Why not stop all that by slipping a family photograph into the pages of *Paris-Match*? Or why not take advantage of this book to answer the question?" This proposal to Jean Ennochi, "Brigitte's" lawyer went unheeded and, in the mind of the presidential couple, placed Emmanuelle Anizon in the category of "people who end up believing in it and who upset your intimacy".

Eventually, during the promotion of her book, Emmanuelle Anizon was the first journalist to write in the mainstream press, after ten years of media coverage of the couple, that Emmanuel Macron was indeed 14 years old when he met "Brigitte": "With this couple, who met when Emmanuel Macron was 14 [...], the fight against paedophilia has been superimposed on Natacha Rey's obsession"[18].

After three years of nagging questions about the real identity of "Brigitte", the mainstream press finally conceded on the 14 years, with Emmanuel Macron's age at the time of the meeting made official by *Le Monde*, traditionally somewhat considered as "the reference daily", in a series of articles published in December 2024 and entitled *Le Président et son double*. In one of the articles in this series, *Le Monde*[19] reveals that at the same time as I was publishing for the first time Jean-Michel Trogneux's childhood photographs, Patrice Faure, a former member of the *Direction Générale de la Sécurité Extérieure* (DGSE) [secret services], was recruited as Chief of staff to the French presidency, with a special responsibility for managing the Jean-Michel Trogneux affair, accelerating the judicial agenda against Natacha Rey, and prosecuting host of the @zoesagan account and Candace Owens. It seems clear that the strategy adopted against me was to trigger an international letter rogatory (on February 29, 2024, two weeks after the publication of Jean-Michel Trogneux's childhood photos) as part of the (unrelated) prosecution initiated by the National Prosecutor's Office for Combating Online Hate[20]. This strategy also consisted of increasing pressure on the majority shareholder of *Faits & Documents*, who dismissed me at the beginning of October 2024…

---

1. Despite Elon Musk's takeover of *X*, keywords relating to the case are constantly being dereferenced from general trends by *X France*. This is why, despite very large flows, the affair remains mostly within niches.

2. *L'Affaire Madame, le jour où la première dame est devenue un homme, anatomie d'une fake news*, Emmanuelle Anizon, StudioFact Éditions, 2024.

3. Emmanuelle Anizon, interviewed by Christophe Barbier on the Jewish community radio station *Radio J*, April 15, 2024.

4. They include Joe Rogan, Andrew Tate, Patrick Bet-David and Jackson Hinkle. NSA repentant Edward Snowden sent a signal to Candace Owens on this topic on *X*, March 13, 2024.

5. Emmanuel Macron, interviewed by Jake Tapper on *CNN*, September 23, 2022.

6. *60Minutes*, Rossiya 1, August 31, 2022.

7. See Chapter 18.

8. Excerpts from the judgment were published by Emmanuelle Anizon on *nouvelobs.com* (September 12, 2024) under the title: *Procès en diffamation envers Brigitte Macron: Natacha Rey condamnée.*

9. This wave of censorship included the closure by X France of Aurélien Poirson-Atlan's @zoesagan account, the closure by Youtube of writer Lionel Labosse's *Coccyx Grue* channel (jokes about "Brigitte"), and the sentencing on April 30, a 76-year-old homeless pensioner was sentenced to 6 months in prison for sending his social worker a photomontage depicting Emmanuel Macron's head on a spike (a representation that is consubstantial with the "values of the French Republic"), along with a message describing "Brigitte" as a "transgender slut". On the press front, editorialist Natacha Polony will be relieved of her post at the helm of *Marianne* magazine after a cover story on "La Rumeur qui inquiète l'Élysée" (The Rumor that Worries the Élysée) (March 28, 2024). Two years earlier, within the same press group (Czech Media Invest), the journalist Myriam Palomba had been dismissed from the management of the weekly magazine *Public* after sending journalists to Amiens to investigate the affair. Internationally, Candace Owens has been fired from the *Daily Wire*, Ben Shapiro's media company that had previously employed her, and will see her Youtube channel partially censored and suspended. In the run-up to the trial, the three-year-old son of François Danghléant, Natacha Rey's lawyer, taken away from her and placed with the Children's Social Welfare Agency (ASE). At the beginning of the affair, in March 2022, the French Internet had gone wild following the discovery of the drowned body of Isabelle Ferreira under the Rance dam in Saint-Malo; on Gilets Jaunes online groups, she had explained that she had found that the "statutory rape" potentially committed by "Brigitte" was, according to the Schiappa law of 2018, not time-barred, as the statute of limitations had been shifted to 30 years after the minor's majority, i.e., concerning Emmanuel Macron, December 21, 2025.

10. Four posts on X by Aurélien Poirson-Atlan were targeted for "cyber-harassment" in relation to "Brigitte":

November 28, 2023: "In Rothschild & Cie's secret documentation, you can discover (but don't tell anyone) that Emmanuel Macron's marital status changes like that of his drama teacher."

March 15, 2024: "Brigitte's sexual crime against Emmanuel Macron will not be time-barred until December 21, 2025. A good opportunity for the judiciary (Smagistrature, @USM_magistrats, @SnmFo) to prove its independence".

September 2, 2024: "My interview with Xavier Poussard reached 600,000 views in one day. The Brigitte Macron affair is a shocking state secret involving State-sanctioned pedophilia" accompanied by a photograph of Candace Owens wearing a t-shirt with an image of Madame Macron on the front page of *TIME* with the headline "MAN OF THE YEAR".

September 11, 2024: "Brigitte Macron is not Brigitte Macron".

11. Quoted by Emmanuelle Anizon in *L'Affaire Madame*, StudioFact Éditions, 2024.

12. *Sud Radio*, April 11, 2024.

13. In *L'Affaire Madame*, Emmanuelle Anizon describes Natacha Rey as follows: "I recognize the slim figure, the blond braid across the chest. I discover a delicate face and green eyes, which this time not behind her big black glasses. Jeans, low heels, black lace top, fitted orange jacket, she's feminine. And what you would call a pretty woman. She's fifty-one, and looks ten years younger at least. It's hard to imagine, looking at her, that she's the source of the whole story. [...] For twenty-four hours, we exchange ideas. Natacha turns out to be voluble and cheerful. She often laughs at what she says, over her organic teas and roasted vegetables with spirulina. Natacha is vegan. [...] Natacha grew up in a modest, loving family, perfectly integrated into the "system", as she calls it. Parents who've managed to afford a small bungalow in a rural village, and a quiet life for their children. They wouldn't let her go teenagers' parties, and education was rather strict, so she relished in old movies from the 1950s and 1960s and in books. Lamartine, Musset, Zola, "but not the best known, I loved *Le Rêve, La Faute de l'abbé Mouret, Le Docteur Pascal, Pour une nuit d'amour...* and then Oscar Wilde, Flaubert, and Anouilh's theater...". Her eyes sparkle as she lists the authors who fed her precocious child's hunger. "Reading saved me, and it has a lot to do with what's happening to me today. "Natacha has the temperament of an artist. In her drawers, she keeps blackened notebooks of poems and song lyrics". During the promotion of *L'Affaire Madame*, *Europe 1* listeners (March 22, 2024) were told that Natacha Rey is "a pretty woman, who has read a lot, is quite cultured, and is very committed to the animal cause".

14. In *L'Affaire Madame*, Emmanuelle Anizon describes Xavier Poussard as follows: "In the months following the publication of the investigation, the *Faits & Documents* journalist continued to pursue the subject and publish. I talk to him regularly on the phone, using Signal's encrypted messaging system. His profile intrigues me. The son of left-leaning secondary-school teachers ["*agrégés de gauche*"], he grew up in a Parisian apartment studded with books [...] and now, at the age of thirty-five, he is a hunter of the elite for a confidential newspaper that some consider to be far-right. I am astonished by this trajectory. he dodges, questions the questioner, e.g.: "What is the far right today?" He is cultured, quotes a bunch of authors, speaks with a mixture of sarcastic brutality and deadpan detachment, details his research with that particular meticulousness of the obsessive investigator, who methodically archives everything every day, and keeps detailed files on everyone. His mind is engraved with a meticulous political-economic-sexual cartography of the entire elite, including its genealogical and historical ramifications. He says he's "happy to have reversed the load of bullshit in this story. Now it's France laughing at them. For him, "Natacha Rey is somewhat like a sniper who shoots one inch from the target. She has an intuition, she came very close to the truth, no doubt, and that's why she's been so harassed, with the police custodies and the legal action. She has also confused us all a lot with her false leads. What remains to be seen is what she missed, what they didn't want her to know." [...] Xavier refused to come to France, so I left to meet him in Italy in early December 2023. I am not sure what he looks like; he is

very discreet and doesn't show his face [...]. In the café where he's arranged to meet me in Milan, I discover a tall, lanky guy with a student look, jeans and thin glasses. He takes me to *Faits & Documents*'s office, a small apartment "belonging to my wife's family". In the corridor, large cupboards are crammed with little cards carefully handwritten by the magazine's founder, Emmanuel Ratier. When the latter passed away in an accident, Xavier Poussard, who was twenty-seven years old and had been working with him for a short time, decided to take over the title's editorial management. He does not write cards by hand, but the method is the same: he produces files on everything and everyone. In his computers, he keeps hundreds of files, photos, videos and telephone conversations, rigorously archived. On his screen, I even spotted one with my name, probably created after our exchanges".

15. In *L'Affaire Madame*, Emmanuelle Anizon describes Aurélien Poirson-Atlan as follows: "Obviously, I would like to meet him. Several times in his tweets, I see that he refers to *Faits & Documents*' work on the Brigitte affair. I call Xavier Poussard, who confirms that the two of them talk regularly on the phone. A former banker turned gallery owner connected them. They are both thirty-somethings, but their profiles differ on about everything. On one side Aurélien Poirson-Atlan (a name of Jewish origin), close to the far-left lawyer Juan Branco; on the other Xavier Poussard, editor-in-chief of a far-right magazine sometimes accused of anti-semitism. The alliance would have been unthinkable twenty years ago, but seems obvious to them today. They hit it off immediately, on the phone, one in Italy, the other in the South of France. Same fast mind, same generation, same life as the dad who takes his kids to school in the morning before going off to destroy the established order, alone in front of his computer. He is active in the same denunciation of the elites and their deviances, supposed or otherwise, particularly sexual, even pedocriminal. In this alliance, the journalist from *Faits & Documents* brings the investigation, the memory, the archives, and @zoesagan, the audience, the impact capacity, the "pop" approach, as he likes to say. The first blows confidential information, which the second stages theatrically. Their cooperation mutually reinforces their power and visibility. [...] So here's the terror of X, thirty-nine years old, slim, dark, lively, laughing. We spend seven hours talking, on the quiet patio of a restaurant he "obviously" didn't choose by chance: *La Cachette*, i.e. *The Hideout*. Never miss an opportunity to turn up your nose. Aurélien explains that he and @zoesaganhave created a "punk social sculpture". The concept was directly inspired by his mentor Steve Oklyn, a New York fashion activist and founder of the *"Not Vogue"* website, a critical, post-situationist counterpoint to *Vogue* fashion magazine".

16. Interview with *Télé-Loisirs*, July 3, 2022.

17. Interview on *Sud Radio*, March 18, 2024.

18. *Jean-Michel Trogneux now Brigitte Macron? An obsession that affects "people of all ages, from all walks of life"*, Libération, March 16, 2024

19. In *Un président et son double. Emmanuel Macron, l'art du secret*, Le Monde, December 24, 2024, reads: "But protecting his image is another matter. At the Élysée palace, the chief of staff, Patrice Faure, is in charge of it, in addition to his other duties. This former member of the DGSE regularly brings together the Élysée

military command and the Presidential Security Directorate to monitor rumors and threats affecting Emmanuel Macron and his family. Neither an *énarque* (from the highly prestigious *École Nationale d'Administration*) nor an alumnus of the *grandes écoles*, but with years of experience in the special forces: Patrice Faure, who is also close to Alexandre Benalla and has worked in New Caledonia and French Guiana, is used to difficult situations. Alerts from prefects and gendarmerie services come to his desk. All heads of State have been targetet by slanderous campaigns. During the Stevan Markovic affair, an employee of Alain Delon (1935-2024) whose murder made headlines in the late 1960s, Georges Pompidou's wife, Claude Pompidou (1912-2007), was the victim of a photo montage designed to make people believe she was taking part in swinger parties. But never have a president and his wife suffered so many attacks as Emmanuel and Brigitte Macron. That is the problem with secretive beings: they give rise to all kinds of fantasies. Patrice Faure calls this "managing reputational risk". And it is against such attacks that he must build a bulwark. Since 2021, an insane hoax has been circulating in conspiracy circles and far-right circles, claiming that "Brigitte Macron is a man". There, the First Lady is renamed Jean-Michel Trogneux, after her brother, as if the two were the same person! However extravagant, the case is being closely monitored by the Presidency: Emmanuel Macron knows that his wife is suffering. He also knows that the hoax is relayed by Turkish and Russian national televisions, and even in the United States, by Candace Owens, a figure of the Trumpist and Holocaust-denying alternative right, whom Marion Maréchal and Éric Zemmour invited to a meeting in 2019. In short, once again, foreign networks are getting involved. In the presidential security jargon, this is called "projected threats". On September 12, the two women behind the hoax targeting Brigitte Macron – one a "medium", the other a "self-taught freelance journalist" – were convicted of defamation. The "Zoé Sagan" case also came up at meetings chaired by Patrice Faure, in charge of coordinating legal action. This pseudonym hides a publicist from Arles (Bouches-du-Rhône), Aurélien Poirson-Atlan, who, under the pretext of telling the comedy of power, spreads false information and scurrilous accusations against the elites. He seems obsessed with the presidential couple. On August 27, 2024, Brigitte Macron filed a complaint for cyberstalking; on December 10, four men were arrested, including "Zoé Sagan", who was held in police custody for 36 hours. At issue were "numerous malicious remarks about Brigitte Macron's gender and sexuality, as well as her age difference with her spouse, from an angle that likened her to a pedophile", as summed up the Paris public prosecutor's office. When it comes to "reputational risk", photographs are the most sensitive material".

20. See *Chapter 21*.

PART V

LOOKING FOR JEAN-MICHEL TROGNEUX

"I'm not upset that you lied to me, I'm upset that from now on I can't believe you."

Friedrich Nietzsche, *Beyond Good and Evil*, 1886.

"- They'll tell you what they want to... Lots of people lie, you know, it's human nature. -Maybe, but not everyone will lie about the same things. I'll be able to cross-check."

Pierre Schoendoerffer, *Là-haut*, Grasset, 1981.

"Fires will be kindled to testify that two and two make four. Swords will be drawn to prove that leaves are green in summer. [...] We shall be of those who have seen and yet have believed."

G.K. Chesterton, *Heretics*, 1905.

"A man's truth is first and foremost what he hides."

André Malraux.

25

THE FAMILY PHOTOGRAPH

A buzz and a lawsuit for a matter of civil status

How do you retrace Jean-Michel Trogneux's life? On the face of it, this is an ordinary man, in his seventies, who has left little or no trace on the Internet. An ordinary individual, but who had potentially become, under a different identity an important, politically exposed person. In addition to the lack of sources, a survey of Mr. Everyman involves the typical difficulties in a neighborhood survey. Writing the biography of a politically exposed person implies an abundance of sources, but may also subject you to political pressure... These are two very different exercises, each with its own difficulties. From the outset, our search combined the difficulties of both settings.

In fact, Natacha Rey, who had contacted the registry of Amiens by post to obtain a copy of Jean-Michel Trogneux's birth certificate without filiation, was twice told, in letters with letterhead of the municipality of Amiens signed by a registrar (dated April 15 and May 5, 2021), that as the birth certificate without filiation for Mr. Jean-Michel Trogneux "is not in our possession, we invite you to contact the municipality of Jean-Michel Trogneux's birthplace, which holds this record."[1]

As I had established that Jean-Michel Trogneux had indeed been born on February 11, 1945 in Amiens, Natacha Rey concluded that there had been a "falsification of civil status documents". It is essentially on this point, exposed on the YouTube channel of medium Amandine Roy, that Natacha Rey was convicted of defamation in September 2024.

In the meantime, the city of Amiens had deigned to deliver the document which would be the main piece of evidence provided by the civil party to convict Natacha Rey… Looking at the document, we notice that at the bottom, part of it seems to have been cut out, or crossed out…

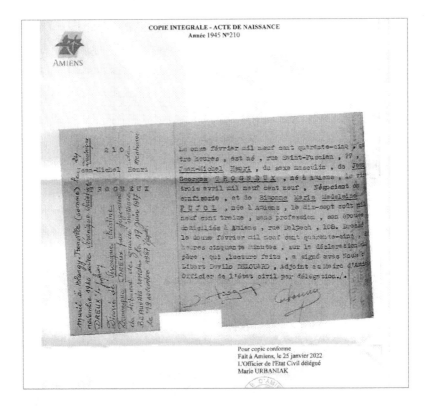

It took an international buzz and a lawsuit to obtain a copy of this birth certificate, which is legally available to anyone who requests it. Were the city of Amiens's double refusal in the spring 2021 simply a double mistake, or was it based on instruction not to issue any information about, specifically, Jean-Michel Trogneux? In any case, our investigation was going to be complicated.

We could now write the first lines of his biography. Jean-Michel, Henri Trogneux was born on February 11, 1945 at 4am at number 77 rue Saint-Fuscien in Amiens (Somme). He is the fifth child of Jean, Georges Trogneux, a confectionery merchant born on April 23, 1909 in Amiens (Somme), and his wife Simone, Marie, Madeleine Pujol, born on August 17, 1913 in Amiens (Somme), living at 108 rue Delpech in Amiens.

The mystery of the lampshade

At this stage, the only physical trace of Jean-Michel Trogneux's past we had was the Trogneux family photograph shown in Viginie Linhart's 2018 documentary. The photo was unedited. We can assume that the photo featured the parents, Jean and Simone Trogneux, in the front row, holding the latest addition, Brigitte Trogneux, on her lap. Alongside them are their other children: from left to right, Jean-Michel, Maryvonne, Jean-Claude, Anne-Marie and Monique.

But the first problem arose: when the photo was published on the Internet for inclusion in "Brigitte's" personal album, it had been amended. The edit was not in the area of the photo featuring Brigitte Trogneux, but the one where her brother Jean-Michel is standing. The large lampshade which draws the attention to the little boy's face had been removed.

Brigitte Macron intime : ses secrets les mieux gardés - Gala

This version of the photograph was featured in the documentary *Brigitte Macron l'influente*, on September 16, 2019 on *BFMTV*.

In 2022, after the first suspicions about "Brigitte's" identity, *VSD* magazine[2] republished it, but Jean-Michel Trogneux was cut out of it. The magazine also published the photograph of Brigitte Trogneux at her First Communion.

A year later, the situation has evolved. The family photo is republished in its original version (lampshade included). For the first time, this photo is captioned by Sylvie Bommel in *Paris Match*, May 25, 2023…

We also knew that Bestimage, Michèle Marchand's agency that manages the presidential couple's public image, tends to edit photographs. In this case, it was established that the family photo had been edited, precisely in the area where little Jean-Michel is standing…

Since I could not draw any conclusions from a single photograph, and an altered one at that, I had to proceed chronologically and logically. At the time, in the microcosm of the Amiens bourgeoisie, girls attended Sacré-Cœur, and boys went to La Providence, the high school where "Brigitte" would later become a teacher.

---

1. See chapter 18. Natacha Rey did not have Jean-Michel Trogneux's exact date of birth when she made her requests, but usually the registrar either replies that he "cannot satisfy the request without the exact date of birth", or, if diligent, carries out the search himself and provides the document. In any case, her good faith could have been upheld at her trial, since she had two official documents on Amiens letterhead stating that the document "is not in our possession". What's more, such a document "without filiation" can be freely communicated to a third party without any limitation period. Unlike the birth certificate "with filiation" (full copy, reproduced above), which can only be disclosed to a third party 75 year after the entry in the register. If the person concerned is deceased, this period is reduced to 25 years from the date of death. In the case of Jean-Michel Trogneux, born in 1945, the 75-year delay was completed in 2020: Natacha Rey was therefore entitled to a copy of the birth certificate, even with filiation, from the city of Amiens.

2. *VSD* n°2173, April 2022.

26

LA PROVIDENCE (PREQUEL)

To check whether Jean-Michel Trogneux had actually attended La Providence, I contacted the *Archives jésuites de France*, based in Vanves, south of Paris. Their highly efficient documentation service provided me with La Providence's student register, with the precise names of those enrolled, year by year.

Here we see Jean-Michel Trogneux, who attended La Providence between 1950 and 1957. He seems to have left the school during his 5ᵉ (*cinquième*) year. My first request for information to the school received no response, so I set out to find the lists of Jean-Michel Trogneux's classmates and contact them one by one, hoping to find out where Jean-Michel Trogneux went after the 5ᵉ. Maybe I could also recover class photos, or at least testimonials – in short, get background information. But no one knows where Jean-Michel Trogneux went after La Providence. In addition to the omerta situation as already with Brigitte Trogneux, I quickly understand that it is pointless to ask aging non-technical people to find, scan and mail class photos to a stranger who called them up.

PROFESSION	ADRESSE	R	1941 1912 1913 1914 1915	1916 1917 1918 1919 1920	1921 1922 1923 1924 1925	1926 1927 1928 1929 1930	OBSERVATIONS
7¹	Condellier Jacques	7¹ CPC					
	Daniel	8¹ 7¹ 6¹¹¹				
	Maurice		8¹ 7¹¹			
	Croullé J.-Claude		6¹ 5¹			
	Michel		8¹ 7¹ 6¹			
	Crancart Gonzague					10ᵉ 10ᵉ 9ᵉ 8¹
	Crentesaux Xavier 2ᴵᴵᴬ					
	Crentesaux Ignace (à Maurecourt) 7ᴵᴵ					5¹ 4¹ᵃ
	Cricot Jacques					
	Criquet Michel 1ᴵᶜ ME					St Martin a peu... off. marine Aurait perdu la foi
	Crouvé, Jean-Luc						11
	Crouvé Claude					11ᶜ 10ᵉ 9ᵉ 8¹¹ 7¹
	Crentesaux Henri			2¹¹ 1ᴵᶜ ME		
	Philippe			2¹ᴮ 1¹ᴮ		Ph
	Crouvain Julie			8ˣ		7¹¹ 6¹ 6¹¹
9¹ 8¹	Crogneux J.-Claude 7ᴵ 6ᴵᴵᴵ	4¹ᴬ 3¹ᴬ 2¹ᴬ 1¹ᴬ 1¹ᴬ		CP ICAM		
	J.-Michel				1¹ᶜ 1¹¹ 10¹ 9¹ 8¹ 7¹¹ 6¹¹¹ 5¹¹
	Tueux Jacques			9¹	9¹ 8¹¹ 7¹
	Curpin Frédéric			9ᶜ 9¹	8¹¹¹ 7¹ 7¹¹ 6¹¹¹ 5¹¹¹ 4¹ᴬ 4¹¹¹
	Tueux Jean Pierre				10¹ 9ᶜ 8¹ 8¹¹
	Crancart Jean Michel (de Lucheux)					6¹

Still, I managed to compile a list of persons who once shared school benches with Jean-Michel Trogneux and seem to have remained close to him. This list, which I submitted to journalist Emmanuelle Anizon on June 14, 2023[1], includes two names that were on the class lists and in Jean-Michel Trogneux's social networking contacts, before they were deleted (Christian Tant and Jean Lemaître). Two others are related to Véronique Dreux (Emmanuel Bougon and Gilles de la Simone), whom, I discover, are the mother of Jean-Michel Trogneux's children[2] and, at the top of the list, Alexis Brunet. As well as having attended classes with him in 9ᵉ and 7ᵉ, and sitting on the board of *Amitiés culturelles picardes* with other Trogneux relatives, he has a sister-in-law who attended school with Brigitte Trogneux. An opportunity for a double hit?

256

Alexis Brunet[3] will present Emmanuelle Anizon with two class photos featuring him and Jean-Michel Trogneux, the 9ᵉ and 7ᵗʰ grades. The question here is whether Jean-Michel Trogneux has become a "chubby guy", as the Elysée suggests, or "Brigitte", as a growing number of French people think. When the first photos are released, the result is visually stunning. "Brigitte" is immediately recognizable, even if the little boy is slightly different from the one in the family photograph. When I share these photos with relatives more or less in the know, simply asking them if they recognize anyone, they all point (with a mixture of confidence and disbelief) to the same little boy, i.e. Jean-Michel Trogneux. The probability of recognizing someone you have never seen before in a group photo from the 1950s is null... unless you have remained acquainted with that face and that body.

I requested facial recognition on the three photos I now had : family, *neuvième* and *septième*. The family photo was unproductive (we will see why later)[4], and the two school photographs gave respectively a small, and a very clear advantage to "Brigitte" over the "chubby guy"[5]. Both visually and in terms of facial recognition comparison score, the result was so clear that I wondered : What if Emmanuelle Anizon had been manipulated by her source ?

We still had to cross-check, find other versions of these photos (the copies supplied to Emmanuel Anizon had been digitized in poor quality) and, why not, the other photos of Jean-Michel Trogneux's schooling. I contacted La Providence again, with more insistence, reached the archivist, and after some negotiation[6], succeeded in visually reconstructing Jean-Michel Trogneux's schooling, this time with good quality scans. Here are class photos from *neuvième* (1952-1953, age 7), *huitième* (1953-1954, age 8), *septième* (1954-1955, age 9) and *sixième* (1955-56, age 10).

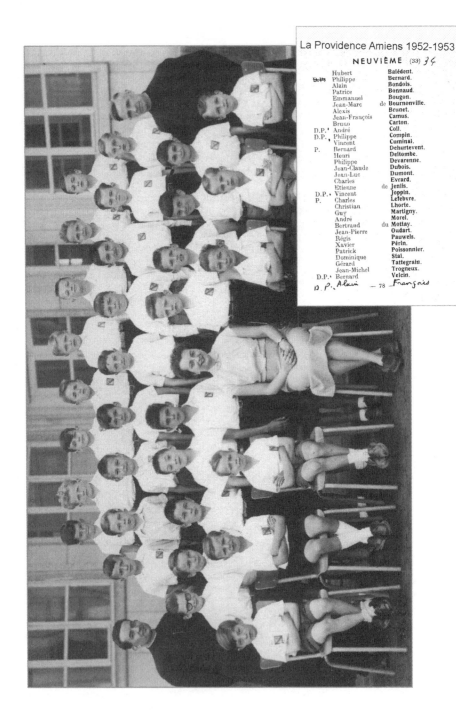

La Providence Amiens 1952-1953

NEUVIÈME (33) 34

Hubert	Baléedent.	
Philippe	Bernard.	
Alain	Bondois.	
Patrice	Bonnaud.	
Emmanuel	Bougon.	
Jean-Marc	de Bournonville.	
Alexis	Brunet.	
Jean-François	Camus.	
Bruno	Carton.	
D.P. André	Coll.	
D.P. Philippe	Compin.	
Vincent	Cuminal.	
P. Bernard	Dehurtevent.	
Henri	Deltombe.	
Philippe	Devarenne.	
Jean-Claude	Dubois.	
Jean-Luc	Dumont.	
Charles	Evrard.	
Etienne	de Jenlis.	
D.P. Vincent	Joppin.	
P. Charles	Lefebvre.	
Christian	Lhorte.	
Guy	Martigny.	
André	Morel.	
Bertrand	du Mottay.	
Jean-Pierre	Oudart.	
Régis	Pauwels.	
Xavier	Périn.	
Patrick	Poissonnier.	
Dominique	Stal.	
Gérard	Tattegrain.	
Jean-Michel	Trogneux.	
D.P. Bernard	Velcin.	

D. P. Alain — 78 Français

258

1953 1954
HUITIEME (1° Section) (29)

	Hubert	(Balédent.) —
D.P.	Patrick	Benoît.
	Philippe	(Bernard.) +
	Alain	Bondois.
	Emmanuel	Bougon.
	Jean-Marc	de Bournonville.
	Alexis	Brunet.
D.P.	Philippe	Compin. —
	Vincent	Cuminal. —
D.P.	Dominique	Defrance. +
	Guy	(Delahoche)
	Henri	Delfombe.
	Philippe	Devarenne.
	Jean-Claude	Dubois.
	Jean-Luc	Dumont.
	Charles	Evrard. —
P.	Marc	Lanthiez.
P.	Jean-Claude	Lefèvre. +
	Yves-Marie	(Lucas.) +
	Guy	Martigny.
	Jean-Pierre	Oudart.
	Régis	Pauwels.
	Xavier	Perdu. +
	Patrick	(Poissonnier.)
P.	Claude	Roux.
	Dominique	Sial. ? ?
	Gérard	Taffegrain.
	Jean-Michel	Trogneux. +
P.	Guy	Véret.

Noël   Vandevot

259

1954 1955
SEPTIÈME (2ᵉ Section)   (32)

	Philippe	Bernard.
	Jean-Charles	Bloc.
	Jean-François	Bloc.
	Alain	Bondois. — R o
	Patrice	Bonnaud.
	Alexis	Brunet. — R '
P.	Christian	Canaple.
	Bruno	Carton. — François Charvet
D.P.	André	Coll. —
	Jean-Marie	Colloche. ?
	Régis	Delaroière. ? R
	Jean-Luc	Dumont.
P.	Xavier	Duquesne. ?
	Charles	Évrard.
P.	Bernard	Gleed.
P.	Patrick	Houdant.
P.	Nicolas	Laroche. — R '
	Gilles	du La Simone.
P.	Christian	Lcont.
P.	Dominique	Louat.
	Yves-Marie	Lucas.
P.	Jean-Guy	Mallet.
	Xavier	Perdue
	Patrick	Poissonnier.
	Alain	Roger. quitte
P.	François	Roose.
P.	Philippe	de Rosny.
P.	Patrick	Sauvage.
	Christian	Tant.
	Jean-Michel	Trogneux.
P.	Guy	Véret.
P.	Alain	Voisin.

Bernard CAZIN. 25-2-89

5 R 5 Ex.

260

1955-1956
SIXIÈME (3ᵉ Section) (35)

	Hubert	Balédent.
P.	Philippe	Bonne
D.P.	Emmanuel	Bougon.
D.P.	Bernard	Cazin.
P.V.	Dominique	Defrance.
P.	Jean	Delahaye.
	Guy	Delahoche.
	Philippe	Devarenne.
	Jean-Luc	Dumont.
P.	Xavier	Duquesne.
P.	Alain	Gheerbrant.
P.	Thomas-Régis	Gronier.
D.P.	Roger	Grossin.
P.	Patrick	Houdant.
	Etienne	de Jenlis.
D.P.	Vincent	Jeplin.
	Gilles	de La Simone.
P.	Christian	Lecat.
P.	Alain	Leclercq.
D.P.	Jean	Lemaître.
P.	Pierre	Massiani.
P.	Roger	Masurel.
P.	Daniel	Miette.
	André	Morel.
P.V.	Pierre	Mulle.
P.	Philippe	Normand.
	Jean-Pierre	Oudart.
	Régis	Pauwels.
	Patrick	Poissonnier.
	Christian	Poulain.
P.	Jean-Louis	Rebour.
P.	Philippe	de Rosny.
P.V.	Christian	de Torcy.
	Jean-Michel	Trogneux.
P.	Guy	Véret.

dence - Amiens

J. RATIVET
3, RUE DE LARMORIQUE
PARIS-XVᵉ

261

The archivist did not have the photo of *onzième* (1950-51). Jean-Michel Trogneux was absent on the day the photos of 10ᵉ and 5ᵉ were taken, so we are not publishing them here. The photo of *huitième* (reproduced here) does not meet the conditions for reliable facial recognition, because the head is too tilted downwards. We prefer photographs that are as close as possible to those required for identity documents[7]. As for Jean-Michel Trogneux's school file, which would have shed light on the boy's personality, the archivist explains that the document disappeared when the school was cleaned of asbestos…

The key finding is: the *neuvième* and *septième* class photos sent to Emmanuel Anizon were authentic. The copies sent by the archivist of La Providence were identical to them, with much better digitization. To these two documents, fully exploitable by facial recognition, I added the *sixième* class photo. As part of this identity control approach, I would ask the *Face++* visual artificial intelligence software: Has Jean-Michel Trogneux become a "chubby guy" or has he become "Brigitte"?

Analysis of the photo of neuvième (1952-1953)

The reference values used to read the assessments here are the results obtained on other schoolmates for whom some adult photos are available on the Internet. By setting reference values, we can see that even though the use of childhood photo lowers the results for boys more than for girls, facial recognition still enables us to identify students on the basis of their current physical appearance, without making any mistakes.

Low - 60,025 %

Low - 56,681 %

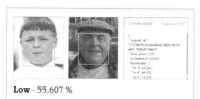

Low - 55,607 %

Normal - 64,037 %

With a result averaging 56.607 % (low) on a panel of 15 photos, facial recognition assesses that it is not unlikely that Jean-Michel Trogneux has become the "chubby guy"; his result are only slightly below the average on the students in this class.

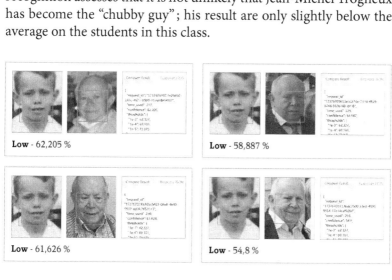

Low - 62,205 %

Low - 58,887 %

Low - 61,626 %

Low - 54,8 %

On the other hand, the evaluation of the probability that Jean-Michel Trogneux has become "Brigitte" (panel of 60 photos) is extremely high, with a result of 67.133 % (normal), i.e. more than 10.526 points higher than the "chubby guy".

High - 70,497 %

Very hight - 75,611 %

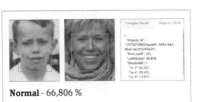

Normal - 66,806 %

High - 70,927 %

High - 72,305 %

High - 69,965 %

Normal - 67,91 %

Normal - 64,643 %

Analysis of the photo of septième (1954-1955)

Here the pupils are two years older. As with the previous photograph, we identified many of the students using facial recognition. Here are a few examples of evaluations obtained on those who were in *septième* with Jean-Michel Trogneux.

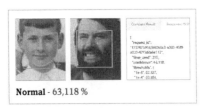

Normal - 63,118 %

Normal - 67,558 %

Low - 60,638 %

Low - 60,454 %

On a panel of 15 photos, facial recognition evaluated the match between the student Jean-Michel Trogneux and the "chubby guy" at 57.739 % (low), a score at the low end of what we observe for students in this class. Here are the highest scores obtained in the tests.

Normal - 63,586 %

Low - 61,401 %

Normal - 66,976 %

Normal - 63,094 %

On a panel of 60 photos, facial recognition gave a 62.2 % (low) match between the student Jean-Michel Trogneux and "Brigitte", 4.461 points higher than for the "chubby guy", and placed "Brigitte" in the middle of the results for the other classmates identified.

Normal - 66,308 %

Normal - 66,375 %

Low - 57,581 %

Normal - 68,29 %

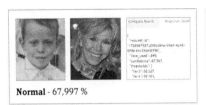

Normal - 67,997 %

Normal - 66,26 %

Normal - 67,473 %

Normal - 63,322 %

Analysis of the photo of sixième (1955-1956)

As with the previous photographs, we identified many of the students using facial recognition. Here are a few examples of evaluations obtained on Jean-Michel Trogneux's former *sixième* classmates.

Normal - 64,434 %

Normal - 62,759 %

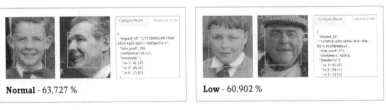

Normal - 63,727 %

Low - 60,902 %

On a panel of 15 photos, facial recognition evaluated the match between the student Jean-Michel Trogneux and the "chubby guy" at 56.626 % (low), below the average for other students.

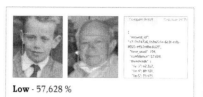

Low - 57,628 %

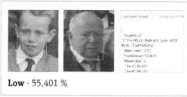

Low - 55,401 %

Normal - 63,67 %

Low - 56,607 %

On a panel of 60 photos, facial recognition evaluated the match between the pupil Jean-Michel Trogneux and "Brigitte" at 62.86 % (normal), 6.234 points higher than for the "chubby guy", and put "Brigitte" at the high end of the results obtained for the other classmates I had identified.

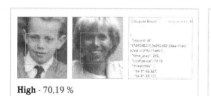

High - 70,19 %

High - 71,894 %

Low - 62,003 %

Normal - 68,498 %

Normal - 66,43 %

Normal - 67,628 %

{
"request_id":
"1736668440.ee6e5e8a-5c50-46cc-
95d1-2b76e049b632",
"time_used": 240,
"confidence": 69.803,
"thresholds": {
"1e-3": 62.327,
"1e-4": 69.101,
}
}

High - 69,803 %

{
"request_id":
"1726069517.f7feb742-1e54-44d3-
8b28-457d7e22850f",
"time_used": 271,
"confidence": 64.798,
"thresholds": {
"1e-3": 62.327,
"1e-4": 69.101,
"1e-5": 75.975,
}
}

Normal - 64,798 %

---

1. Reproduced in *Chapter 23*.

2. See *Chapter 18*.

3. Contacted by the author on January 17, 2024, Alexis Brunet confided that he had given his photos to Emmanuelle Anizon. He died a few days after my call, on January 29, 2024.

4. On the family photo, facial recognition gives a fairly low score of just under 55% (low) on both "Brigitte" and the "chubby guy".

5. On the version of the 9e photo digitized by Emmanuelle Anizon, we obtain 62.853% (normal) for the "chubby guy" (average of a panel of 15 photos) vs 65.657% (normal) for "Brigitte" (average over a panel of 60 photos) (i.e. 2.804% more for Brigitte). With the same panels, on the photo of *septième* (taken two years later), the gap widens to 54.185% for the "chubby guy" against 67.799% (normal) for "Brigitte" (i.e. +13.614% for "Brigitte").

6. La Providence complied with the opinion issued in the author's favor by the *Commission d'accès aux documents administratifs* (Opinion n° 20243646 of July 18, 2024) and, provided the requested photographs.

7. Although neither "Brigitte" (panel of 60 photos) nor the "chubby guy" (panel of 15 photos) exceeded 55% (low) for Jean-Michel Trogneux in the *huitième* photo, the result was still 6.2 points higher for "Brigitte".

27

A MATTER OF TEETH

Above all, consulting photos of Jean-Michel Trogneux's schooling provided a crucial clue – some would say a "proof". In 2018, echoing Virginie Linhart's documentary which visually reconstructed "Brigitte's" teaching career, Closer[1] noted that "Brigitte used the services of an orthodontist to rectify the alignment of her teeth and make it just perfect." However, upon close inspection of the family photo, Jean-Michel Trogneux's teeth are well aligned, whereas on the class photos, dated from the same period, the dental alignment corresponds to that of young "Brigitte".

The family photo had been edited to match Jean-Michel Trogneux's teeth to "Brigitte's" current teeth. A trait of coquettishness that, years later, would betray the secret...

---

1. Closer n° 677.

28

ERASED FROM MEMORY

How do you trace Jean-Michel Trogneux after he left La Providence in his *cinquième* year? One of his former classmates told me that his family had withdrawn him from the school as a disruptive pupil, and that perhaps (as was customary at the time) he had been registered at Institution Saint Jean in Douai (Nord). But upon checking in this school's registers, I found no trace of Jean-Michel Trogneux. Strangely, his name seems to have been erased from collective and even family memory, as suggested by the fact that he was no longer mentioned in the family notebook of the *Bulletin des Anciens de La Providence* in the 1960s and 1970s. This is the case here, in 1963, when the marriage of Jean-Claude Gueudet and Monique Trogneux, shown here as Jean-Claude Trogneux's sister, was announced. The absence of Jean-Michel Trogneux is surprising, especially considering that all relatives with La Providence are mentioned, even when quite distant, for exemple François Bonnemaison, brother of the canon (*chanoine*) Bonnemaison who gave the nuptial blessing at Monique Trogneux's wedding...

Or here, in June 1973, when the *Bulletin des Anciens de La Providence* mentions the death of Marguerite Charlier ("Mme Jean Trogneux, Jean-Claude's grandmother"). And yet, like his brother Jean-Claude, Jean-Michel is an "alumnus of La Providence". But Jean-Michel Trogneux has disappeared from the register, which systematically lists all the siblings of former students. As if he had been erased.

DECES

1. Anciens Elèves :

98- Maurice BLOTIERE, père de Bernard(26) et d'Yves (28)
08- Philippe CARON, beau-père d'Emmanuel LINE (40)
12- Louis CREDOZ, père de Jean-Paul (54) et de Philippe (56)
32- André CHARVET, frère des Pères Pierre et Paul (27) et d'Etienne (36)
      beau-frère de Joseph LEQUAI (28)
34- Pierre POULAIN, frère de Jacques (33)
52- R.P. François-Marie LEFEBVRE

2. Parents d'Anciens Elèves :

20- Mme Henri DEQUEN, mère de Pierre e grand-mère de Dominique DEQUEN (
      et de François (43) et Bernard VASSELLE (44)
27- Mme Henri GAILLARD, mère de Dom Jean GAILLARD et de Joseph GAILLARD
30- Mme Ferdinand DUDAY, mère de Maurice, grand-mère de Paul-Marie (61)
      et de François-Marie (62)
33- Mme Charles LAMBRY, mère de Guy, grand-mère de Paul(69) et Jean (70)
34- M.Patrice VEZIER, père de Louis et de Joseph (36)
39- Mme du MESNIL GAILLARD, mère de Tanguy et d'André (41)
39- M.Paul VASSEL, père d'André et de Pierre (40)
39- Mme Maurice LE GENTIL, belle-mère de René LE NOIR de BECQUINCOURT
      et grand-mère de Xavier LEFRANT
44- M.Pierre VITOUX, père de Jacques, Jean-Pierre (48) et Alain (51)
46- Colonel Marcel OLLAGNIER, père de Bernard
     et Alain CHAVENON (65), soeur(?) à Amjahid (54), Ghis
50- Mme Jean TROGNEUX, grand-mère de Jean-Claude
59- Mme Adrien DESCHRYVER, mère de Gérard
61- Mme Charles ROUSSEAU, mère de François
66- Mme Camille NOTTELET, grand-mère de Patrick
66- Mme Pierre DUGAS, mère de Bernard
71- Mme d'AVOUT, grand-mère de Jacques d'AVOUT.

273

29

ALGIERS

He had just turned 18

Military service was a good way of tracing Jean-Michel Trogneux. At the time, in every canton, all men aged 18 were required to report to a *conseil de révision* (draft review board) for military service. On February 12, 1963, the day after Jean-Michel Trogneux's 18th birthday, his father Jean Trogneux performed the military registration of his son (class of 1965) for the Canton Sud-Ouest d'Amiens, in order to draw up his individual identification form (218 S.O.).

The census file contains three types of information. The first two are trivial: Jean-Michel Trogneux is presented as a "confectioner" (the family business) and invokes Article 23 of the Military Code to obtain a deferment of drafting renewable tacitly up to the age of

25 for professional reasons or to pursue studies. The third piece of information is far more surprising. Jean-Michel Trogneux was residing in… Algiers. Seven months after independence, at a time when the *Pieds-noirs* had given way to the *Pieds-rouges* [the communists who had come to help build the new Algeria], the presence of an 18-year-old son of the Amiens bourgeoisie at 87 boulevard Saint-Saëns (today's boulevard Mohamed V, leads to Algiers' *Faculté centrale*) was surprising…

Brigitte's Algerian past

At first glance, Algiers never appears in the biographies of "Brigitte". But if we scratch around, we discover that she resided in this city, as mentioned by the Algerian press in December 2017. At the time, Emmanuel Macron was preparing an official visit to Algeria. Besides the official components, a visit was scheduled (reported in the Algerian daily *L'Expression*[1]) to the *Faculté centrale d'Alger*, where "Brigitte Macron is said to have memories. [...] This information, which has been circulating for several a few days now, has been 'given credibility' by the university's enhancement work".

Two days later, in France this time, the "Africa" section of *Le Point*'s website[2] echoed "the Algerian rumour [claiming] that the First Lady,

Brigitte Macron, will be visiting this illustrious university, which she is said to have attended in the past". In its Arabic edition, the Saudi women's weekly *Sayidaty*[3] states that "the French First Lady does not belong to the *pieds noirs* category [...] but her father was posted to teach in Algeria, ten years after the country's independence, where she grew up and studied contemporary literature at the Arts Institute of the Central Faculty of Algiers. During this period, Brigitte Macron's family lived on rue Larbi Ben M'hidi [Author's note: formerly rue d'Isly] near the university, a pedestrians-only street since the mid-80s." Where does this narrative come from? Either the author of the article has let his imagination run wild, or he has reported what officials had told during the preparations for this visit or during Emmanuel Macron's previous trip to Algiers, when the French President said French Algeria was guilty of a "crime against humanity"[4]. Two days before the visit to Algiers, *Algérie Patriotique*[5] (close to Algerian intelligence circles) details the program: "Mr. Macron's plane will land in Algiers on December 6 at around 10 a.m. During his visit, the French head of State will hold talks with President Abdelaziz Bouteflika and several Algerian officials, including Prime Minister Ahmed Outyahia. As part of his visit, Emmanuel Macron, accompanied by his wife Brigitte, will take a walk down rue Larbi Ben M'hidi. After the stroll, the presidential couple will visit the *Faculté Centrale d'Alger*, where Mrs. Macron has fond memories".

In fact, on December 6, 2017 Emmanuel Macron traveled alone for a visit reduced to a few hours. *Jeune Afrique*[6] reports: "His Algerian tour was cut short by one stage. The French head of State was due to visit the Central Faculty of Algiers (Université Benyoucef-Benkhedda) before moving on to the large Place de l'Emir Abdelkader. This visit was cancelled for security reasons. Possibly a risk of attack?

The French and Algerians are reluctant to discuss the reasons for the cancellation. Yet the programming was appreciated among teachers and students. To celebrate the occasion, Algiers town hall had embellished and refurbished the sidewalks, staircases and walls of the buildings…".

"Under the sway of his 'wife' Jean-Michel Trogneux"

Two years after this visit, the story of "Brigitte", a student at the *Faculté centrale d'Alger*, will be rewritten in Naoufel Brahimi El Mili's book, *France-Algérie, 50 ans d'histoires secrètes -Tome 2 (1992-2017)*[7]. It reads: "On this December 5, 2017, the event went unnoticed by the French media. Yet Emmanuel Macron was expected there as a friend, after he described colonization as a crime against humanity. Now President of the Republic, he believes he no longer wishes to revisit this shameful past. This was followed by declarations, a meeting between presidents and, above all, to the delight of Algerian students, the official delivery of the work in the central faculty, entirely repainted white. Brigitte Macron, who was to accompany her husband to Algiers, had expressed the wish to visit the capital's university, where one of her great-aunts[*grande tante*[8]] had studied. "While we were unable to identify any of "Brigitte's" "great aunts" in Algiers, Jean-Michel Trogneux's presence there was confirmed.

From repeated declarations of love on the French side (with Algerian immigration to France facilitated), to humiliations of Paris by Algiers, this very special relationship between Emmanuel Macron and Algeria has raised questions among all those familiar with the case[9], and commentators[10]. Translating what many had sensed, journalist Marc Endeweld wondered whether Emmanuel Macron was being blackmailed by Algiers[11], without finding out the subject of this blackmail... In any case, this Algerian tropism had finally irritated neighboring Morocco. So, in a vitriolic article entitled "Part man, part woman, he assumes nothing: who is Emmanuel Macron really?", *Maroc 360*, a medium considered to be a conveyor belt for the Palace, had mentioned "Brigitte Macron, 24 years older than him and who, on the way, did not escape doubts about her sexual identity"[12].

When Emmanuel Macron moved closer to Morocco, it is *La Nouvelle République*, the mouthpiece of the Algerian army and security services, which described him as "a cocaine-addicted, psychopathic president, under the sway of his 'wife' Jean-Michel Trogneux, who runs France without having been elected"[13]...

1. *La fac centrale se prépare à recevoir une visite de marque, L'Expression*, 3 décembre 2017.

2. *Algérie : quand les jeunes scrutent Macron, lepoint.fr*, 5 décembre 2017.

3. *Sayidaty*, 6 décembre 2017.

4. *Echorouk News*, 14 février 2017.

5. *Ce que l'Algérie attend de la prochaine visite du président français*, Algérie patrio-tique, 4 décembre 2017.

6. *En Algérie, Emmanuel Macron a fait l'impasse sur la fac, Jeune Afrique*, 6 décembre 2017.

7. *France-Algérie, 50 ans d'histoires secrètes -Tome 2 (1992-2017)*, Naoufel Brahimi El Mili, Fayard, 2019.

8. "Brigitte" is making a provocative pun: "tante", in a colloquial sens, means a male homosexual - a "fag".

9. See, for example, *L'Enigme algérienne*, by Xavier Driencourt, a former French ambassador to Algiers, published by Éditions de l'Observatoire in 2022.

10. *Off Investigation, Macron l'Algérien*, 15 mars 2022.

11. *Le Grand Manipulateur*, Marc Endeweld, Stock, 2019.

12. *"Un peu homme, un peu femme", mais il n'assume rien: qui est vraiment Emmanuel Macron ?, Maroc 360*, 21 septembre 2023.

13. *Le Makhzen marocain recrute Jacques Sapir dans sa croisade contre l'Algérie, La Nouvelle République*, 30 mars 2024.

30

PARIS

Jean-Michel Trogneux's documentation for military service states that he was granted a delay on November 30, 1963, nine months after the first census and that his place of residence was in Algiers: a boarding house called *Pension Mon Foyer*.

But when we consult the document associated with the registration number (231), we discover that the individual was no longer in Algiers when the delay was granted. He had returned to mainland France to study in the preparatory course for the *"École TP"* in Paris Vᵉ.

281

His return seems to have occurred at the end of the 1962-63 school year, as Jean-Michel Trogneux was located on September 20, 1963 in Amiens (Somme) by the draft review board handling the military class of 1965.

Conseil de Révision — Classe 1965
Convocations
Canton Sud Ouest

NOM et PRÉNOM		ADRESSE	ACCUSÉ RECEPTION
ALEXANDRE	Jacques	rue Lescouvé, 114	C 12/9/63
ANDRÉ	Jean-Louis	rue Albéric de Calonne, 52	C 12/9/63
ANDRIEUX	Gilbert	rue Béranger 100	C 14/9/63
TROGNEUX	Francis	bd Faidherbe, 8t B appt 14 cité relais	c 17/9/63
TROGNEUX	Jean-Michel	rue Delambre, 1	C 20/9/63
TROUCHE	François	cité Jean Petit, 2H	c 14/9/63
VAQUETTE	Francis	rue Dargent, 119, Apou u tin Beau Te/Ega	a 19/5/63 Nord
VARLET	René	rue d'Elbeuf, 9 Bt 1	C 13/9/63
VASSEUR	Jean-Marie	rue Larivière, 12	C 19/9/63

This "*École TP*" was interesting. A school curriculum evokes academic records, student photo tables (*trombinoscopes*), former classmates etc. – a nest of information potentially easier to use than the Algiers trail, since the Algerian authorities had, anyway, already publicly exposed "Brigitte" by describing Jean-Michel Trogneux as Emmanuel Macron's "wife".

We need to establish what this "École TP" is. Does TP stand for *Travaux Publics*, i.e. public works? Cachan, south of Paris, is home to the *École spéciale des travaux publics* (ESTP). On the phone, on April 18, 2023, the reception agent confirmed that there was indeed a file for Jean-Michel Trogneux in the school archives. "But to consult the document,

I need the approval of the executive assistant"... who denies it, arguing that the school is private and that only family members can consult the documents, invoking "privacy". Yet this track deserves to be pursued – especially as the law, in this case the *Code du Patrimoine* (Heritage Code) is on my side. First, the 50-year legal deadline for disclosure has been exceeded. Second, even though the school is private, it is still subject to the law because it provides a public service. Once again, I brought the matter before the *Commission d'accès aux documents administratifs* (CADA), the authority responsible for ruling on disputes between the French and their administrations.

In its opinion n° 20240874 issued on March 7, 2024, CADA wrote: "Mr. Xavier POUSSARD contacted CADA following the refusal of the director of the *École spéciale des travaux publics, du bâtiment et de l'industrie* to disclose the following documents in digitized regarding the preparation of a press portrait: 1) the academic record of Mr. Jean-Michel, Henri, TROGNEUX, born February 11, 1945 in Amiens, enrolled in the integrated preparatory program during the 1963-1964 year; 2) his class photograph.[...] In the light of these elements, the Commission considers that the École spéciale des travaux publics, du bâtiment et de l'industrie, in view of the general interest of its activity, the conditions of its organization and operation, the obligations imposed on it and the measures taken to verify that the objectives assigned to it are achieved, must be regarded as a private-law entity entrusted with a public-service mission. The documents relating to the school's students are thus part of the public service provided by this establishment, and are therefore public archives as per Article L211-4 of the French Heritage Code. [...] In the present case, the commission notes that, although the school records requested and the photo album for the year 1963-1964 necessarily contain information covered by the secrecy of the private lives of the students concerned, the afore-mentioned fifty-year period has expired. The documents requested, if they exist, are now freely available to anyone who requests them. [...] Consequently, the commission issues a favorable opinion on the request for disclosure of the solicited documents, using the means chosen by the applicant".

But the ESTP's director refused to comply with CADA's decision on political grounds, arguing that the author was from the "extreme right" and that the documentation requested would "damage the honor of the presidency"[1]. So I decided to activate my contacts in the mainstream (i.e. largely. "left-wing") press to retrieve these documents which, after all, would have been a good way to debunk the affair. None agreed. One of them confided to me that he was "afraid of reprisals". While the proceedings against the ESTP were following their course, I wondered what Jean-Michel Trogneux had been doing, on his return from Algeria, in a preparatory class for a public works school. The only link between this engineering school and the Amiens confectioner's family was Jean-Claude Trogneux's father-in-law, Henri Courbot, who graduated from ESTP before becoming a leading figure in the building and civil engineering sector, notably as president of the *Syndicat Professionnel des Entrepreneurs de Travaux publics de France et d'Outre-Mer*, but also as president of the *Société des Ingénieurs diplômés ETP*. This hypothetical explanation did not help us in our search for the documents, so we headed for the ESTP Alumni association: Jean-Michel Trogneux is not listed among the school's graduates, explains the manager, who points out that "a large part of [their] archives burned down in 1989 in our former house on rue Thénard"…

If the trail seems sterile, I remember that at the beginning, the reception agent assured me that a "Jean-Michel Trogneux" file was indeed present in the school archives. My lawyer Fabrice Delinde, took the case to the Administrative Court. After a first formal notice (*mise en demeure*), the ESTP management eventually explained to me that they no longer had the requested photo table in a letter dated June 24, 2024, yet attaching Jean-Michel Trogneux's school record. Problem: the space dedicated to the portrait is… empty!

The twenty-page document shows that Jean-Michel Trogneux, then aged 18 (the age at which, typically, the *baccalauréat* is awarded in France), had not attended school for the previous three years, and had no diploma, not even the BEPC normally awarded at the end of the class of *troisième*. Jean-Michel Trogneux was enrolled in this

N° d'inscription :

284 034

NOM : *Trogneux*

PRENOMS : Jean-Michel

NÉ LE : 11 Février 1945

À Amiens DÉP. Somme

NATIONALITÉ : Française

ÉTUDES FAITES AU COURS DES DEUX ANNÉES SCOLAIRES AVANT L'ENTRÉE A L'ECOLE

19

19 Brevet de trois années

DIPLOMES OBTENUS (Titre du Diplôme et année de l'obtention)

NOM ET ADRESSE DES PARENTS
M. Trogneux Jean
1 rue Delambre Amiens (Somme)

	Entré au cours le	ANNÉE SCOLAIRE
	26 septembre 1963	19 63 — 19 64
	Passé en .... le :	**T.S.** 1/2
	Radié le :	
	Entré au cours le 28 septembre 1964	ANNÉE SCOLAIRE 19 64 — 19 65
	Passé en .... le :	**T.S.** 2/1
	Radié le :	
	Entré au cours le :	ANNÉE SCOLAIRE 19 — 19
	Passé en .... le :	
	Radié le :	
	Entré au cours le :	ANNÉE SCOLAIRE 19 — 19
	Passé en .... le :	
	Radié le :	
	Entré au cours le :	ANNÉE SCOLAIRE 19 — 19
	Passé en .... le :	
	Radié le :	

program for two years, but his file describes a mediocre student with "insufficient results", but "admitted out kindness to the next class". During his second year, "passable" results became "quite insufficient" and his count of unmotivated absence grew sharply each term : 4, then 41, then 139…

Perhaps the precise references of the classes to which he belonged would help us in our search for the photo table(s). On this point, the ESTP director was not necessarily lying. After all, the reception agent had simply mentioned a "file"… Since the address of the preparatory class for the *École TP* in the military documentation was "Paris V^e", we tried our luck at the *Archives de Paris*, but no documentation relating to the ESTP is kept there. So we tried the *Archives départementales du Val-de-Marne*, the department of Cachan, the town where the ESTP is located. There, we looked up an "ESTP photo library 1877-1970" containing "photographs of groups of students with lists of names", arranged by school year. But when we got to the archive center, the

ANNÉE SCOLAIRE 1963-1964

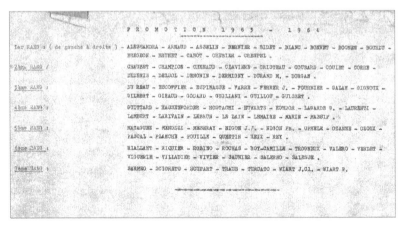

librarian told us that "these archives are private, and can only be consulted with the ESTP's authorization"... When we mentioned CADA's opinion, the librarian complied and handed us an envelope containing a photo table and its corresponding list of names.

While the wide-rimmed, thick eyeglasses make the photograph largely unusable for AI facial recognition, we note at least two distinctive features that further confirm that the individual born Jean-Michel Trogneux is not today a "chubby guy" but has indeed become "Brigitte": the snub nose and the overall shape of the mouth, especially the lower lip border (muco-cutaneous line).

---

1. Letter sent by ESTP Director Joël Cuny to CADA on March 4, 2024.

31

SPEYER

A first conclusion

Before moving on to Jean-Michel Trogneux's biography, we can already draw a first conclusion. We examined four clear photos from Brigitte Trogneux's past: the communion photo, the wedding photo and their respective cross-checks by journalist Emmanuelle Anizon. All four show that "Brigitte" was not born Brigitte Trogneux on April 13, 1953 in Amiens, and that she did not marry André Auzière on June 22, 1974 in Le Touquet. This is why "Brigitte", who had promised to certify that it was really her on Brigitte Trogneux's wedding photo, did not do so during the Auzière trial: this would have constituted perjury.

The eight photos from Jean-Michel Trogneux's past confirm that "Brigitte" is indeed this individual, born on February 11, 1945 in Amiens: the family photo as edited (lampshade, teeth), which can only be explained if Jean-Michel Trogneux became "Brigitte"; the six class photos (cross-checked with two copies held by Emmanuelle Anizon) and their concordant facial recognition analyses; the photo of Jean-Michel Trogneux at age 18 at the ESTP, which features at least three indisputable distinguishing marks.

Therefore we can conclude that Jean-Michel Trogneux has been living under the civil birth identity of his sister Brigitte Trogneux since at least 1986. Logically, Sébastien, Laurence and Tiphaine Auzière are administratively his nephews. Overall, "Brigitte" scrubbed her past (Jean-Michel Trogneux) and told her sister's past as her own when presenting herself to the French. For the moment, the details are a family secret. Maybe the story is not infamous (potential scenario: a sister doomed by a serious illness entrusts the custody of her children, and her identity, to a brother to whom she is very close and who has always felt like a woman), but this is still a case of identity theft.

As in the case of statutory rape, the notion of consent does not apply for identity theft. In addition, a marriage entered into as part of an ongoing (hence not time-barred) identity fraud – such as the one with Emmanuel Macron in 2007 – is an aggravating circumstance. This marriage, which could be qualified as forgery and fraud, should then be declared null and void. At this point, the further back we go into "Brigitte's" past, the more we understand that her real resume falls under the Penal Code...

Blau-Weiß Speyer

Following the military track, we have established that Jean-Michel Trogneux was again granted a delay (again under Article 23) at the 1965 *Conseil de Révision* (review board) for the canton of Amiens Sud-Ouest. The following year, Jean-Michel Trogneux turned 21, so there was an additional way to trace him: voting registration lists. They indicate a registration in Amiens in 1967, with her father Jean Trogneux at 1 rue Delambre. However, his presence on site is not confirmed, especially as the vote tally tables show that he did not vote in the legislative elections of March 5 and 12, 1967, nor in the cantonal elections of September 24 and October[1,] 1967. Meanwhile, the mention "E. 19.5.67" was added in the margin. "E" stands for "*enquête*" (inquiry), usually about a change of address.

An absence was indicated on May 19, 1967., coinciding with Jean-Michel Trogneux's potential presence in Germany, in Speyer (Rhineland Palatinate; Spire in French). This track soon proved promising. One of the few open online sources relating to the individual when we began our investigation was an article in *Die Rheinpfalz* on May 9, 2019[1]. Shortly after the existence of Jean-Michel Trogneux had just been revealed by journalist Sylvie Bommel[2], this local daily reported that Brigitte Trogneux's brother had been a non-commissioned officer in Speyer, also playing field hockey[3] as a right half-back in the B team of the local club, HC Blau-Weiß Speyer: "The former player Roland Weich, who lives in the wine-growing village of Königheim (Heilbronn-Franconia), wrote to his former club colleague Franz-Joachim Bechmann in Speyer about the stay in northern France of this descendant of the founder of the Trogneux chocolate dynasty from Amiens. The letter reads: 'I was friends with Jean-Michel. One day, he invited me to his parents' home in Amiens, Picardy. I met the whole family with the six children, including Brigitte Marie-Claude, alias Bibi. At the dinner table, she always sat in front of me'".

We contacted HC Blau-Weiß Speyer, which confirmed that Jean-Michel Trogneux was present in Speyer during the 1967-68 season. The club sent me a team list dated September 30, 1967, showing Jean-Michel Trogneux on the roster for a match against neighboring Mannheim.

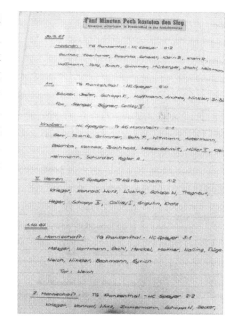

However, neither the club, nor the local or national federations, nor the Land's Ministry of Sport are able to provide us with a copy of the individual's sports license.

Contacted via *Die Rheinpfalz*, the main witness, Roland Weich, did not respond to our requests.

There was still the military option. The Speyer Historical Museum, which has organized an exhibition in 2021 on the French Forces in Germany (FFA), sent me its digitized collections. But they included no trace of Jean-Michel Trogneux. On-site, Speyer's municipal archives explain that the FFA holdings have been transferred to France, to the *Service Historique de la Défense* in Vincennes (Val-de-Marne).

In the meantime, the collection of testimonies on social media shows an itinerary that does not really match the Amiens electoral rolls: Jean-Michel Trogneux has supposedly trained in 1965 in Angers (Maine-et-Loire), at the Verneau barracks, before joining the 3rd Engineer Regiment then stationed in Speyer, where he joined Captain Pelabon and Second-Lieutenant Nicolas 2nd company. Unfortunately, the witnesses who mentioned this "Trogneux" in their memories on their *Facebook* or *Copains d'avant* pages have either passed away or are not responding to our requests. And within the *Amicale du 32e Régiment du Génie*, none of those we contacted could recall a Jean-Michel Trogneux. The *Établissement de communication et de production audiovisuelle de la Défense* (ECPAD), which manages the armed forces' audiovisual archives, has no documentation relating to conscripts in the FFA between 1965 and 1970.

We headed for the Bernadotte barracks in Pau (Pyrénées-Atlantiques), which houses the CAPM military personnel archives, including files on conscripts. Jean-Michel Trogneux's military file, which would enable us to cross-check the information gathered, is kept there under the reference 6580001874. I sent a request directly to the Ministry of the Armed Forces, whose Directorate of Memory, Culture and Archives "reject[ed] it on the grounds that disclosure of the file would unduly infringe privacy interests"[4].

For the fourth time in the course of this investigation, I referred the matter to the *Commission d'accès aux documents administratifs* (CADA), the authority that adjudicates disputes between the French and their administrations. In its opinion n° 20245437 issued on October 10, 2024, CADA stated that "In response to the request for observations sent to it, the Ministry of the Armed Forces specified that Mr. TROGNEUX's military file, closed in 1981, contained information infringing privacy and medical secrecy. For these reasons, the time limit for communicating these files is set at fifty years from their closure, and, for the medical information contained in Mr TROGNEUX's file, at twenty-five years from the date of his death, or one hundred and twenty years from his birth, if the date of death is unknown. [...] CADA therefore issues an unfavorable opinion on the disclosure of the aforementioned documents,"

In response, we suggested that the Ministry of the Armed Forces comply with CADA's recommendations by "sending digitized reproductions of the documents; in which information relating to medical secrecy and information after the 50-year communicability period, i.e. information published after 1974, would be crossed out?"[5]. We have not received any reply to this.

For now, we can date Jean-Michel Trogneux's return to France in the early summer of 1968, thanks to the electoral rolls. The individual signed up for the legislative elections of June 23 and 30, 1968. Always registered at the same polling station and still living with his parents, he never registered between 1970 and his application to be struck off the register on December 21, 1973, which became effective on February 7, 1974. We are now entering the period when, legally, under the French Heritage Code, documents whose disclosure would undermine the protection of privacy are no longer freely communicable, as the fifty-year period has not expired as we are investigating...

---

1. *Einfach tierisch gut*, Die Rheinpfalz, May 9, 2019.

2. Her book, *Il venait d'avoir 17 ans* was published a week earlier, on May 3, 2019.

3. Field hockey, a sport practised by the Amiens bourgeoisie, was played at a high level by Antoine Choteau, Tiphaine Auzière's father-in-law, who founded TAC Hockey in Le Touquet in 1985 and was later the main driving force of the national

elite level of this sport. He was a general practitioner in Étaples-sur-Mer. He committed suicide at his home in Le Touquet on October 9, 2013.

4. Mail dated July 12, 2024.

5. Mail dated November 15, 2024.

32

BLANGY-TRONVILLE

What did Jean-Michel Trogneux do between June 1968 and 1973? Although little is known about this period of his life, "Brigitte" has always claimed to have watched the 1969 American moon landing on TV from the US... Be that as it may, at the beginning of 1974, the 29-year-old individual registered to vote in Blangy-Tronville (Somme), remaining there until 1982. Our investigation continues in this small village (500 inhabitants at the time) located 10 km south-east of Amiens, home of one of the most famous peat marshes in the Somme valley: the *Grand Marais de la Queue.*

At the western end of Blangy-Tronville, at the end of rue du Mail, Picardie Metal was set up on June 12, 1973, with Jean-Michel Trogneux as manager. The purpose of this company was "the shaping, transformation and sale of all materials, particularly iron", according to the advertisement published at the time in the *Bulletin officiel des annonces civiles et commerciales* (Bodaac). However, in 2021, during the first research on Jean-Michel Trogneux, this advertisement in the *Bodaac* contained an error from a digitization bug on *Google Book* (overlapping columns), suggesting that "Jean-Michel, Henri Trogneux is acquiring the Gallice jewelry store located at 25, rue des Boucheries in Toulon (Var), the address of residence"[1]. Natacha Rey in December 2021 did not notice; but far from leveraging it to permanently discredit our investigation, the Trogneux's entourage had given credence to this false lead. So the person contact who initially told me he had never met Jean-Michel Trogneux called me back three hours later to assure me that it was a "chubby guy"[2], also (wrongly) confirming the (false) Toulon lead...

Endeavoring to sort things out, we established that on June 12, 1973, SARL Picardie Metal was set up in Blangy-Tronville, with Jean-Michel Trogneux as its director. The clerk's office of the Amiens Commercial Court, which we contacted on April 27, 2022, sent us "the only document still available in our archives concerning Picardie Metal." On reading the documentation submitted (two pages, but no articles of association), one suspects that Picardie-Metal may have been a ghost company. Indeed, on May 21, 1974, less than a year after its creation, the SARL recorded a "continuation of the company despite the loss of net assets of more than ¾ of the share capital". Following a formal suspension of payments on November 20, 1977, the company was wound up and earmarked for liquidation. A bankruptcy judge (*juge-commissaire*) was appointed: Lucien Jodoche[3]. Picardie Metal was automatically closed by the Amiens Commercial Court on March 23, 1982, "due to insufficient funds obtained from the liquidation of the company's assets".

What was the company's real economic standing? What role did Jean-Michel Trogneux play? Was he just a figurehead for his father, Jean Trogneux, in this affair? On June 13, 1973, the day after Picardie Metal was founded, Jean Trogneux purchased business space at 3-5 rue de la République in Amiens. This is the address of the engineering office of a Patrice Caron, active in the installation of sports infrastructures, and more particularly tennis courts. At the time, Jean Trogneux was the president of the Regional Tennis League of Picardie (1964-1976).

However, there is nothing in the two pages submitted by the Amiens Commercial Court to establish any link between the business of the Trogneux and of Patrice Caron. But the documentation available seems to us to be extremely weak, and apparently expurgated. So we tried our luck with the *Institut national de la propriété industrielle* (INPI), which this time returned a 53-page file from... the Amiens commercial court! Picardie Metal's articles of incorporation confirm our intuition. Although Jean-Michel Trogneux is the company's managing director (in the articles of association, he usurps the title of "engineer", which he never was), the partners are none other than Jean Trogneux and... Patrice Caron[4], who sold his shares on October 26, 1973. Picardie Metal's commercial purpose was to provide fencing for the tennis courts installed by Patrice Caron, when Jean Trogneux was president of the Tennis League of Picardy.

This brings us back to our original question: Was Jean-Michel Trogneux just a cover for his father in this affair? In 1970, a telephone line was registered at this address in the name of Jean Trogneux, as can be seen from the Somme directory ("TROGNEUX J confiseur, av Mail... 25"). From 1972, this line refers to Jean-Michel Trogneux ("Trogneux J.-M. confiseur, av Mail") until 1978, with a few variations, as in 1975, when the line refers to *Picardie Métal, clôtures*. It includes the contact details of a "representative" (*representative*): Jean Delarue, now deceased. On October 6, 1978, when Picardie Metal had stopped all activity and its name had disappeared from the Blangy-Tronville telephone directory, Jean-Michel Trogneux acquired several plots of land in the commune. These plots were resold in December 1984... In Blangy-Tronville, nobody remembers Jean-Michel Trogneux. At best, the old-timers tell us that at the Avenue du Mail address, young people from Amiens used to come and party.

On June 22, 1977, Jean Trogneux and Simone Pujol donated Jean-Michel Trogneux, on the inheritance, 102 shares in Picardie Metal (10,200 francs) and of their current account in the company (102,159.93 francs), for a total of more than 120,000 francs –at the time, a nice sum of money securing some financial autonomy. Three months later, on *Antenne 2*'s *Aujourd'hui Magazine*, the anonymous testimony of a transsexual under the pseudonym "Véronique" was broadcast. The voice, diction and phrasing are very similar to those of the current "Brigitte"...

1. See *Chapter 18*.

2. See *Chapter 19*.

3. Lucien Jodoche, born on September 14, 1929 in Amiens (Somme) and died on June 17, 2007 in Rang-du-Fliers (Pas-de-Calais), was related to the Trogneux family. He was an alumnus of La Providence, and married Édith Boulogne on April 7, 1957 in Amiens (they had two children, Catherine and Sophie), who was none other than the sister of Gérard Boulogne, head of Etablissements Boulogne, to whom Jean Trogneux married his eldest daughter, Anne-Marie. In addition to their family ties, Lucien Jodoche and Jean Trogneux served together on the *Comité économique et social de Picardie* created in September 1973.

4. Patrice, Henri, Marie, Maurice, Claude Caron was born on January 15, 1939 in Amiens (Somme) in a family of nurserymen. A landscape gardener, on January 29 1963 he founded Parcs et Jardins de France, a public works company specializing in the creation of parks and gardens. Over the years, the company's turnover exploded, and the creation of parks and public gardens was gradually relegated. Patrice Caron owes his success above all to his "all-sports" floors. He benefited from the boom in municipal gyms and stadiums, tartan tracks, outdoor sports arenas, gymnasium floors and artificial turf grounds. His specialty: the construction of synthetic tennis courts; an innovative technology at the time, with suppliers all located in West Germany (FRG). A flourishing business, as shown in his company's balance sheet for 1971. That year, Entreprise Caron built eleven athletics tracks, two soccer fields and no fewer than one hundred and thirty tennis courts. At the time, he was the exclusive importer and applicator for France and its overseas territories of the production processes of Porplastic Andeck (thermoplastic materials) and Kunststoff (synthetic materials) from Godel et Von Cramm, of synthetic turf from PolyGras (now Polytan), and of the sports carpet and the Lasting Tennis soil from Moketennis. Business was booming, as the list of customers for Patrice Caron's sports floors (document published in May 1973) reveals, including municipalities, major government departments, sports complexes and luxury hotels, as well as wealthy individuals, all over France… In the months following Jean-Michel Trogneux's registration of Picardie Metal and Jean Trogneux's purchase of Patrice Caron's business premises, Parcs et Jardins de France was under suspension of payments (*cessation de paiement*) on March 15, 1974. Meanwhile, Patrice Caron sold his shares in Picardie Metal on October 26, 1973, then announced in *Picardie La Gazette* (December 18, 1973) the launch of a new entity, Société de commercialisation des sols sportifs Patrice Caron (SSPC). Located at 3 rue Saint-Germain in Amiens, this limited liability company (SARL) with a capital of 100,000 francs was registered on March 12, 1974, with the object of "distributing and marketing all processes for the construction of sports fields in special materials, and acquiring or leasing out all businesses for this purpose". In the same year, Patrice Caron associated with Jean-François, Marie Jullien, born August 8, 1942 in Amiens, nurseryman in Dury-les-Amiens, and René Zuppardo, born September 7, 1941 in Saint-Gaudens (Haute-Garonne) and died January 10, 2007 in Nîmes (Gard). The business continued to

flourish until the early 1980s. In 1985, the company's head office was closed, and on February 6, 1987, the Amiens Commercial Court performed the compulsory liquidation of SSPC, which was deregistered from the Amiens Commercial Court on April 5, 1995. In the meantime, Patrice Caron had moved his business to the West Indies… So, on July 28 1983, Société de Diffusion et d'Environnement des Antilles (SODEA) was registered in Amiens. The following year, Patrice Caron sold his shares in SODEA to his brother, Jacques Caron, born in Amiens on October 1st, 1934. In 1985, Patrice Caron was back in Fort-de-France with this SARL with a capital of 100,000 francs, associated with Paul Vincent, born December 25, 1938 in Paris, Robert Penet, born on September 13, 1947 in Paris and Jean Mulleman, born on February 6, 1941 in Agen (Lot-et-Garonne). On December 23, 1989, SODEA was transformed into a limited company (SA: *société anoonyme*) with a capital of 400,000 francs, and its head office moved to Schoelcher (Martinique), where Patrice Caron is now domiciled. The Board of Directors includes René Zuppardo, his partner in SSPC, who has also moved to Schoelcher (Martinique), as well as his son, Emmanuel Caron, born on July 25, 1964 in Neuilly-sur-Seine (Hauts-de-Seine), of a first marriage celebrated in Moreuil (Somme) on September 22, 1962 with François Bédier. On July 10, 1992, in Petit-Bourg (Guadeloupe), Patrice Caron also associated with the Giraud-Castaing family from Bordeaux to form the Société Aménagement Rénovation Habitat (ARH), with a capital of 250,000 francs. In the summer of 2023, while we were investigating this track, a photograph featuring Patrice Caron with the "chubby guy" was posted on *Facebook*. I was later contacted by someone claiming to know a woman, Odile Bouthors, who said she had dated the "chubby guy" and had seen a private photo of him in the early 90s. The person could not supply the document, but told us that Jean-Michel Trogneux had become, in 1976, the catholic godfather of Bertrand Caron, the son of Odile Bouthors and Patrice Caron. When we contacted Bertrand Caron, he assured us that Jean-Michel Trogneux was present at Emmanuel Macron's inauguration event at the Élysée Palace, but refused to provide any photographs from this period, even against the promise, if they were conclusive, not to divulge them and to publish an article closing the whole affair.

33

"VERONIQUE"

"Becoming completely a woman"

When the question of "Brigitte's" identity was first raised in 2021, there were mentions of a 1977 interview on public television with a transgender woman with her face hidden, presenting herself under the pseudonym "Véronique"[1]. His voice, diction, phrasings in particular, recurrently saying "c'est-à-dire" (equivalent of "that is to say", or "like...") and the sound – overall very similar to "Brigitte's" vocal characteristics. The similarities were confirmed by the audio software *Audacity*: The professional account of the Brussels studio IGMaudio explained on *Twitter*, also providing a graphic: "I can attest that these are two identical voices. Same prosody, only age separates them. The "Brigitte" and "Véronique" samples are not at the same pitch, but

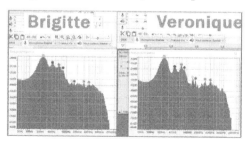

their fundamentals and partials are well demonstrated. I work in audio processing, especially of voices, and it would be the same person without searching any further."

Only a short excerpt is available on the INA public website (archives of public broadcasting). However, the excerpt from this September 27, 1977 program has been cut from the version available on *InaMédiapro*, the archive database used by journalists. The full version is at the *Inathèque*, the full archive of French public broadcasting, which is only accessible in research libraries. We therefore present the full content here:

"François Desplats - I can only guarantee the authenticity of Véronique's testimony. Véronique, I'd like to know if, when you had this operation, which is the one you've had, it was a difficult moment for you or was it just the culmination of something that had happened before?

Véronique - I don't think there's any transformation because the psyche is already feminine and the individual, in this case me, is already prepared for this kind of mutation out of necessity, in the sense that we feel like women, and we merely normalize a situation. There's no transfer, there's normalization.

FD - So you're completely a woman (*Vous êtes complètement femme*). How long ago did you have the operation?

V - [NB: Not answering to the point] I don't really like the words "completely a woman". In other words, we become a kind of woman who can copulate, but cannot procreate. Hence the legal problems we'll be talking about later. In other words, integration goes smoothly on an individual level. They only exist on a social level.

FD - You have a job that we're not going to reveal here. Let's just say it's a job that's about the public.

V - That's right, I'm a craftsman. I have regular contact with the public. I am in close contact with customers. I don't have any problems. I used to, because I had a phenotypic gender, meaning an ambiguous appearance. They took me for what I wasn't, i.e. a homosexual, which wasn't the case, either in my behavior or in my way of thinking. But unfortunately, this image resulted in non-integration. And actually I normalized a situation for my integration. And I live very legally and honorably. For civil status purposes, it is possible to change your first name to an ambiguous one. This is very important, because it enables integration, or pseudo-integration, into society, in the sense that there are always problems, but they can be solved administratively, i.e. by mutual agreement. But legally, there's no solution, unlike all foreign legislation except the Belgian legislation, which is modeled on ours.

FD - Do you feel that you are now completely yourself? And you don't have any problems identifying yourself since your operation?

V - To tell the truth, I only had identification problems towards others, not with myself. I saw myself as what I was: a woman with a body that didn't belong to her. It's very difficult to conceive for someone who's comfortable in one's own skin. I use the term "comfortable in one's skin" because it's the typical image – because I didn't have any problems; but people created problems. Now I don't have any problems. To tell the truth, this operation, i.e. the removal of an organ that is useless in our case because it is both unusable and unused...

FD - Do you live alone?

V - I'm not with anyone, but I've lived with a woman. And conceived this union in the style of George Sand and Chopin. Chopin was probably a transsexual. His style of melody, the way he plays, makes this quite clear. [...] I think the image that has been given of the Rimbaud/Verlaine union is a distorted, caricatured image that doesn't correspond at all..."

Here, the presenter chips in and the interview ends.

We note that "Véronique" remains vague and never answers when the precise date of her "reassignment" is requested by François Desplats, who insists in his preamble on "guaranteeing the authenticity of Véronique's testimony". Was "Véronique" really a transsexual woman at the time? Or still a man? Or, like the Chevalier d'Éon, an androgynous individual capable of embodying a different persona depending on needs and situations? The individual

"Véronique" offers a well-honed discourse, appearing as a seasoned campaigner for a cause to which he brings lends an intellectual veneer. In this interview, we note a reference to Chopin that echoes the "official legend" of the presidential couple, in which Emmanuel Macron plays the piano, but only when he is alone with "Brigitte"… with a predilection for the works of Frédéric Chopin: "Thanks to Emmanuel, or rather Brigitte, there is again a piano in the Élysée Palace, because it seems that Manu plays Chopin too", explained the musician André Manoukian in 2021[2]. As for the couple formed by Arthur Rimbaud and Paul Verlaine, Emmanuel Macron had considered admitting them to the Pantheon as a homosexual couple, but Arthur Rimbaud's family objected to the poet being reduced to the status of a "gay icon". Finally, "Véronique's" testimony shares with "Brigitte's" official biography the unequivocal proclamation of a form of sexual abstinence, with, on the one hand, the reference to the couple formed by Frédéric Chopin and George Sand, and, on the other, the university dissertation that "Brigitte" is said to have devoted to *L'amour courtois* (Courtly love).

Le Carnet du Courrier

Madame Jacques DREUX
Monsieur et Madame
Jean TROGNEUX
sont heureux de vous faire part du
mariage de leurs enfants
Véronique et **Jean-Michel**
Celui-ci a eu lieu dans la plus
stricte intimité, le 24 novembre
1980, à BLANGY-TRONVILLE.
Allery, 21, rue de Merelessart.
Amiens, 1, rue Delambre.

Brigitte Trogneux, witness in Jean-Michel and Véronique's wedding

In an astonishing redundancy, Jean-Michel Trogneux married a Véronique Dreux[3] at the same time, on November 24 1980 in Blangy-Tronville. This union was only announced retrospectively in *Le Courrier Picard*, specifying that the wedding had taken place "in the strictest privacy"[4].

When we retrieved the documentation of this union and made it public in December 2021, the Blangy-Tronville town hall issued a full copy of the marriage certificate to journalist Jonathan Moadab on January 7, 2022, who posted a crossed-out version on *Twitter*.

His aim was to debunk the affair by revealing that Brigitte Auzière had been Jean-Michel Trogneux's wedding witness, and that they couldn't possibly be the same person... But far from torpedoing our investigation, this information on the contrary documented the great closeness between Brigitte and Jean-Michel Trogneux. Indeed, we now knew that they had been witnesses to each other's weddings. So Brigitte Trogneux was the key to Jean-Michel's life, and vice-versa. This made not only Jean-Michel Trogneux's disappearance from "Brigitte's" official biography all the more incomprehensible, but also the fact that, when recounting her life, "Brigitte" had shifted all family events in time, with the effect of making this hidden brother untraceable...

Above all, giving a journalist the full version of this marriage certificate was a very special, even exceptional, form of treatment, because it was against the law. A town hall can only issue this type of document - a copy of a full marriage record - to a third party after a period of 75 years has elapsed (2055 in this case) or 25 years from the date of death of one of the spouses, whichever is shorter (which is not the case here). Obtaining this document was therefore totally abnormal and its sole purpose was to strike a blow against Natacha Rey's thesis by including Brigitte and Jean-Michel Trogneux in the same document (while not showing any image of them together in the past)... And when, one of my correspondents made the same request a month later, he was refused a full copy of the document, in accordance with the law. In the conversation that my correspondent recorded at Blangy-Tronville town hall that day that day, the town hall employee reveals the conditions under which she issued the document for debunking purposes: "When we called the Amiens town hall, they told me to do it this way. I've even got one person in charge of this request only." So the Blangy-Tronville town hall had acted on the orders of Amiens town hall, where someone was specifically in charge of the Trogneux file?

The Trogneux saga's forgotten boutique

In his marriage certificate, Jean-Michel Trogneux, whom we have known as a "confectioner" or an "engineer", declares this time that he is a "commercial agent"... After this marriage, Véronique Dreux briefly moves into an apartment in downtown Beauvais (Oise), at no. 4 rue Saint-Pierre, a stone's throw from the cathedral. In the white pages of the Oise newspaper, a line appeared in 1982 (for that year only) with the name "Trogneux Jean-Michel, Beauvais, 4 rue Saint-Pierre". Across the street, Véronique Dreux has opened her own boutique, Tentations. Although Véronique Dreux is the statutory manager, the boutique is in fact a Jean Trogneux boutique, having been entirely funded by her parents-in-law[5]. Although called Tentations, this store, like all the others in the family, is a franchise of La Maison des Baptêmes, the parent company of the family confectionery group. Advertising inserts in the Yellow Pages and local press at the time made no secret of the fact that Tentations was indeed a Jean Trogneux boutique, and even used it as an advertising point.

However, like everything related to Jean-Michel Trogneux, the Trogneux boutique in Beauvais was completely erased from the official biography of "Brigitte" and from the Trogneux saga[6]. But for the time being, the boutique at 17 rue Saint Pierre seems to be doing well, and a second Tentations boutique is even opening in Beauvais, rue d'Amiens. Whatever the materiality of the couple they formed, Véronique Dreux and Jean-Michel Trogneux declared two children, Jean-Jacques[7], born November 12, 1982, in Amiens, and Valérie, born February 20, 1984[8]. Upstream, Véronique and Jean-Michel

Trogneux had purchased a house[9] at 10 rue Boulanger in La Neuville-sur-Oudeuil (Oise), a village of 300 inhabitants located 20 kilometers north of Beauvais and 50 kilometers south of Amiens. Jean-Michel Trogneux and Véronique Dreux were granted a divorce by the Beauvais (Oise) Regional Court on June 17, 1987. Closed on April 30, 1987, Tentations was struck off the register of the Beauvais Commercial Court on December 27, 1989.

Jean-Michel Trogneux, the erased marriage

Véronique Dreux remarried on January 30, 1998 in Toulon (Var) to Alain l'Eleu de la Simone, a major insurer from Amiens[10]. Surprisingly, in 2008, when Véronique Dreux and Alain de la Simone set up an SCI [*Société civile immobilière* – an arrangement to manage real estate collectively] to house their property in Corsica, the document issued by a notary in Amiens listed them as united by "first marriage", whereas in fact Alain de la Simone was marrying for the second time, and Véronique Dreux had already been married twice. In short, Jean-Michel Trogneux had (again) been wiped out.

STATUTS DE SOCIÉTÉ CIVILE IMMOBILIERE

A la requête de :

1°) Monsieur Alain Bernard Marie Joseph **L'ELEU de la SIMONE**, Retraité, et Madame Véronique Christine Dominique **DREUX**, sans profession, son épouse, demeurant ensemble à AMIENS (80000), 202 rue Jean Moulin,
Nés savoir :
Monsieur **L'ELEU de la SIMONE** à PARIS 17ÈME ARRONDISSEMENT (750~~17~~)~~ le 22 ~~ ~~1925~~,
Madame **DREUX** à AMIENS (80000) le 22 septembre 1952,
~~Mariés, Monsieur et Madame en premières noces sous le régime~~ de la séparation de biens pure et simple défini par les articles 1536 et suivants du Code civil aux termes de leur contrat de mariage reçu par Maître Cyril NEVIASKI, Notaire à AMIENS, le 22 décembre 1997, préalable à leur union célébrée à la mairie de TOULON (83000), le 30 janvier 1998.
Ce régime n'a subi aucune modification conventionnelle ou judiciaire depuis.
Monsieur est de nationalité française.
Madame est de nationalité française.
Résidents au sens de la réglementation fiscale.
Sont présents à l'acte.

In the same way, this marriage to Jean-Michel Trogneux literally erased Véronique Dreux from her life, including the administrative aspects. In this tax document dated January 4, 1992, relating to a *Groupement foncier agricole* (farming collective) located in Airaines, only her first marriage, to Serge Franchois is mentioned.

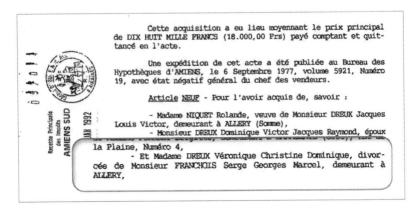

"Brigitte told me not to get involved"

So I was looking to contact Véronique Dreux. What was the materiality of her marriage to Jean-Michel Trogneux? Who was he? How and when had they parted? After marrying a Trogneux, Véronique Dreux continued her upward social mobility by marrying a la Simone, now listed in the *Bottin mondain*. That is where I found her phone number. Contacted on WhatsApp, she agreed to get back to me the next day, and did so. Our conversation lasted half an hour. Even though she repeats the wording often heard from the Trogneux entourage (e.g. "Those women are crazy!", referring to Natacha Rey and Amandine Roy), she first pretends not to know what the call is about: "About Jean-Michel becoming Brigitte, right? Listen sir, I don't know; it's ridiculous anyway, because I have two children with Jean-Michel. I saw on *Youtube* that they made a family tree where they even put that I might be Macron's mother". Véronique Dreux is referring to questions raised by Internet users about the uncanny physical resemblance between Emmanuel Macron, husband of "Brigitte", and Jean-Jacques Trogneux, son of Jean-Michel Trogneux.

In his civil status, Jean-Michel Trogneux is not Emmanuel Macron's wife. If this had been the case, he would have been known as Jean-Michel Macron. However, Jean-Michel Macron is not Emmanuel Macron's wife, but his father... "Listen sir, I have been divorced from Jean-Michel Trogneux for many years. Listen sir, I have remarried, and my children are here, I don't want any problems. But I can tell you that Jean-Michel is not Brigitte; that's ridiculous. [...] I had two chocolate stores in Beauvais. Well, I had two children, it didn't work out so well, so I went back to live with Mom, and that's all. But I can tell you that Jean-Michel is not Brigitte". I take her at her word and ask her for photos of her shared past with Jean-Michel Trogneux, promising, if they are conclusive, to close the case without even publishing them: "Brigitte told me not to get involved. I don't want any trouble about my children, or about uh... it's not relevant to the family any more". As I argue that she should hold Brigitte Macron to account, because it's because of her silence that her own photo, as well as those of her children (Jean-Jacques in particular) are circulating on social networks, she cuts me off and inexplicably blurts out: " and also, I know Macron's father... Well, I don't know him very well. He was a surgeon at the Amiens hospital. But I didn't even know Macron. We lived in Toulon, I didn't even know him, I saw him at my daughter's wedding. First time

I'd ever seen him." I can hear another person on the line. Véronique Dreux stops, visibly embarrassed, as if she's gone too far. She pulls herself together and asks me, "Well, and what is your name?"…

1985-86

In March 1985, Jean-Michel Trogneux was allocated the 550 000 francs in the current account of Tentations when his parents, Jean and Simone Trogneux, made a shared donation to their notary, Me Hervé Laudren. Tentations closed in October 1985 when Véronique Dreux resigned. In September 1986 "Brigitte" began her teaching career at the Lucie Berger school, and Véronique Dreux returned to Amiens at 14, rue André Chénier. Problem: this address does not refer to her mother's address, as she told me over the phone, but to a property belonging to her future ex-father-in-law Jean Trogneux…

----

1. An excerpt is available on INA's website as *Véronique et Martine, transexuelles dans les années 1970*. This video is just a short excerpt from the *Aujourd'hui Magazine* program broadcast on Tuesday, September 27, 1977, produced and aired on *Antenne 2*, presented by François Desplats (who died in 1999), with Jacques Samyn and Gilbert Kahn at the helm and, as other living guests, make-up artist Charly Koubesserian, singer Nicole Croisille and singer Michel Marceau, the eldest son of the mime Marceau.

2. *C à vous*, France 5, June 21, 2021.

3. Véronique, Christine, Dominique Dreux was born on September 22, 1952 in Amiens (Somme). His father, Jacques, Victor, Louis Dreux, born on April 26, 1918 in Mézidon (Calvados) to Louis Théophile Dreux (1876-1942) and Antoinette, Charlotte, Léontine Ducrocq (1883-1970), was taken prisoner at Décize (Nièvre) on June 18, 1940, interned in Stalag III-B at Fürstenberg-sur-Oder (Brandenburg) and released in early 1943. He died on August 28, 1958 in Airaines (Somme), where he had taken over the family farm before developing a business as a merchant of heating systems. Fatherless, Véronique Dreux was raised by her mother, Rolande Niquet, who was born on May 22, 1920 in Allery (Somme) and died on July 3, 2011 in Amiens. Véronique Dreux's mother came from a family of jute cloth producers, and she is the granddaughter of industrialist Raymond Niquet (Tissage R. Niquet), who was mayor of Allery, president of the Société de Secours Mutuel and honorary president of the Union Laïque. Before marrying Jean-Michel Trogneux, Véronique

Dreux had married Serge, Georges, Marcel Franchois on December 16, 1972 in Allery, Somme. Contacted by the author on January 18, 2024, Véronique Dreux describes this brief marriage (divorced on December 6, 1974 by the Tribunal de Grande Instance d'Amiens) as a "youth error". During her youth, Véronique Dreux lived in the United States, in Scarsdale (New York), where she was an au pair with an American family, while studying English at Hunter College in New York, as she indicated on her Facebook page in 2021 (those data were deleted following media coverage of the case). Her elder brother, Dominique, Victor, Jacques, Raymond Dreux, born May 30, 1944 in Paris VIIIe married Brigitte Furodet, born March 3, 1944 in Thiers (Puy-de-Dôme) to Raoul, Gabriel, in Airaines (Somme) on July 17, 1965, Etienne Furodet (1920-1987), a PTT (postal system) technical controller who became a porcelain, glassware and silverware retailer in Paris and Amiens (Laloue Cadeaux), and his wife Gabrielle, Paulette, Sylvanie Leclercq (1920-2014). Brigitte Furodet, Véronique Dreux's sister-in-law, will be her witness when she marries Jean-Michel Trogneux. Based in Lamorlaye (Oise), Dominique Dreux and Brigitte Furodet will have two children (Guillaume and Sophie). Between 1997 and 1999, Dominique Dreux ran a catering business in Amiens (Au Cornet de Frites), which closed shortly before her divorce on September 16, 1999. Brigitte Furodet later moved to Soissons (Aisne)- where she is still on the electoral roll - but we were unable to contact this valuable witness. Dominique Dreux, who married Saïda Affdal on December 30, 2002, passed away on April 21, 2016 in Morocco.

4. The wedding was celebrated in Blangy-Tronville (Somme) by Louis Warmé, who was the mayor of this commune between 1959 and 1983. His daughter-in-law, Véronique Warmé, current First deputy mayor of Blangy-Tronville, sits on various Amiens-Métropole committees.

5. Véronique Dreux is the statutory manager of this limited liability company with capital of 50 000 francs, divided into 500 shares of 100 francs each, whose registered office is at the address of the main boutique, 17 rue Saint-Pierre. Although the company was registered in the Beauvais Trade and Companies Register under number 321 629 336, it was first incorporated in Amiens under the auspices of the Trogneux family's notary, Me Hervé Laudren, on March 24, 1981. Although their son, Jean-Michel, appears in the articles of association, it was Jean and Simone Trogneux who provided the start-up capital; the securities belonged to Mme Trogneux Pujol (the groom's mother) and were deposited at Banque Lenoir et Bernard in account n° 14449-003. Jean and Simone Trogneux therefore "paid" for a store in Beauvais for their daughter-in-law.

6. In *Il venait d'avoir 17 ans* (JCLattès, 2019) Sylvie Bommel recounts the Trogneux saga: "Bold and cautious at the same time, Jean Trogneux limits his export market to the Nord-Picardie region, as the only attempt outside this area, in Nantes, ended in failure. For Arras, his first conquered territory, he invented "« Les cœurs d'Arras", an orange-peel cookie that revisits a local gingerbread specialty. For Saint-Quentin, he created a praline chocolate bearing the effigy of Quentin de La Tour, as this painter was born in Arras. The same strategy applies to Lille, the regional capital, with the fleur-de-lis on its coat of arms. Once the locals have been won, the merchant can quietly impose his Amiens macaron at €0,80 euro each (2019 price).

Swallowed in two bites, but excellent value for money." In addition to the fact that the Beauvais boutique has been erased from history, its short active period has been transferred to the Nantes boutique, which is said to have been "a failure". Although the boutique closed on December 31, 2016, La Maison des Baptêmes at no. 5 rue Guépin was quite an institution in Nantes, operating successfully for over 60 years. Strictly speaking, it is not a failure, as confirmed by the announcement of the store's closure published in *Ouest France* on December 20, 2016.

7. Jean-Jacques Trogneux is a computer scientist working as an *auto-entrepreneur* (a status for independents) in Amiens (registered in March 2016). On his *LinkedIn* profile, he presents himself as a communications and project management consultant with Honet Communication (since May 2016). Previously, he was a project manager and webmarketer at Oblady, a local IT services company (April 2013-March 2016). As part of the family, he was in charge of *Gueudet.fr*'s referencing within the Gueudet Group between 2008 and 2009, when he graduated from the École Supérieure de Commerce in Reims. Jean-Jacques Trogneux did not respond to our requests. His partner Loretta Rizzuto (civil partner since March 24, 2016) is a journalist with the regional daily press *(Courrier picard, Picardie la Gazette, etc.)*.

8. Born Valérie Anne-Catherine Trogneux, she married Frank, Paul, Freddy Limpens on June 21, 2008 in Amiens. Born on April 20, 1985 in Albert (Somme), and residing in Maucourt (Somme). He is the son of Michel Georges, Paul Limpens, born on April 10, 1953 in Maucourt (Somme) and his wife (union celebrated in Maucourt on June 28, 1980) Chantal, Jeanne, Germaine Jacquemont, born March 6, 1962 in Montdidier (Somme). Based in Roye (Somme), the couple have two other children, including William, Freddy, Frank Limpens, born on December 15, 1990 in Corbie (Somme), married to Nelly Thoumire (born on October 6, 1987 in Enghien-les-Bains). The latter diversified the family business into wholesale turf (Les Gazons des Hauts-de-France). In this family of farmers (EARL Limpens), the business goes back at least to Michel Limpens' parents, André Limpens and Odette Billebaud. Valérie Trogneux, a former pharmaceutical delegate and mother of three, bought the from Béatrice Marquis in September 2019 Instant Couturea, a haberdashery located on Place Léon Debouverie in Amiens, but whose head office (SAS B. Marquis) is located on rue de Grosville in Rivière (Pas-de-Calais).

9. In the presence of Me Vandermeersch, associate notary in Marseille-en-Beauvaisis (Oise), the property was acquired on July 27, 1982 for 350 000 francs from Claude Perreau and his wife, Odile (née Fernandez-Rodriguez), who moved to Touraine. The funds for this purchase appear to have been provided by Jean Trogneux. After Jean-Michel Trogneux and Véronique Dreux divorced, Amiens notary partner Me Laudren recorded a community division on May 4, 1988, followed by the resale of the property on December 19, 1990 for 425 000 francs. At this address, a telephone line in Jean-Michel Trogneux's name appears in the White Pages of the Oise department between 1983 and 1988.

10. Alain, Bernard, Marie Joseph L'Eleu de la Simone, born February 28, 1935 in the 17th arrondissement of Paris, died February 5, 2022 in Amiens. Alain de la Simone comes from a Picardy bourgeois family with pretensions of nobility (allied to the Guillebon family in particular), and graduated from HEC business school in

1959. He is the eldest of six children of Daniel l'Eleu de La Simone (1905-1969) and Geneviève Lalande (1909-2011), including jazz clarinettist Christian de la Simone (1938-2009) and his son, singer Albin de la Simone. From a previous marriage to Domitille Bougon (1941-2011), Alain l'Eleu de la Simone is the father of Stéphanie (Mrs Olivier Drevon, four children) and Éric, married to Isabelle Bidart (one child).

EPILOGUE

THE BLOOD OF THE ROTHSCHILDS

The forgotten first name

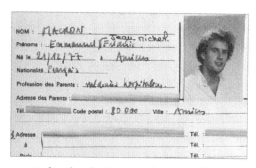

The embarrassment felt by Véronique Dreux when discussing Emmanuel Macron's childhood, with his unspoken physical resemblance to her son Jean-Jacques Trogneux, was a reminder that little or nothing was known about Emmanuel Macron's childhood. What did Françoise Noguès, in charge of the 'gender reassignment' program at the Caisse Nationale d'Assurance Maladie (*Social Security*), mean when she declared that, for her, "Brigitte is not a daughter-in-law"? What if, inside embedded levels – a *mise en abyme* –, the theater workshop had in fact consisted in... staging the meeting between "Brigitte" and Emmanuel Macron in front of witnesses? What forces had brought this dark story to power, combining family secrets, pedophilia and transsexualism, hinting at what the mysterious "+" in the acronym LGBTQIA + might stand for... In his application form for Sciences-Po Paris, Emmanuel Macron had forgotten to mention his middle name... "Jean-Michel".

Rothschild & Cie played a key role in what the *Wall Street* Journal called "The calculated rise of Macron"[1]. Surprisingly, an error also crept into the family bank's internal documentation. Until 2011, Emmanuel Macron was described as "born on December 21, 1977 in Paris (75)"; as here, in the minutes of the Extraordinary General Meeting of January 22, 2010:

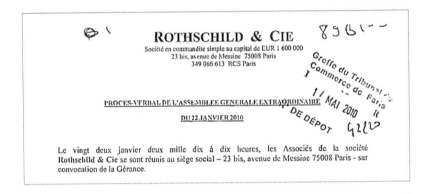

Or here, in this transfer slip dated February 11, 2011:

Then in 2012, when he left the bank to join François Hollande at the Élysée Palace, we read that Emmanuel Macron was "born on December 21, 1977 in Amiens (80)".

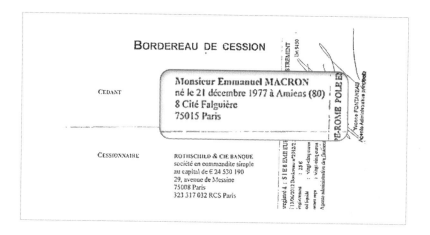

"You're sort of a prostitute"

The Rothschild bank's role in promoting the Macron political product (i.e. the couple formed by the young man and his mentor "Brigitte") has been claimed by the interested party himself on numerous occasions. What is to be understood when, in 2012, Emmanuel Macron declared: "I had a very unintelligible background. No one could understand him outside of Rothschild"[2]? When he became the economic advisor to Socialist President François Hollande, he said: "David [de Rothschild] knows about my commitment, I'm his hedge, his cover. When the left is in power, I'll be his protector"[3].

Surprisingly, whenever the Macron-Rothschild association was mentioned, it was always laced with references to prostitution. Alain Minc, who claims to be Rothschild & Cie's unofficial HR director, explained on public television: "I said to David de Rothschild, we must take him at any cost. An investment banker has to be smart, flexible, fast and if he can be charming – because after all it's a bitch's job. These are the qualities of an investment banker, and they had them all"[4]. Emmanuel Macron said no different when he told the *Wall Street Journal*: "You're sort of a prostitute. Seduction is the job."[5]. François Henrot, David de Rothschild's right-hand man, openly praised Emmanuel Macron's ability to "manipulate opinion"[6].

Within the bank, Emmanuel Macron's progress surprised many. Cyrille Harfouche explained that he "had been identified as a very singular personality, with a lot of contacts", and Sophie Javary, who trained him at Rothschild & Cie, reports that "he had very high-level contacts for our files with links to the State". According to her, her most experienced colleagues were surprised by his "supports at the top level of the bank, notably David de Rothschild and his right-hand man François Henrot", who occasionally allowed him to "bypass his immediate hierarchy"[7]. This support enabled him to become, at the age of 32, the youngest managing partner in the bank's history, even though, according to the other employees, he was a "poor technician": "Macron doesn't know much about it". "In meetings, we giggle and think ardently: 'Here's another Macron gem'"[8]. Reporting on confidences from Rothschild & Cie executives, journalist Marc Endeweld confirms the bitterness aroused by his accelerated promotion: "At Rothschild, he has the reputation of never having written an equation"; "he didn't know what an EBITDA is – the operating profit of a company"; "David de Rothschild had to violate them to appoint him managing partner"[9].

No doubt the change in Emmanuel Macron's place of birth in the Rothschild & Cie documentation was simply a clerical error. This is just one more of the countless anomalies that have marked Emmanuel Macron's career during his studies and beyond. Here is a summary:

1- In 2002, Emmanuel Macron was admitted to ENA without having answered the question asked during the oral exam[10];

2- He joined the *Inspection générale des finances* thanks to his ENA exit ranking, which "surprised, even displeased"[11] his fellow classmates off the Senghor promotion, whose mobilization led to the cancellation of the year's ranking (an unprecedented event in the school's history) by the *Conseil d'État* in 2007. In 2021, Emmanuel Macron announced the suppression of the ENA itself and of the *Inspection générale des finances*, while his fellow Senghor graduates, over time, were assigned all the top jobs in the Republic.

3- In September 2008, his recruitment by Rothschild & Cie was accompanied by an exemption from the compulsory procedure for placement on leave from the civil service (in accordance with article 44b of Decree 85-986), i.e. without publication of the order signed by the Minister in the *Journal Officiel*.

4- Consequently, he was not reinstated to the civil service when he was appointed to François Hollande's presidential team in May 2012: "I've never seen anything like it," explains Jacques Arrighi de Casanova[12], deputy chairman of the Conseil d'Etat's Legal section and chairman of the Civil service ethics commission.

The Rothschilds and the Oise track

Yet the shadow of the "Rothschild connection" hangs over all his dealings. Henry Hermand, who was his generous patron and witness at the wedding with "Brigitte" (celebrated in Le Touquet but prepared in his villa in Tangier, Morocco), had long been linked to Élie de Rothschild, having made his fortune in the 1960s by operating the Saint-Maximin (Oise) commercial hub built on a land property owned by Alain and Élie de Rothschild. The latter's daughter, Elisabeth de Rothschild, an architect in Singapore, married Marc Leland, who heads the German Marshall Fund of The United States, a transatlantic program that will sponsor Emmanuel Macron in New York[13].

It was also during an internship in New York for Rothschild & Cie that Emmanuel Macron became involved with the power couple formed by financier Henry Kravis (KKR) and economist Marie-Josée Droin[14]. In Senlis (Oise), where he lived, Henry Hermand was a member of the fonds de dotation du Patrimoine [Heritage Endowment Fund] of

Senlis, alongside diplomat Jean-Marc Simon, who was, as a member of the French embassy in Nigeria, Emmanuel Macron's first mentor in his curriculum at ENA. Emmanuel Macron's second internship will be at the Oise prefecture in Beauvais. It is here that he is said to have linked up with Pierre Donnersberg, insurance broker and Chairman of Siaci Saint-Honoré (a subsidiary of Compagnie Financière Edmond de Rothschild), which will provide the insurance policy enabling Emmanuel Macron to finance his election campaign in 2017[15]. In particular, Henry Hermand had financed and hosted Terra Nova, a think tank created in conjunction with the Center for American Progress, the organization founded by John Podesta, whose vice-president Christophe Bejach, former European managing director of Monument Capital Group[16], was convicted in 2016 in the United Kingdom for possession of child pornography[17].

"Savior of Europe"

Jacques Attali, who was Guy de Rothschild's right-hand man at the *Fonds Social Juif Unifié* before taking on the role of HR Manager in French politics, said: "Emmanuel Macron? I'm the one who spotted him. I even invented him."[18] In fact, it was his twin brother Bernard Attali (closely linked to the CIA[19]) who organized a secret meeting in 2012 during which the support of financial circles for the Socialist candidate François Hollande was conditional upon the hiring of Emmanuel Macron as economic advisor at the Élysée Palace[20]. When François Hollande came to power, he set the condition for being a minister of having been elected by universal suffrage. In fact, in 2014, Emmanuel Macron was appointed Minister of the Economy without ever having been elected. Heralded as a "surprise" by the French press, this appointment came as no surprise to Jake Sullivan. He had announced this back in 2012 in a memo to Hillary Clinton as Director of Policy Planning for the Obama Administration.

At the Ministry of the Economy, Emmanuel Macron will multiply the sales of French industrial and strategic flagships abroad, in constant liaison with the Rothschild bank. Journalist Martine

Orange sums up the general impression: "Beyond the Alstom case, which is likely to return to haunt the presidency for a long time, examples abound of these operations desired by Emmanuel Macron which – mere chance, really? – were carried out to the detriment of French interests, even when the French positions were the strongest. [...] When every major maneuver systematically results in the stripping of France's activities, there is some reason to wonder"[21].

But *The Economist*, the weekly magazine controlled by the Rothschild and Agnelli families, has constantly been glorifying Emmanuel Macron, sometimes painting him as almost walking on water as "savior of Europe"[22], sometimes as the incarnation of a "New European Order"[23], even comparing him to Charlemagne[24]...

"A great eschatological project"

In Paris, some suspect that the Macron product ("Brigitte and Emmanuel") is simply David de Rothschild's instrument for making France pay for François Mitterrand's nationalization of the bank in 1981[25]. 'Many are wondering about the strangely tactile complicity between David de Rothschild and "Brigitte", which raises many questions about the true nature of the relationship between the presidential couple and the Rothschilds...

Although publicly acknowledged, this relationship is implicitly taboo in public debate in France. Anyone who dares broach the subject is immediately accused of antisemitism, and his career would be immediately destroyed. This is what happened to the economist Gaël Giraud, until then a "*directeur de recherche*" at CNRS[26]. On the *Thinkerview Youtube* channel[27], this well-connected economist had broken the ban by declaring: "Emmanuel Macron's arrival at Rothschild was decisive for him. He was under the aegis of David de Rothschild, the former CEO of this major bank, which [...] has a revenge to take for the nationalizations of 1981. And who, for his part, has a grand eschatological project for the end of time [....]. This is my take on a report circulating in Paris. Emmanuel Macron is David de Rothschild's hitman. [...] So, in a way, the person Emmanuel Macron, so much in the public focus, is not very interesting. He's a boy who carries out a program dictated to him by others, notably David de Rothschild".

What was the link between the Rothschilds' "eschatological project" and the Macron couple? Amanda Lear, a reference point for transsexual biographies, was perhaps a key to understanding the relationship between "Emmanuel" and "Brigitte". "Amanda" had "married" in Las Vegas Alain Philippe Malagnac, who had been the lover of writer Roger Peyrefitte from the age of 12. And, a few weeks after his death, Alain Philippe Malagnac died in murky circumstances, in a fire that ravaged Amanda Lear's *mas* [farmhouse] in Saint-Étienne-du-Grès (Bouche-du-Rhône). Amanda Lear was a familiar face at the Rothschilds' receptions. According to her, the most memorable evening[28] she had attended was the Bal Surréaliste given on December 12, 1977 at Château de Ferrières by Guy and Marie-Hélène de Rothschild. The costumes and ambience were supervised by her then companion Salvador Dali. The table decorations were baby dolls that had been dismembered and had their skulls smashed...

"Because it stays in the family"

But behind the "artistic" façade, there was a darker side. In 2022, it came to light that David de Rothschild's personal bodyguard, Christian Giroud, had been commissioned to silence a victim of insurer Jacques Bouthier (Vilavi Group), who was accused of recruiting teenage girls, including a 14-year-old Romanian, to satisfy his pedophile tastes. The operation consisted of "covering up the affair, recovering the [compromising] video and finding Kenza [one of Jacques Bouthier's "sex slaves"] to take her by force to a foreign country. A criminal mission.", according to *Le Parisien*[29].

When the Epstein affair broke out, the name of Edouard de Rothschild, David's half-brother, appeared in the *Black Book* of 2004. Then Edmond de Rothschild's name in the *Black Book* of 1997, found in July 2021 by *Business Insider*. In May 2023, the *Wall Street Journal* revealed that after Edmond de Rothschild's death, ties had persisted with his daughter-in-law and current president of the Edmond de Rothschild Group, Ariane de Rothschild. This was an extensive relationship (a dozen meetings between 2013 and 2019), ranging from help in recruiting a multilingual assistant to a $25 million contract signed in 2015 with Jeffrey Epstein. For Ariane de Rothschild, Epstein was also the intermediary who introduced her to Joshua Cooper Ramo, director of FedEx and Starbucks and a senior executive at Henry Kissinger's geopolitical consulting firm, and to Kathy Ruemmler, former White House counsel to Barack Obama, now General Counsel at Goldman Sachs. The British branch's doings are at a comparable level. In addition to Hannah de Rothschild, daughter of Baron Jacob de Rothschild, Jeffrey Epstein and Ghislaine Maxwell were close friends of Evelyn de Rothschild and his wife Lynn Forester. It was the latter who introduced the couple to Bill Clinton at the White House. These names are the tip of an iceberg of personalities related to or affiliated with the Rothschilds who fill the documentation relating to the Epstein affair. Foremost among them was Robert Maxwell, one of the Rothschilds' main associates. The World Jewish Congress (WJC), whose current

Chairman of the Board of Directors is none other than David de Rothschild, has two of its most senior representatives at the heart of the "Epstein system": current WJC Chairman Ronald Lauder, who allowed Jeffrey Epstein to obtain an Austrian passport, and his predecessor Edgar Bronfman, who co-founded the Mega Group, one of the main channels of funds for the operation led by Jeffrey Epstein and Ghislaine Maxwell.

Notoriously, the Rothschilds' longevity and the preservation of their fortune are based on an extensive practice of endogamy and alliances between cousins. At a conference at the *Musée d'art et d'histoire du judaïsme* (MAHJ)[30] Nathalie Rheims, David de Rothschild's cousin, went further, declaring: "A very common practice in such families: 'vice is nice but incest is best because it stays in the family'. We're simply raised to be silent, so that nothing comes out. [...] We're brought up with this weight to make sure – and it works – that we never speak out." Words that echo what we encountered throughout our investigation of "Brigitte": a family cloistered in silence, jealous to protect a family secret that has become a state affair...

---

1. The Calculated Rise of Macron, The Wall Street Journal, April 29, 2017;

2. Quoted by Martine Orange in *Rothschild, une banque au pouvoir*, Albin Michel, 2012.

3. Quoted by Marc Endeweld in *L'Ambigu Monsieur Macron*, Flammarion, 2015.

4. *Rothschild, le pouvoir d'un nom*, France 2, December[1,] 2016.

5. *Quoted in France Casts Its Fate With Ex-Banker, Wall Street Journal*, March 9, 2015.

6. *Emmanuel Macron, la stratégie du météore*, France 3, November 24, 2016.

7. *The French Exception*, Adam Plowright, Icon Books, 2017.

8. Quoted in *Society*, April[1,] 2016.

9. Quoted by Marc Endeweld in *L'Ambigu Monsieur Macron*, Flammarion, 2015.

10. In *Le Traître et le néant* (Fayard, 2021), journalists Gérard Davet and Fabrice Lhomme recount the circumstances surrounding Emmanuel Macron's entry into the ENA: "Prefect Joseph Zimet, who would become his communications director at the Élysée Palace twenty years later, was present at this admission oral exam. Like other students, in fact. Zimet, whom we met, did not wish to comment publicly on

his former comrade, but everyone, including him, remembers the question asked by a learned professor about Turkish influence in Central Asia. Clearly, Macron had not sufficiently studied this geopolitical issue. He could or should have gone blank, blushed and stammered. This is not Macron. His answer, more or less? "Look, I'm sorry, I'm not quite see the point… Do you have another question?"

11. In *Les Macron* (Fayard, 2017), Caroline Derrien and Candice Nedelec report that"in 2004, Emmanuel Macron came out *'dans la botte'* [in the boot, ENA slang for: among the top students]. Bronze medal on the podium. [...] His exit rank makes some jealous. Nicolas Sarközy's future advisor, Sébastien Proto, would have been surprised, if not displeased, by such a success. He's not the only onealthough second in the exit rankings.

12. Quoted in *Marianne*, October 24, 2014.

13. *Quand Emmanuel Macron découvrait l'Amérique, JDD*, 22 avril 2022.

14. Marie-Josée Kravis is a Canadian economist and co-chair of the Bilderberg Group, one of the world's leading globalist groups.

15. Présidentielle 2017: l'assurance au secours du candidat Macron, L'Argus de l'assurance, June 28, 2017.

16. Based in Washington and chaired by Joël André Ornstein, the investment company Monument Capital Group is the result of a joint venture between the French branch of the Rothschild family via Euris-Rallye (then associated with Robert Maxwell) and The Carlyle Group, the American giant of unlisted equities closely linked to the CIA.

17. *Former advisor to France's finance minister avoids jail despite admitting trying to organise an 'erotic nudes' photoshoot with three sisters aged eight to 12, Daily Mail,* January 3, 2017.

18. Quoted by Anne Fulda in Un jeune homme si parfait, Plon, 2017.

19. On this subject, see *Europe/USA, la guerre économique secrète* (CAPA, *Canal+*, March 28, 2005), and *La Puce et le Morpion: Les dessous du raid de la CIA sur la première Licorne française* (Bruno Charlaix and Marc Delassus, Librinova, 2019).

20. This meeting was revealed by journalists Gérard Davet and Fabrice Lhomme in an article, *La Dévorante ambition d'Emmanuel Macron*, published in *Le Monde* (August 31, 2019): "January 2012. François Rebsamen, close friend and future minister of François Hollande, is invited to a secret dinner at Bernard Attali's home. A former boss of GAN insurances and Air France, Jacques' brother is a fan of these kinds of gatherings, where careers are made and unmade among elite business leaders. Although he was not physically present that evening, Macron was on the discussion menu. Invited guests included Gérard Mestrallet (Suez), Jean-Pierre Clamadieu (Rhodia), Jean-Pierre Rodier (Pechiney), Serge Weinberg (Sanofi) and others… "A discreet bridge between bosses and political friends", confirms Bernard Attali. In short, left-wing industrial powers with XXL networks at the service of a promising budding politician. And a fine investment in the future. On his return, Rebsamen gave Hollande clear instructions: "The message they give me is: If Hollande is elected, tell him we have only one request: that Macron be General

Secretary for the Economy. I see François Hollande; he says to me: Is that the only message they gave you? I reply: Yes, the only one..." The request is unambiguous: the young Macron needs a position of influence. He himself is of the demanding sort. A mere economic advisor at the Élysée Palace? He deserves better than that. He projects himself as deputy general secretary. "If Hollande doesn't want, I'm not going,", he tells Minc. But Hollande is willing."

21. *Macron en naufrageur de l'industrie, Médiapart*, May 31, 2019.

22. *The Economist*, June 17, 2017.

23. *The Economist*, September 30, 2017.

24. *The Economist*, October 31, 2021.

25. Although Guy de Rothschild protested vigorously by publishing a thunderous column in *Le Monde* (October 30, 1981) in which he described himself as "a Jew under Pétain, a paria under Mitterrand", the real reason for the nationalization of the Rothschild bank would be revealed a few years later by Jean Peyrelevade, who was in charge of nationalizations in Prime Minister Pierre Mauroy's cabinet: "Financially, the nationalization was a blessing for the Rothschild family. Around 500 million francs in compensation when the bank was worth nothing" (Rothschild, le pouvoir d'un nom, France 2, December 2, 2016).

26. *Gaël Giraud, l'éclipse d'une étoile montante, Le Monde*, March 25, 2023.

27. *Crise financière: la descente aux enfers?, Thinkerview*, 23 octobre 2022.

28. *Le dîner idéal d'Amanda Lear, Point de vue*, 11 février 2020.

29. *Le Parisien.* May 25, 2022.

30. February 7, 2013 conference.

SOMMAIRE

PARTIE I - "BRIGITTE" IN POWER **5**

1 - 2017 7
2 - "BRIGITTE", THE RED THREAD OF EMMANUEL MACRON'S REIGN 19
3 - BRIGITTE AND THE CONSERVATIVE RIGHT: AN ACT OF SOCIAL SLEIGHT OF HAND 29
4 - THE MACRONS' TASTES 37

PARTIE II - THE ENCOUNTER **43**

5 - BOY, 14 45
6 - THE MYTH OF MACRON AS A WRITER 49
7 - BALZACIAN YOUNG WOLF OR EXFILTRATED TEENAGER? 55
8 - THE SHADOW OF THE PEDOPHILE LOBBY 59
9 - WHAT WAS BEHIND THE MATHIEU GALLET RUMOR ? 63
10 - A PEDOCRIMINAL NEBULA AROUND THE MACRONS ? 67
11 - THE AUTHORS OF THE "OFFICIAL LEGEND" 93
12 - "MIMI", "BRIGITTE" AND *LA LÉGENDE DES SIÈCLES* 101

PARTIE III - THE INACCESSIBLE PAST OF THE PRESIDENTIAL COUPLE **109**

13 - MACRON BEFORE BRIGITTE 111
14 - «MANETTE» 121
15 - FRANÇOISE MACRON-NOGUÈS AND THE TRANSGENDER TRACK 127
16 - "BRIGITTE" BEFORE MACRON (I) 131
17 - "BRIGITTE" BEFORE MACRON (II) 143

PARTIE IV - THE JEAN-MICHEL TROGNEUX AFFAIR **157**

18 - NATACHA REY 159
19 - A "CHUBBY GUY" 173
20 - #JEANMICHELTROGNEUX 181
21 - THE AUZIÈRES AND THE BALD MAN IN A SWIMSUIT 187
22 - THE DISAPPEARANCE OF BRIGITTE TROGNEUX (1 – THE COMMUNICANT) 203
23 - THE DISAPPEARANCE OF BRIGITTE TROGNEUX (2 – THE BRIDE) 219
24 - " THOSE WHO END UP BELIEVING IT " 235

PARTIE V - LOOKING FOR JEAN-MICHEL TROGNEUX **247**

25 - THE FAMILY PHOTOGRAPH 249
26 - LA PROVIDENCE (PREQUEL) 255
27 - A MATTER OF TEETH 269
28 - ERASED FROM MEMORY 271
29 - ALGIERS 275
30 - PARIS 281
31 - SPEYER 289
32 - BLANGY-TRONVILLE 295
33 - «VÉRONIQUE» 301

EPILOGUE - THE BLOOD OF THE ROTHSCHILDS **315**